Preservation, Sustainability, and Equity

Preservation, Sustainability, and Equity

Edited by Erica Avrami

TABLE OF CONTENTS

Addressing Equity in Place

Reimagining Preservation's Purview

Appendices

► Introduction

1
See appendices for a literature review further examining spatial exclusion research.

2
There is ongoing debate around the capitalization of "White." The choice to capitalize it in this essay is in support of scholars, activists, media professionals, and others who have argued that not capitalizing it "frames Whiteness as both neutral and the standard." Ann Thùy Nguyn and Maya Pendleton, "Recognizing Race in Language: Why We Capitalize 'Black' and 'White,'" Center for the Study of Social Policy, 2020, https://cssp.org/2020/03/recognizing-race-in-language-why-we-capitalize-black-and-white. As sociologist Eve Ewing argues, "When we ignore the specificity and significance of Whiteness—the things that it is, the things that it does—we contribute to its seeming neutrality and thereby grant it power to maintain its invisibility." Eve Ewing, "I'm a Black Scholar Who Studies Race. Here's Why I Capitalize 'White,'" 2020, https://zora.medium.com/im-a-black-scholar-who-studies-race-heres-why-i-capitalize-white-f94883aa2dd3.

Preservation's New Horizon

Erica Avrami

Heritage occupies a privileged position in the built environment, spatially and conceptually. Most municipalities in the United States, and nearly all countries around the world, have enforced laws and adopted policies meant to preserve heritage in situ, seeking to protect particular places—sites, buildings, districts, and landscapes—from physical loss and the market forces of change. But the idea of heritage is not limited to the formal and spatial dimensions of place. The values and historic narratives associated with heritage places are inherently understood to serve important community-building functions within society. Through physical and spatial encounters with the past, choices about what and how to preserve reinforce—or challenge—certain narratives, shared identities, and reflections of self. The perpetuation of these heritage places and their associated stories is believed to support social resilience by reinforcing notions of shared values and endurance through time. In this sense, preservation is not simply an end state but also an iterative vehicle for collective agency.

At the same time, contemporary research is bringing to light how the built environment creates, compounds, and evinces inequality within and between communities.1 The legacy effects of unjust policies like the dispossession of land and culture, forced relocation, racially restrictive covenants, redlining, and urban renewal are embedded in geographies and built forms, contributing to the systemic recurrence of social and spatial exclusion. Architecture itself can be exclusionary, physically manifesting barriers related to race, gender, economic status, disabilities, religion, and more.

Heritage places, as well as the preservation enterprise, often echo these legacies of injustice. As cities across the United States review what exactly is being memorialized by their monuments, the public debates around them highlight the ways in which historic elements of the built environment can exacerbate social inequities by privileging some—such as White male figures or Confederate histories—and disprivileging others.2 As the discourse around spatial justice evolves, these debates are extending beyond statuary to similarly examine the sites, landscapes, buildings, and districts that memorialize the past. Public policies like designation and listing promote heritage places as the most socially valued and "fixed" elements of our spatial context. This recognition codifies the intention (on the part of government and the body politic) that these places should endure as markers of collective memory.

When the aggregate histories associated with heritage places center the narratives of certain publics and underrepresent or marginalize others, preservation policy does not simply overlook and perpetuate exclusion; it valorizes it. This is not simply a problem of representation—that is, whose story gets told. In shaping and managing built environments and landscapes, preservation policy affords privileges beyond narrative recognition. As a regulator of social-spatial relationships, the built environment constrains and empowers certain communities and individuals—physically, economically, ecologically, socially, and culturally. When a particular site or district is officially deemed historic, it engenders additional layers of regulation and at the same time affords access to additional privileges. For example, buildings that are listed on or determined eligible for the National Register of Historic Places can qualify for historic tax credits or for exemptions from energy code compliance. Designation alone can also create benefits, such as increased property values.

Who wields the tools of preservation policy, and whom do these tools benefit? These questions are ever more salient as polities confront the inequities of the built environment and the policies employed to design, plan, and manage it. While preservation practice and discourse over the past quarter century reflect efforts toward more diverse and robust public participation in what and how to preserve, emerging research on the distributive and longitudinal effects of preservation policy raises critical issues. The inclusive engagement of diverse publics in heritage decision-making is essential, and the field still has much work to do on this front; but just processes do not ensure just outcomes.[3] The distributive effects of preservation policies are correspondingly integral to advancing equity in and through preservation. Such effects are informed by the socioeconomic characteristics of those who inhabit heritage places; in New York City, for example, the demographics of historic districts are by and large Whiter, wealthier, and better educated.[4] This population is thus disproportionately advantaged by preservation policy, meaning these racial and economic disparities are apt to be repeated, if not intensified, in the benefits and exemptions afforded by historic designation.

The climate crisis compounds the inequities associated with the built environment and preservation policy. Environmental conditions—such as flooding along coasts and inland waterways, extreme heat, and desertification—and energy transitions away from fossil fuels will necessitate increasingly complex decisions about buildings and their communities as the climate emergency escalates. In the same way that government-backed decisions about resettlement, mortgage lending, highway construction, and urban renewal have often negatively affected marginalized and vulnerable publics, decisions about which communities receive government resources and support for adaptation or relocation incur new or exacerbate existing inequalities of power and agency.

The government-recognized value of heritage places may privilege those landscapes and built environments, and thus their populations, in climate responses. For example, a coastal historic district might be prioritized in resilience planning or receive funding for flood adaptation because of its heritage value, while another community is displaced due to a lack of disaster preparedness or through a buyout or managed retreat program. Research has already demonstrated significant racial disparities in postdisaster funding through the Federal Emergency Management Agency (FEMA).[5] FEMA also provides supplemental support for historic structures. If the demographics of historic districts lean White, as they

3
Susan Fainstein, *Just City* (Ithaca, NY: Cornell University Press, 2010).

4
Ingrid Gould Ellen, Brian McCabe, and Eric Stern, *Policy Brief: Fifty Years of Historic Preservation in New York City* (New York: Furman Center, New York University, 2016).

5
FEMA has recognized these inequities and committed to ensuring that existing or new FEMA programs, policies, and practices do not exacerbate them. See National Advisory Council Report to the FEMA Administrator, November 2020, https://www.fema.gov/sites/default/files/documents/fema_nac-report_11-2020.pdf.

6
Erica Avrami, Jennifer L. Most, Anna Gasha, and Shreya M. Ghoshal, "Energy and Historic Buildings: Toward Evidence-Based Policy Reform," *Journal of Cultural Heritage Management and Sustainable Development* (forthcoming).

7
See appendices for the literature review examining the preservation-equity-sustainability nexus, which was shared with participants as a point of departure.

do in New York City, policies intended to preserve heritage in the face of climate challenges could amplify existing inequities. Similarly, state energy codes across the country provide waivers for historic structures, while other property owners must retrofit their buildings for greater energy efficiency and carbon reductions. A study in New York City found that census tracts with higher percentages of energy code-exempt built area due to historic status were likely to be Whiter and wealthier.6 Policies intended to protect historic fabric may contribute to energy injustice by privileging some populations with exemptions while others bear the burden of reducing energy use.

Some argue that it is not the responsibility of preservationists to dismantle inequities within the built environment writ large or those compounded by the climate crisis. However, the adaptive strategies and green transformation required to confront the climate crisis are inextricably entwined with questions of equity, and preservation action is not detached from those dynamics. As a profession so dedicated to learning from the past, historic preservation is uniquely positioned to root out and reflect upon these inequities and the disparities they engender, and to ensure that preservation policy works to counter them. At its core, historic preservation should be about instrumentalizing heritage, broadly defined, to sustain communities and promote resilience. Many heritage places and projects are confronting injustice and climate in innovative ways, but systemic change toward equity and sustainability requires looking beyond site-by-site efforts and considering the outcomes of preservation policy—operationalized through laws and guidelines, regulatory processes, and institutions—across time and larger sociogeographic scales.

In this spirit, this volume extends a threaded dialogue of the collaborative research project Urban Heritage, Sustainability, and Social Inclusion. The Columbia University Graduate School of Architecture, Planning, and Preservation, the Earth Institute–Center for Sustainable Urban Development, and the American Assembly established the project, supported by the New York Community Trust, with the aim of examining historic preservation as an integral element of urban policy in the United States. Through a series of invitational symposia and related publications, this initiative has explored the social, environmental, and technological factors that are shaping and challenging the evolution of preservation policy. By forging stronger connections among researchers, policy makers, and practitioners in the field, the initiative has sought to create a forum for imagining the next generation of preservation policy.

This volume was preceded by a symposium in February 2020, in which participants were invited to consider how equity and sustainability might induce and undergird preservation policy reform.7 Two previous symposia and publications laid the foundation for this dialogue. The first, *Preservation and the New Data Landscape*, explored how the preservation enterprise is engaging, shaping, learning from, and capitalizing on new urban data resources and analytics to forge evidence-based research, coproduce knowledge with communities, and inform policy agendas. The second, *Preservation and Social Inclusion*, centered on questions of justice and exclusion by examining how multiple publics are—or are not—represented in heritage decision-making, geographies, and policy structures. A critical theme of this second symposium and publication was the need to reckon with preservation's own past and practices to decenter dominant narratives and more justly represent and engage excluded publics.

Questions of justice extend into this volume, which takes a decidedly more future-oriented approach by examining the agency of the field in championing equity and sustainability—social, economic, and environmental. While preservation discourse is pivoting toward climate concerns, it largely focuses on the objectification of heritage as a victim of climate change and the inherently green qualities of heritage. But preservation can complicate as well as advance justice and climate action; effective alignment of shared goals and outcomes involves explicit shifts in the field's intentions. This compendium thus frames preservation as an enterprise of ideas, methods, institutions, and practices that must reorient toward a new horizon, one in which equity and sustainability become critical guideposts for policy evolution.

Soon after contributors to this volume shared initial ideas around a table in New York City, the COVID-19 pandemic upended our lives and laid bare a raft of social and economic inequities. Long-standing injustices associated with White supremacy and systemic racism received renewed and much-warranted attention with the tragic killing of George Floyd and the amplification of Black Lives Matter protests. Anti-Asian hate crimes escalated. The US Capitol was the scene of a violent insurrection. The contributions to this volume reflect and reflect upon these sobering realities and the work to be done in and through the preservation enterprise, but at the same time point to our capacity for change and collective action.

The following themes resonate across the chapters of this volume and signal areas of preservation policy reform that seek to harness that collective agency toward equity and sustainability.

▶ ENERGY RETROFITS

The relationship of buildings and energy became a focus of public policy in the United States during the 1970s oil crisis. Codes regulated energy efficiency, government assistance promoted weatherization, and tax reform incentivized building rehabilitation in recognition of the embodied energy invested in existing buildings. Preservationists capitalized on embodied energy as further justification for conserving historic buildings, but at the same time successfully argued that historic buildings should not be required to comply with energy codes, which regulate operating energy and may incur modifications to building envelopes and systems.[8] This contradiction underscores the way in which preservationists finessed the policy opportunity to prioritize its primary intention: protecting historic fabric.

Widespread exemptions for historic buildings persist today in model energy codes at the national level, as well as in state- and municipal-level codes. This inconsistency in preservation policy undercuts what Amanda L. Webb and David Moore refer to as "a virtuous cycle in which energy retrofits make an older building more desirable, desirability is more likely

8 Advisory Council on Historic Preservation, *Assessing the Energy Conservation Benefits of Historic Preservation: Methods and Examples* (Washington, DC: prepared by Booz, Allen, and Hamilton for Advisory Council on Historic Preservation, 1979); Advisory Council on Historic Preservation, *Preservation and Energy Conservation* (Washington, DC: Advisory Council on Historic Preservation, 1979); Baird M. Smith, "Information Structure of Building Codes and Standards for the Needs of Existing Buildings," in *Selected Papers Dealing with Regulatory Concerns of Building Rehabilitation*, ed. Patrick W. Cooke (Washington, DC: US Department of Commerce, National Bureau of Standards, 1979), 17–54.

to preserve the building by keeping it in use, and keeping it in use is a sustainable act." In the face of today's climate crisis, the disruption of that cycle has critical ramifications for equitably reducing carbon-based energy consumption. Webb and Moore discuss the different dimensions of energy justice, exploring how compounding benefits, lack of access to energy information, and "rigidity toward energy retrofits" in preservation practice and municipal review processes may privilege some publics and create energy burdens for others. Sara C. Bronin underscores the need to reconcile energy retrofits, like energy-efficient windows and solar panels, with preservation policies, a point examined in her climate-focused critique of the Secretary of the Interior's Standards for the Treatment of Historic Properties. Bronin echoes concerns about inflexibility and advocates for revisions to the Standards and Guidelines as a critical step in explicitly aligning preservation law and policy with climate action. Beyond shifts in regulatory guidance, Jennifer Minner notes the need to augment preservation's knowledge base to address "low-cost, less resource-intensive, and effective means of energy retrofitting across a spectrum of building types." After decades of energy code exemptions, the preservation field arguably has yet to build a robust foundation of research, practice, and policy regarding energy retrofits. Developing this proficiency—in ways that incorporate technical, environmental, economic, and social implications—constitutes a critical need in evidenced-based policy reform that is both climate and equity oriented.

▶ REUSE

New greenhouse gas laws in many parts of the United States are advancing energy efficiency and net zero operating emissions in the built environment in response to the climate crisis. The need to further reduce carbon-based emissions has brought renewed attention to the embodied energy, and more specifically the embodied carbon, of buildings. The extraction, manufacture, transport, and installation of materials as part of the construction process incurs fossil fuel-based energy consumption and carbon emissions. James B. Lindberg explains how the reuse of existing buildings maximizes the time value of carbon by avoiding the emissions associated with new construction. He argues that preservation's ethic of reuse serves as a model for existing buildings, not just historic ones, which could be scaled up to sharply and rapidly reduce the cumulative effects of carbon emissions and thus mitigate climate change.

Lindberg counsels that ambitions for widespread building reuse must be coupled with shifts in land use policies and regulations, as well as in preservation practice, to "collaborate more fully and intentionally with allied organizations and interests." He uses Chicago as an illustration of how advocates for affordable housing, community development, energy retrofitting, and preservation coalesced around the shared goal of rehabilitating smaller apartment buildings in the city's older neighborhoods. Stephanie Ryberg-Webster explores the collaborative imperative of reuse in three Ohio case cities: Cleveland, Cincinnati, and Columbus. Examining municipal programs related to housing rehabilitation, lead abatement, sustainability, and historic preservation, she identifies opportunities ripe for intersection and cooperation, but finds that preservation professionals and policies are too disconnected from these broader urban agendas. Ryberg-Webster argues that it is incumbent upon preservationists to actively engage in "synergistic policy goals such as affordable housing, environmental justice, and sustainability," while recognizing, as Lindberg also does, that such engagement will incur difficult decisions and trade-offs.

▶ DECONSTRUCTION

Realigning preservation policies around issues of sustainable reuse complicates some of the core practices of preservation in the United States. For example, carbon emissions can also be avoided through the recycling and reuse of building materials, not just entire structures. As circular economies mature within the construction industry, deconstruction will become an essential facet of reuse within the built environment. Lindberg makes the case that preservation practice and policy must evolve to recognize deconstruction as part of preservation's toolbox, even though deconstruction seems antithetical to preservation values such as architectural integrity.

Bronin brings this point directly to the regulatory arena, recommending the addition of deconstruction as a form of preservation treatment to the Secretary of the Interior's Standards, though as a last resort (the Standards currently cover four approaches to treatment: preservation, rehabilitation, restoration, and reconstruction). And Minner challenges contemporary perceptions of deconstruction as contradictory to preservation's primary goals, contending that deconstruction is an age-old practice of building care and material thrift. Reestablishing it as a valid preservation option can more deliberately align the field and its policies with those of sustainable design and planning.

▶ REINVESTMENT

Beyond buildings and materials, the broader agenda of reuse also involves reinvesting in communities. The inextricable dynamics of physical and social fabric make people central to decisions about places and their heritage. Several authors explore the use of preservation as a tool for redevelopment and revitalization in marginalized communities, but one that must more purposefully address legacies of injustice, systemic racism, and the risks of displacement. Culture, they argue, is fundamental to sustainable and equitable reinvestment processes and policies.

Claudia Guerra describes how the Shotgun House Initiative of San Antonio's Office of Historic Preservation aligns goals of conserving climate-responsive vernacular architecture, retaining affordable housing, preventing displacement of working-class residents, and enabling the intergenerational transfer of traditional practices, local knowledge, and community bonds. At its core, the initiative "is rooted in the idea that

9
Newport, Rhode Island, was among the first municipalities to issue standards for elevating historic buildings in response to flooding. See its Policy Statement and Design Guidelines for Elevating Historic Buildings: https://www.cityofnewport.com/en-us/city-hall/departments/zoning-inspections/historic-preservation/elevating-history. Charleston, South Carolina, adopted similar Design Guidelines for Elevating Historic Buildings in 2019. See https://www.charleston-sc.gov/DocumentCenter/View/18518/BAR-Elevation-Design.

10
These guidelines were illustrated, updated, and reissued in June 2021. See https://www.nps.gov/orgs/1739/upload/flood-adaptation-guidelines-2021.pdf.

culture and social well-being are vital parts of sustainability." In the context of Detroit, Randall Mason discusses equitable redevelopment that seeks to counter or defuse gentrification, noting that "the act of building on existing cultures, no matter how tattered, is a foundation for hopeful acts of sustainable and equitable development." He maintains that preservation can serve as an integrative agent in reinvestment processes precisely because of its focus on culture. Lisa T. Alexander's work similarly seeks to valorize the culture produced by disadvantaged publics and to enable them to benefit from reinvestment without being displaced by it. She finds that "historic preservation law has done a poor job of seeing those forms of culture that are produced at the root level, when they are not attached to buildings." Alexander advocates for reforms to policy and practice that better recognize the geographic and spatial dimensions of culture beyond the formal qualities of architecture.

Vicki Weiner extends this critique of the field's emphasis on material form by asking rhetorically, "Can saving the buildings also save everything else about the place?" Weiner and Ryberg-Webster contend that preservationists must work toward centering people and orienting their work within complex community development agendas to counter the potential inequities of reinvestment. Minner furthers this case with the concept of "equity preservation," which can serve as a framework for orienting "preservation and community development policies toward social equity, the use of sweat equity, and retaining local community control and ownership of land."

▶ ADAPTATION AND RELOCATION

The call for preservationists to engage more robustly in the complexities of people-place relationships is inexorably complicated by the climate crisis. Concepts of equitable reinvestment are inherently place contingent. The specter of intensified heat and desertification, coastal and waterway flooding, and extreme weather events signals a future of climate-related risk and displacement for many, if not most, communities. When people-place connections face rupture, what is preservation's role?

Adaptation is, in many respects, the go-to response for preservation. It incurs loss or alteration of historic form and fabric, which challenges preservation norms; but unlike with energy retrofits, the imperative for change is more directly experienced. The tangible damage of repeated flooding, for example, makes the need to elevate a historic structure readily apparent. In response, municipal preservation agencies, including those in Newport, Rhode Island, and Charleston, South Carolina, have started to develop local guidelines for elevating and flood-proofing buildings. 9 The National Park Service issued Guidelines for Flood Adaptation in late 2019 to supplement the Secretary of the Interior's Standards for Rehabilitating Historic Buildings. 10

Bronin observes that the federal flood guidelines mark an important and positive shift in aligning the Standards and Guidelines with climate action, but further reform is needed. She advocates for augmenting the Standards' existing four treatment approaches by adding relocation. Once part of a long history of building care and reuse, relocation is discouraged by contemporary preservation principles, which uphold original context as integral to heritage values. Anticipating that many heritage places will be at risk due to the climate crisis, preservationists should consider relocation part of preservation's remit.

Adaptation and relocation nonetheless encompass far more than the technical work of altering or moving historic buildings. As in the case of reinvestment, culture plays a critical and complicating role. A. R. Siders and Marcy Rockman elucidate how "heritage creates sense of community and attachment to place, which promote disaster recovery and collective action. Yet heritage may also be an anchor that prevents us from moving or restricts our available options." Siders and Rockman argue that the triage mindset and methods employed by preservationists "to identify priority areas for preservation in place and to develop creative ways to preserve meaning even without physical objects" constitute a critical point of intersection with adaptation practitioners. The value-laden nature of decisions about whether and how to adapt or relocate necessitate multiexpert and community-engaged processes, which should incorporate heritage in ways that acknowledge past injustices and prevent the protection of privilege.

▶ MIGRATION AND GROWTH

Climate adaptation sometimes incurs the relocation of buildings and infrastructure, but it inevitably involves the movement of people. While many locales are beginning to grapple with the prospect and the magnitude of climate-induced retreat, Robin Bronen reminds us that for far too many communities—especially Indigenous peoples and descendants of formerly enslaved peoples—forced migration and resettlement has a long and fraught history that cannot be untangled from climate vulnerability. She elucidates how the climate crisis constitutes yet another chapter in a legacy of repeated cultural trauma for Alaska Native communities, who have been at the front line of climate-forced relocation for decades. Protecting their culture and lifeways, Bronen argues, is inseparable from protecting their right to self-determination and requires "decolonizing the structural and institutional systems that continue to subjugate Indigenous communities."

Bronen explains how the lack of coordinated government policies, agencies, and resources to address relocation further exacerbates injustice and inaction, even in cases of entire communities committing to relocation. Victoria Herrmann echoes this critique, noting that the national programs that "support disaster displacements and hazard-induced buyouts do not aim to maintain the social and economic cohesion of communities." She sheds light on the need for policies and practices regarding emplacement of climate migrants in receiving communities, since the climate crisis incurs not only displacement but also critical changes to existing communities to better support new and growing populations more justly. Herrmann observes that "the spatial dimension of climate emplacement into new cities is multidimensional and includes connections to both a new place-based identity and retention of an existing community." Understanding heritage values, places, and practices—of both the displaced and the receiving communities—can inform co-location planning and enable migrants to thrive in their new locales. This constitutes a new ambit of preservation policy and practice in its alignment with sustainability.

The concept of emplacement is connected in important ways to sustainable growth policies, especially to meet affordable housing needs. Accommodating more people in towns and cities, without unsustainably consuming more undeveloped land, requires infill development and/or redevelopment in existing built environments. Louise Bedsworth and Ken Bernstein discuss the emerging use of accessory dwelling units (ADUs)—familiarly known as granny flats—in California, specifically in Los Angeles, to introduce more population density into single-family neighborhoods. Preservation and densification have historically been at odds in many cities, often over increased formal density through the introduction of high-rises, which does not necessarily create population density and can negatively alter the context of historic buildings and districts. To enable sustainable and equitable growth, Bedsworth argues, "density needs to be thought of in a much more contextual way. It's about accessibility. It's about social networks, cohesion, and connection." Interestingly, these qualities characterize many of the local historic districts in Los Angeles. Bernstein refers to findings from recent analyses of these districts, known as Historic Preservation Overlay Zones (HPOZs), which determined that their residential density is 50 percent higher than that of the rest of the city and that twenty-one of the thirty-five HPOZs have a higher percentage of BIPOC residents than the citywide average. Bernstein notes that many of these residents "sought historic designation not only to protect and enhance their neighborhood's architecture but also as a way of preventing erasure of their community's unique cultural identity."

▶ REALIGNMENT

The concomitant interests of preservation, equity, and sustainability suggest ripe opportunities for intersection. Lindberg notes that preservation brings unique value to the work of climate adaptation, as few other fields can claim preservation's knowledge of how to intervene in older and existing buildings. However, Ryberg-Webster cautions that simply demonstrating preservation's value is insufficient. Mobilizing around common goals and shared policy agendas requires the preservation field to more proactively redirect its ambitions and adopt new ways of working, at structural and institutional levels. Most preservation agencies have limited resources to support major shifts in policy and scope; trade-offs are inevitable if preservation is to redress social injustice and meet the climate crisis head-on.

Bernstein and Bedsworth, for example, discuss the tensions among preservation, sustainable growth, and climate action policies and the importance of more purposeful and coordinated alignment between

17

municipal- and state-level entities, as well as across agencies in Los Angeles. Bronen, Herrmann, and Siders and Rockman all point to significant gaps and lack of coordination in climate adaptation and relocation policy, as well as to important intersections with culture and heritage, signaling potential avenues where the preservation enterprise could augment its triage approaches and serve the aims of equitable resilience.

Central to these opportunities and threaded throughout this volume is the need to reorient preservation practices and policies toward people. Webb and Moore caution that the diversity of inhabitants of older and historic buildings is neglected when preservation fails to adopt energy justice frameworks. Bronin argues that the Secretary of the Interior's Standards and Guidelines "are overly focused on the materials they protect rather than the people, neighborhoods, and communities that preservation is for." Minner highlights the opportunities for preservation to align with the Green New Deal to serve communities and advance societal transformation. Alexander, Guerra, Weiner, and Mason see opportunities to ensure sustainable and equitable reinvestment, prevent cultural displacement, and redress social injustice if, as Mason notes, preservation professionals and organizations choose to be "forceful agents for change." Despite the immensity of the task ahead, these authors find hope and potential in the capacity of preservation institutions and professionals to learn and unlearn, to pivot and persevere, in service to a better future.

► Confronting Adaptation and Relocation
▷ Reorienting toward Climate and Justice
▷ Addressing Equity in Place
▷ Reimagining Preservation's Purview

Connecting Cultural Heritage and Urban Climate Change Adaptation

A. R. Siders

Marcy Rockman

Confronting Adaptation and Relocation

Environmental forces have always affected cultural heritage and destroyed some elements; no time or place or people has ever had a "full set" of the heritage that came before. It is not possible to save everything, and part of the challenge heritage practitioners have always faced is deciding which elements to preserve. Climate change accelerates, intensifies, and expands this challenge, and climate adaptation as a field has struggled to engage in the triage of preservation in a way that also engages heritage.[1] After all, decisions about what to protect and what not to protect are inherently social and value laden. Although climate adaptation and cultural heritage preservation are often considered separately, they are intimately connected, and managing their complex relationship requires greater coordination.

Consider, for example, the case of Ellicott City, Maryland, a historic mill town set along the Patapsco River near its confluence with four creeks. The first grist mill in the area was built in 1766 and was destroyed by a flood in 1768. Subsequent floods occurred in 1817, 1837, 1868, 1901, 1917, 1923, 1942, 1952, 1972, 1975, 1989, 2011, and, catastrophically, in 2016 and 2018, when lives were lost.[2] Current climate projections anticipate more extreme precipitation and flooding in the region. In response, the local government has proposed removing part of historic Main Street to mitigate future floods by making room for the water. Some residents oppose this decision because of the historic nature of the buildings:

> When you walk through Ellicott City and when you discover what's inside of those buildings, you see where slaves were hidden on their path to freedom. You see a lot of things that connect you to our greater community… Family and very dear friends will say, what are you doing here? Why are you still here? You know, especially if you know what's coming, why are you here?… I tell them this place is worth sticking around and working for.[3]

Other residents feel just as strongly that preserving heritage should not be a reason to avoid adaptation:

> I'm really sad, but I genuinely think that by taking my house down that the people who are upstream from me are going to be safer… my son will need less therapy if we're not living on top of this river all the time… If you pretend that human lives are worth less than historic buildings, you're a despicable person. And I don't have any bones about saying that. You're absolutely despicable.[4]

This drama—the strong and divided opinions, the historic reasons for building in exposed areas, the increased risks posed by climate change, the social trade-offs between preservation and transformation—is playing out in cities and towns across the United States and around the world.

So many urban areas are where they are because of environmental features such as rivers, coasts, and their related ecosystems. As the climate changes, those same environmental features may now present new or elevated risks. At the same time, the development of these urban areas has created *places*: not only centers of dense infrastructure and economic activity but also spaces that are deeply interwoven with the identities,

1
National Park Service, "Policy Memorandum 14-02: Climate Change and Stewardship of Cultural Resources" (National Park Service, 2014); Marcy Rockman et al., "Cultural Resources Climate Change Strategy" (Washington, DC, 2016), http://www.thegoldensieve.com; May Cassar and Robyn Pender, "The Impact of Climate Change on Cultural Heritage: Evidence and Response," *Proceedings of the ICOM Committee for Conservation, 14th Triennial Meeting* (2005), 610–616, http://discovery.ucl.ac.uk/5059; Michelle Berenfeld, "Planning for Permanent Emergency: 'Triage' as a Strategy for Managing Cultural Resources Threatened by Climate Change," *George Wright Forum* 32, no. 1 (2015): 5–12; Tom Dawson et al., "Coastal Heritage, Global Climate Change, Public Engagement, and Citizen Science," *Proceedings of the National Academy of Sciences of the United States of America* 117, no. 15 (2020): 8280–8286, https://doi.org/10.1073/pnas.1912246117.

2
Preservation Maryland, "After Action Report: Ellicott City, Maryland Flood of 2016," 2017, https://www.preservationmaryland.org/wp-content/uploads/2017/07/preservation-maryland-ellicott-city-flood-after-action-report-2017-web.pdf.

3
Rebecca Hersher, "How a Proposal to Reduce Flood Risk in Ellicott City Nearly Destroyed the Community," National Public Radio, October 9, 2019, https://www.npr.org/2019/10/09/768697825/how-a-proposal-to-reduce-flood-risk-in-ellicott-city-nearly-destroyed-the-commun.

4
Hersher, "How a Proposal to Reduce Flood Risk in Ellicott City Nearly Destroyed the Community."

5
United Nations Educational, Scientific, and Cultural Organization (UNESCO), "Cultural Heritage" (2017), http://www.unesco.org/new/en/santiago/culture/cultural-heritage.

6
Rohit Jigyasu et al., "Heritage and Resilience: Issues and Opportunities for Reducing Disaster Risks," in 4th Session of the Global Platform for Disaster Risk Reduction, 19–23 May 2013 (Geneva, Switzerland, 2013), 60.

7
Junia Howell and James R. Elliott, "Damages Done: The Longitudinal Impacts of Natural Hazards on Wealth Inequality in the United States," Social Problems, no. 412 (August 14, 2018): 1–20, https://doi.org/10.1093/socpro/spy016.

8
Jesse M. Keenan, Thomas Hill, and Anurag Gumber, "Climate Gentrification: From Theory to Empiricism in Miami-Dade County, Florida," Environmental Research Letters 5, no. 13 (2018): 054001, https://doi.org/10.1088/1748-9326/aabb32.

9
S. Costas, O. Ferreira, and G. Martinez, "Why Do We Decide to Live with Risk at the Coast?," Ocean and Coastal Management 118 (December 1, 2015): 1–11, https://doi.org/10.1016/j.ocecoaman.2015.05.015; Natasha Kuruppu and Diana Liverman, "Mental Preparation for Climate Adaptation: The Role of Cognition and Culture in Enhancing Adaptive Capacity of Water Management in Kiribati," Global Environmental Change 21, no. 2 (May 2011): 657–669, https://doi.org/10.1016/j.gloenvcha.2010.12.002; Petra Tschakert et al., "Climate Change and Loss, as if People Mattered: Values, Places, and Experiences," Wiley Interdisciplinary Reviews: Climate Change 8, no. 5 (2017): 1–19, https://doi.org/10.1002/wcc.476.

histories, memories, and characters of the people who live and work there. Successful adaptation for urban areas must navigate both the physical realities that climate change has brought and will bring and the values and meanings that are held in and for these places.

The relationship of cultural heritage to climate change is complex. Too often it is simplified: climate change threatens cultural heritage; climate adaptation efforts must address cultural heritage. But such statements omit the messy and multidimensional connections between heritage and adaptation. Navigating this complex relationship requires collaboration between adaptation practitioners and heritage practitioners. By adaptation practitioners, we refer broadly to people working on climate adaptation, emergency response, disaster risk reduction, urban planning, housing, and related fields. In turn, by heritage practitioners, we refer to a broad range of people engaged in the designation, management, preservation, and practice of cultural heritage. Cultural heritage includes tangible sites, such as buildings, structures, monuments, and landscapes, and intangible expressions, such as oral traditions, manners, rituals, practices, knowledge, and techniques that have come into the present from the past. [5] While heritage in urban areas may be most visible in its buildings, most urban areas include many, if not all, forms of cultural heritage.

A place to begin this navigation is recognizing that heritage is an anchor: a lifeline that grounds us and provides security and connection in the midst of change. Heritage creates sense of community and attachment to place, which promote disaster recovery and collective action. [6] Yet heritage may also be an anchor that prevents us from moving or restricts our available options.

For example, exposure to climate-related hazards is the result of a complicated interplay of historic forces (e.g., segregation, redlining, economic pressures) and cultural influences (e.g., beach culture, migrant communities, sense of place). Different communities have come to be in the places they are now through different social and economic trajectories, some purposefully or accidentally inequitable. Histories of inequality, racism, and discrimination and continued disparities lead vulnerable people to live in more at-risk places, often in less safe buildings, with access to fewer resources, so they experience more harm during extreme events and have a harder time recovering afterward. [7] Current practices continue to shape these vulnerabilities. For example, the term "climate gentrification" was first used to describe demographic shifts in Miami, Florida, where wealthy residents move away from the exposed waterfront and displace lower-income residents living in previously undesirable neighborhoods at higher elevations. [8]

Heritage may also shape how people perceive climate change in places they know, visit, and experience. [9] These perceptions shape how they assess risk, experience change, and make decisions, including how they assign responsibility for adaptation and what actions are considered fair. [10] It affects how people learn, whom to trust for information, how well systems are understood, and what resources can be gathered to respond. [11] People tend to prefer actions that maintain the status quo, and those with strong ties to the past might resist change of any type. [12] While this may sound like a critique in terms of logic, it is rather a recognition that strong connections to place may encourage people to remain in places that are extremely hazardous. 13 People who live closer to the water in the United States are more likely to return and rebuild after a disaster because proximity to water is important to their self-identity and sense of place. 14 As John Silk, minister of foreign affairs for the Republic of the Marshall Islands, told the United Nations in 2019, the Marshall Islands is "literally being eaten away" as climate change causes sea levels to rise and ocean waters to warm and acidify, killing the coral reefs that form the nation's atolls. Yet many people remain on the islands because, as Minister Silk quoted from the Marshall Islands Constitution: "All we have and are today as a people, we have received as a sacred heritage which we pledge ourselves to safeguard and maintain, valuing nothing more than our rightful home on the island."15 Island nations that are losing land are one of the most visible examples of the challenges of relocation, but similar struggles of maintaining home and facing loss are playing out at smaller scales in cities and towns across the world.

The qualities that shape the importance of heritage also affect what options are available to address the challenges of climate change, and official designations of heritage play a particularly significant role. 16 For example, historic buildings may lose their designation (and associated funding and protections) if they are relocated, which can keep people in place even if it puts them and the building at greater risk. Protective infrastructure is expensive, so it is often used to protect dense populations or areas with economic importance, including previously designated heritage sites or districts. 17 Charleston, South Carolina, is considering building an eight-mile, $1.75 billion perimeter wall to protect the historic city against rising seas and hurricane surge. But the wall won't protect Rosemont, a historic African American neighborhood in Charleston. 18 Would Rosemont be protected if its history was officially recognized as heritage? When the community of Turkey Creek in Gulfport, Mississippi, was threatened with demolition to address flooding, residents organized to have the community's history officially recognized because official designation provides a level of protection that cultural ties and historic connections to place do not. 19 Both the existence of heritage and the processes by which it is formally recognized (or not) by national registers, by local heritage officials, and so forth may create or exacerbate inequalities in terms of what adaptation options are presented to urban communities.

And yet, if not all places can be saved, if we believe that adaptation resources are finite and a decision to preserve one historic site or to protect one community in place may therefore reduce the resources available to protect other people and other histories, then choices must be made. The questions become: How are those choices made? And by whom?

Heritage practitioners have long experience with the reality that not all heritage will, can, or should be preserved. The mindset and methods used in triage—to identify priority areas for preservation in place and to develop creative ways to preserve meaning even without physical objects—could provide valuable insights for adaptation practitioners. When adaptation decisions involve such difficult questions as "Should this community continue to exist in this place?," they require engagement with complex issues of heritage. As hydrologist Ben Zaitchik notes: "The

10
Daniel Henstra, Jason Thistlethwaite, Craig Brown, and Daniel Scott, "Flood Risk Management and Shared Responsibility: Exploring Canadian Public Attitudes and Expectations," Journal of Flood Risk Management 12, no. 1 (2019): 1–10, https://doi.org/10.1111/jfr3.12346; W. Neil Adger, Tara Quinn, Irene Lorenzoni, and Conor Murphy, "Sharing the Pain: Perceptions of Fairness Affect Private and Public Response to Hazards," Annals of the American Association of Geographers 106, no. 5 (2016): 1079–1096, https://doi.org/10.1080/24694452.2016.1182005.

11
W. Neil Adger et al., "Are There Social Limits to Adaptation to Climate Change?," Climatic Change 93, no. 3–4 (2009): 335–354, https://doi.org/10.1007/s10584-008-9520-z; Kimberley Thomas et al., "Explaining Differential Vulnerability to Climate Change: A Social Science Review," Wiley Interdisciplinary Reviews: Climate Change 10, no. 2 (2019): 1–18, https://doi.org/10.1002/wcc.565.

12
Antonio Ciccone, "Resistance to Reform: Status Quo Bias in the Presence of Individual-Specific Uncertainty: Comment," American Economic Review 94, no. 3 (2004): 785–795, https://doi.org/10.1257/0002828041464425.

13
Brenda Phillips, P. A. Stukes, and P. Jenkins, "Freedom Hill Is Not for Sale—and Neither Is the Lower Ninth Ward," Journal of Black Studies 43, no. 4 (2012): 405–426, https://doi.org/10.1177/0021934711425489; W. Neil Adger, Jon Barnett, F. S. Chapin III, and Heidi Ellemor, "This Must Be the Place: Underrepresentation of Identity and Meaning in Climate Change Decision-Making," Global Environmental Politics 11, no. 2 (2011): 1–25, https://doi.org/DOI: 10.1162/

GLEP_a_00051;
Sherri Brokopp Binder,
Charlene K. Baker, and
John P. Barile, "Rebuild
or Relocate? Resilience
and Postdisaster
Decision-Making after
Hurricane Sandy,"
*American Journal of
Community Psychology*
56, no. 1–2 (2015):
180–196, https://doi.
org/10.1007/s10464-
015-9727-x.

14
Anamaria Bukvic,
Hongxiao Zhu,
Rita Lavoie, and
Austin Becker, "The
Role of Proximity
to Waterfront in
Residents' Relocation
Decision-Making
Post-Hurricane Sandy,"
*Ocean and Coastal
Management* 154
(2018): 8–19, https://
doi.org/10.1016/j.
ocecoaman.2018.01.
002; Timothy F.
Green and Robert B.
Olshansky, "Rebuilding
Housing in New
Orleans: The Road
Home Program after
the Hurricane Katrina
Disaster," *Housing
Policy Debate* 22, no. 1
(2012): 75–99, https://
doi.org/10.1080/105
11482.2011.624530;
Elyse M. Zavar, Ronald
R. Hagelman III, and
William M. Rugeley
II, "Site, Situation,
and Property Owner
Decision-Making after
the 2002 Guadalupe
River Flood," in
*Evolving Approaches to
Understanding Natural
Hazards*, ed. Graham
A. Tobin and Burrell E.
Montz (Newcastle upon
Tyne, UK: Cambridge
Scholars Publishing,
2015), 458–470.

15
United Nations,
"General Assembly
74th Session" (United
Nations, 2019), https://
doi.org/10.1017/
S0020818300010821.

16
Costas, Ferreira, and
Martinez, "Why Do We
Decide to Live with Risk
at the Coast?"; Kuruppu
and Liverman, "Mental
Preparation for Climate
Adaptation"; Tschakert
et al., "Climate Change
and Loss."

17
A. R. Siders, "Social
Justice Implications of
US Managed Retreat
Buyout Programs,"
Climatic Change 152,
no. 2 (2018): 239–257,

question of what you do... about New Orleans is not a rational engineering conversation. It's a conversation about what we want to be as a society, what a place means to us as a community locally and as a country."[20] Heritage practitioners have considered trade-offs and prioritization in the context of parks and site-based tangible heritage, but these tools may provide insights or be translated to address urban and intangible heritage.

In a review of how climate change will affect cultural heritage sites, Tom Dawson et al. note, "Heritage managers need to make conscious and justified decisions about taking action—or not. Loss should not happen by default."[21] The US National Park Service Cultural Resources Climate Change Strategy similarly notes that "taking no action is a decision."[22] The first insight is that outcomes—financial, social, psychological, cultural— will be most effective and fair when decisions are made purposefully.[23] Currently, many adaptation decisions are made without consideration of the whole system, or without consideration of issues of heritage.

Second, just as there are many ways to think about what makes a heritage site or practice "significant," there are many ways to think about what makes a neighborhood a community or what makes it worthy of protection in place. Defining community is a difficult process and should be done with community engagement and consideration of heritage. After Hurricane Sandy, the New York State government offered to purchase homes in the Oakwood Beach neighborhood on Staten Island, an offer that would allow residents to relocate and return the land to open space. Drawing lines around Oakwood Beach, however, became a fraught process. Ultimately, it was unclear how the government decided on the boundaries of the neighborhood, or why Oakwood Beach residents should receive buyout offers while neighboring homeowners were required to rebuild.[24] As a result, these decisions created confusion and distrust. Engaging with the public to understand how people identify their communities, how they connect to place, and why they want to remain or to move can help craft adaptation policies that better respect tangible and intangible heritage.

Decisions about where to relocate and what to protect cannot be made based on purely technical grounds, but they also cannot be entirely a matter of popularity. The archaeologist Jon McVey Erlandson warns that "just as the fight to save endangered species often seems biased towards cuter, smarter, and mostly mammalian species that appeal most to the general public," saving national tourist destinations may come "at the expense of many less scenic, less visited, but no less significant archaeo- logical sites" or heritage sites of less powerful populations.[25] Similarly, climate adaptation decisions should not protect only dense, expensive infrastructure or glamorous destinations. Just as heritage has traditionally focused on significance, adaptation has traditionally focused on cost- effectiveness, despite recognition of the limitations of this approach[26] and the potential for such adaptation to privilege the protection of wealth.[27] Rather than focus on a single criterion, adaptation practitioners need to consider numerous characteristics including uniqueness, local and scientific values, national concepts of fairness, long-term sustainability, alignment with global climate mitigation and environmental goals, and recognition of the historic injustices and systems that have created cur- rent patterns of risk exposure—many of the same elements that should be considered by heritage practitioners when prioritizing.

Third, making these multielement adaptation decisions should involve technical experts and community members at all stages of the decision-making process: both in understanding the risk and in designing strategies to address risk. Technical vulnerability or risk assessments are often conducted by experts. Hydrologists, meteorologists, and GIS experts map the extent of flood risk; engineers consider building vulnerability; sociologists think about social vulnerability to floods and hurricanes. In turn, heritage experts team with GIS analysts to conduct high-resolution scans to determine how coastal erosion will affect heritage sites. [28] In both fields, however, community input is necessary to understand why these risks matter.

Expert knowledge and public input are also needed to design potential strategies to address risk. Engineers are needed to determine the height, width, and material of an effective floodwall, but decisions to remove homes to make space for the wall or to stop the wall before it reaches a vulnerable neighborhood are political decisions that require public discourse. A heritage expert may determine that elevating a historic building is physically feasible, but community input is needed to understand how that physical change will affect the meaning and interpretation of the building. Conversations with stakeholders are particularly important when adaptations threaten intangible practices, like traditional uses of land. Scotland's Coastal Archaeology and the Problem of Erosion (SCAPE) team works closely with communities to understand their values and priorities for local heritage sites before deciding how to manage those sites. The US National Park Service (NPS) has also begun conversations with community members about their values and priorities for cultural heritage in parks. [29] After Superstorm Sandy, the New York City government held community engagement workshops to gain insights from the public as to how they had been affected by the storm and how they wanted to address flood risk in the future. These types of conversations could be even more effective if they were integrated, explicitly considering risk and heritage together.

Heritage practitioners have also developed some novel strategies to engage in these difficult conversations about loss and change. For example, in 2018, SCAPE realized it wanted to understand what it means for communities to lose or face the loss of heritage sites. So with funding from the Scottish Universities Insight Institute, SCAPE, staff from Historic Environment Scotland, Scottish academics, members of the Florida Public Archaeology Network, and the NPS met with community groups across northeast Scotland and the Orkneys to discuss their heritage and their future. These conversations were organized according to the following six questions:

1. What is significant about [place]'s heritage?
2. What are the threats facing this heritage?
3. What would be the impact on [place] if this heritage is lost?
4. If we can't take action at all sites, how should these places be prioritized?
5. What are your aspirations for [place]'s heritage by 2030? What needs to happen to get there?

https://doi.org/10.1007/s10584-018-2272-5; A. R. Siders and Jesse M. Keenan, "Variables Shaping Coastal Adaptation Decisions to Armor, Nourish, and Retreat in North Carolina," *Ocean and Coastal Management* (July 2019): 105023, https://doi.org/10.1016/j.ocecoaman.2019.105023.

18 Chloe Johnson and Mikaela Porter, "Charleston's Peninsula Could Be Walled In under New $1.75B Flood Prevention Plan," *Post and Courier*, April 20, 2020, updated September 25, 2020, https://www.postandcourier.com/business/real_estate/charlestons-peninsula-could-be-walled-in-under-new-1-75b-flood-prevention-plan/article_1da35bd6-80dc-11ea-a07c-279e26d1510d.html.

19 Leah Mahan, *Come Hell or High Water: The Battle for Turkey Creek*, documentary film (USA: America ReFramed, 2014).

20 Hersher, "How a Proposal to Reduce Flood Risk in Ellicott City Nearly Destroyed the Community."

21 Dawson et al., "Coastal Heritage, Global Climate Change, Public Engagement, and Citizen Science."

22 Rockman et al., "Cultural Resources Climate Change Strategy."

23 A. R. Siders, Miyuki Hino, and Katharine Mach, "The Case for Strategic and Managed Climate Retreat," *Science* 365, no. 6455 (2019): 761–763, https://doi.org/10.1126/science.aax8346; Carolyn Kousky, "Managing Shoreline Retreat: A US Perspective," *Climatic Change* 124, no. 1–2 (2014): 9–20, https://doi.org/10.1007/s10584-014-1106-3.

24 Sherri Brokopp Binder and Alex Greer, "The Devil Is in the Details:

Linking Home Buyout Policy, Practice, and Experience after Hurricane Sandy," *Politics and Governance* 4, no. 4 (December 28, 2016): 97, https://doi.org/10.17645/pag.v4i4.738; Sherri Brokopp Binder, John P. Barile, Charlene Baker, and Bethann Kulp, "Home Buyouts and Household Recovery: Neighborhood Differences Three Years after Hurricane Sandy," *Environmental Hazards* 18, no. 2 (2019): 127–145, https://doi.org/10.1080/17477891.2018.1511404.

25
Jon McVey Erlandson, "As the World Warms: Rising Seas, Coastal Archaeology, and the Erosion of Maritime History," *Journal of Coastal Conservation* 16, no. 2 (2012): 137–142, https://doi.org/10.1007/s11852-010-0104-5.

26
Daniel Lincke and Jochen Hinkel, "Economically Robust Protection against 21st Century Sea-Level Rise," *Global Environmental Change* 51, no. April (2018): 67–73, https://doi.org/10.1016/j.gloenvcha.2018.05.003; Camille André, Delphine Boulet, Hélène Rey-Valette, and Benedicte Rulleau, "Protection by Hard Defence Structures or Relocation of Assets Exposed to Coastal Risks: Contributions and Drawbacks of Cost-Benefit Analysis for Long-Term Adaptation Choices to Climate Change," *Ocean and Coastal Management* 134 (December 1, 2016): 173–182, https://doi.org/10.1016/j.ocecoaman.2016.10.003; Sierra Woodruff, Todd K. BenDor, and Aaron L. Strong, "Fighting the Inevitable: Infrastructure Investment and Coastal Community Adaptation to Sea Level Rise," *System Dynamics Review* 34, no. 1–2 (2018), https://doi.org/10.1002/sdr.1597.

27
Siders and Keenan, "Variables Shaping Coastal Adaptation Decisions"; Jeremy

6. In order to achieve these aspirations, where do roles and responsibilities lie? [30]

These conversations started with heritage, but they grew to encompass hopes, dreams, and the economy. Having started by identifying a community's roots, history, and priorities in terms of keeping their stories and knowledge, participants were able to demonstrate flexibility and creativity in terms of where they could see themselves wanting to go in the future.

At a national level, in 2017 the nation of Fiji took on leadership of the UN Framework Convention on Climate Change (UNFCCC) Conference of the Parties and proposed an approach they called the Talanoa Dialogues:

> Talanoa is a traditional word used in Fiji and across the Pacific to reflect a process of inclusive, participatory and transparent dialogue. The purpose of Talanoa is to share stories, build empathy, and to make wise decisions for the collective good. The process of Talanoa involves the sharing of ideas, skills, and experience through storytelling. [31]

The Talanoa Dialogues work through three questions: Where are we? Where do we want to go? How do we get there? The concept of sharing knowledge and experience is central to Talanoa, and it is also the essence of history and heritage, although it may not always be recognized in that way in its recent use for addressing climate change.

While SCAPE focuses on the coastal archaeology of a site, the Talanoa Dialogues were designed to create a common understanding among nations. Both processes, however, use a sense of history as a way to start difficult conversations, to help people process potential loss due to climate change, and to build common ground to support collective action. It is possible that approaches like these could be useful in urban contexts: just as SCAPE asked which heritage sites should be saved and how stakeholders would understand the loss of these sites, urban communities could discuss their shared heritage as a way to think about which neighborhoods should be protected and which relocated and what loss of those neighborhoods would mean. Or, just as a Talanoa Dialogue asks people to reflect on what they want for the future of their community, people in an urban neighborhood could be asked to think about how they want to relocate in a way that preserves their heritage.

Some efforts are already being made to translate these tools from site-based heritage to larger questions of culture and adaptation. The Florida Public Archaeology Network, for example, has begun holding conversations similar to those of SCAPE in communities in Florida. In the adaptation and disaster risk reduction field, "photovoice"—a practice in which stakeholders are asked to take photographs and are then interviewed about their meaning—is gaining traction as a way to help people reflect on their values and to help decision makers understand stakeholder preferences. [32] Many practitioners in many fields are looking for ways to engage in difficult but productive conversations, and the approaches developed by heritage practitioners are worth exploring to see how well they can be translated into the urban adaptation context.

Another lesson that heritage practitioners may be able to offer climate adaptation is to help people think creatively about new ways to understand the meaning of "place" and "community." Does preserving a community mean preserving every building? Does it mean living on the land, or could it involve a broader set of uses: visiting, hunting, having celebrations with past neighbors? Some tangible heritage retains meaning separate from its physical location. For example, the parlor of Appomattox Court House will still be the room in which the American Civil War came to an end, regardless of whether the Court House itself remains in the same place. But—hypothetically speaking—the Statue of Liberty would lose some of its context in relation to Ellis Island and the New York Harbor if either the statue or the structures at Ellis Island were moved. While some heritage sites may lose or change meaning when they are relocated, in some cases relocation may be necessary and can become part of the longer story of heritage. For example, the Cape Hatteras Lighthouse was famously relocated away from its original site; the lighthouse has taken on new meaning as an example of coastal retreat, and the relocation process itself has become part of the building's heritage. Heritage designation and regulations often prevent relocation, based on the assumption that relocation would reduce significance, but this may need to be reconsidered in light of climate change, and heritage regulations may require greater flexibility in thinking about how meaning changes with location.

At first glance, it may appear that intangible heritage is easier to relocate, but cultural practices and values are often tied to specific locations and place-based activities, which can make relocation difficult. Difficult, but not impossible. Communities that retreat from climate-related hazards are already engaged in maintaining their values, practices, and heritage separate from their original physical location. For example, more than twelve thousand Marshall Islands citizens live in northwest Arkansas and nearby US states. For a community with a strong connection to the ocean, living in a landlocked state presents significant threats to their heritage, but they are finding ways to preserve language, dances, and foods. 33 If Marshall Islands citizens continue to move to the United States, future conversations that explicitly address heritage and its preservation could identify ways that the US government and other organizations can support them in continuing these elements of their heritage.

Similarly, people who evacuated New Orleans after Hurricane Katrina often felt displaced in their new homes in faraway cities, cut off from their cultural practices. Many found that food was a way to maintain identity and community in their new cities. Eating red beans and rice "was affirming," wrote one former New Orleans resident, "because it meant that not all had been lost… Through food, a part of the Orleanian culture could still be maintained. There is a kind of security you get from food beyond having your stomach full. Having a food tradition is part and parcel of one's culture."34 Conversations that engaged heritage practitioners, adaptation and emergency response practitioners, and experts in the food industry could imagine creative ways to support future disaster evacuees and migrants—to help them maintain cultural ties and practices even in new locations.

As we consider how to maintain heritage through relocation, we

Martinich, James Neumann, Lindsay Ludwig, and Lesley Jantarasami, "Risks of Sea Level Rise to Disadvantaged Communities in the United States," *Mitigation and Adaptation Strategies for Global Change* 18 (2013): 169–185, https://doi.org/10.1007/s11027-011-9356-0; Thomas Thaler, Andreas Zischg, Margreth Keiler, and Sven Fuchs, "Allocation of Risk and Benefits—Distributional Justices in Mountain Hazard Management," *Regional Environmental Change* 18, no. 2 (2018): 353–365, https://doi.org/10.1007/s10113-017-1229-y; J. A. G. Cooper and J. McKenna, "Social Justice in Coastal Erosion Management: The Temporal and Spatial Dimensions," *Geoforum* 39, no. 1 (2008): 294–306, https://doi.org/10.1016/j.geoforum.2007.06.007.

28
Dawson et al., "Coastal Heritage, Global Climate Change, Public Engagement, and Citizen Science."

29
Erin Seekamp and Malorey Henderson, *Informing Plans for Managing Resources of Cape Lookout National Seashore under Projected Climate Change, Sea Level Rise, and Associated Impacts: Community Member Interviews Report,* Tourism Extension Report Series 2017-CALO-001 (Raleigh, NC: Department of Parks, Recreation, and Tourism Management, College of Natural Resources, North Carolina State University, 2017).

30
Tom Dawson, Joanna Hambly, William Lees, and Sarah Miller, *Proposed Policy Guidelines for Managing Heritage at Risk Based on Public Engagement and Communicating Climate Change, The Historic Environment: Policy & Practice* (2021), doi: 10.1080/17567505.2021.1963573.

31
UNFCCC, "2018 Talanoa Dialogue Platform," UN Framework Convention on Climate Change, 2018.

32
Ronald L. Schumann, Sherri Brokopp Binder, and Alex Greer, "Unseen Potential: Photovoice Methods in Hazard and Disaster Science," *GeoJournal* 84, no. 1 (2019): 273–289, https://doi.org/10.1007/s10708-017-9825-4.

33
Bret Schulte, "For Pacific Islanders, Hopes and Troubles in Arkansas," *New York Times*, July 5, 2012, https://www.nytimes.com/2012/07/05/us/for-marshall-islanders-hopes-and-troubles-in-arkansas.html.

34
Olga Bonfiglio, "Mardi Gras Reflection: Food's Impact on Rebuilding New Orleans," *Resilience*, March 8, 2011, https://www.resilience.org/stories/2011-03-08/mardi-gras-reflection-food%E2%80%99s-impact-new-orleans.

35
Berenfeld, "Planning for Permanent Emergency."

36
Organisation for Economic Cooperation and Development (OECD), Nuclear Energy Agency (NEA), Records, Knowledge, and Memory (RK&M), "Preservation of Records, Knowledge, and Memory across Generations: Markers—Reflections on Intergenerational Warnings in the Form of Japanese Tsunami Stones," 2014, https://www.oecd-nea.org/jcms/pl_19476/markers-reflections-on-intergenerational-warnings-in-the-form-of-the-japanese-tsunami-stones.

37
OECD, NEA, RK&M, "Preservation of Records, Knowledge, and Memory across Generations."

38
A. R. Siders, "Art and Science in the Netherlands' Watersnood Museum," *Europe Up Close* (January 2017), https://europeupclose.com/article/watersnood-museum-netherlands.

may also need to think about the role and impact of creating new heritage. Change is an invitation to be creative, to find ways to create "a future history of that doomed place," as Michelle Berenfeld puts it. [35] Such interpretive histories will make the changes being wrought by climate change visible and understandable to current and future peoples. Provincetown, Massachusetts, placed historic markers on houses that were relocated from their original site on Long Point in the 1850s. In the Japanese village of Aneyoshi, a tsunami stone reads: "High dwellings ensure the peace and happiness of our descendants. Remember the calamity of the great tsunami. Do not build any homes below this point." [36] Learning from their ancestors, residents did not build below the marked line, and were unharmed when the 2011 tsunami struck the coast. More than 317 tsunami stones have been erected across Japan following historic tsunamis. The markers not only serve as physical reminders but have promoted oral histories and formal education about tsunamis and how to prepare and respond safely. [37] In the Netherlands, the Watersnoodmuseum was created to memorialize the 1953 flood that inspired a national water management program. Museum curators have designed the space not only to preserve stories, artifacts, and structures but also to teach new generations about the risks facing their nation and the need for active flood management. [38] Cultural practices can also create new heritage. The NPS and Friends of Portsmouth Island hold a biannual homecoming in Portsmouth Village, North Carolina, a village that was abandoned due to storms and coastal erosion and is now a park, to maintain community. [39]

We must be conscious, however, of how we shape emerging heritage sites. In San Antonio, Texas, for example, a memorial plaque was placed prominently at the entrance to the football stadium that was built on land acquired after major floods destroyed homes in the area. The plaque memorializes the flood and provides a hopeful message, noting that "Community Leaders saw this as an opportunity to turn the devastation brought on by the flood into a rebirth of a community," but fails to mention that the flood displaced the only African American neighborhood in San Antonio, choosing to present a forward-looking narrative rather than memorialize the specific heritage that was lost. [40] As climate change and climate adaptation decisions destroy towns, change their ways of life, and inspire new buildings, heritage and adaptation practitioners have a responsibility to think carefully about the narratives they are privileging and preserving.

Site-based heritage managers have been thinking about creative ways to preserve spaces that cannot be saved, and some of these lessons may be useful for urban planners and adaptation practitioners to consider. The Scotland Coastal Heritage at Risk Project (SCHARP), a project of SCAPE, supported fourteen community-led projects to explore, interpret, or preserve archaeological sites. Efforts included use of digital recordings and creation of 3D models to document sites. [41] Use of 3D models has grown in recent years as an approach to document historic sites and to disseminate them to a wide audience. [42] Even video games have been used to preserve sites and enable exploration. [43] Currently, due to issues of long-term digital file stability and accessibility, 3D models and recording are not recommended as a primary means of preserving heritage in perpetuity. [44]

However, when used in combination with more traditional methods, such as hard copy drawings, field notes, and photographs, 3D methods can be powerful and engaging tools. How could these be translated to urban spaces? Neighborhoods slated for destruction or abandonment could be documented and oral histories collected. Digital models of neighborhoods, towns, or the natural land could be collected and linked to photographs, maps, and other documents. What steps should we take now to ensure that the history of a place can be maintained after the place is gone?

To think back to Ellicott City, Maryland, where residents were fiercely divided about the plan to remove historic buildings: Would residents feel more willing to let go of the physical buildings if records about those buildings were created, preserved, and displayed somewhere else? Would it ease the pain of those who have decided to leave? Heritage and adaptation practitioners should work together to explore new tools for documenting soon-to-be-lost places and helping citizens grieve the loss or carry elements of the heritage with them to new places or use them in new ways. Creative strategies like this move beyond recognition that "heritage matters" for adaptation or that climate change will affect heritage. Rather, they provide a space for truly integrated conversations to help both heritage management and adaptation practice.

If we cannot stay here, and we cannot stay as we are, what are the most important things to carry with us into the future? What kind of future do we want to create? Climate change is challenging more and more people and communities with these questions, and heritage can and should play a central role in answering them. Heritage managers and adaptation practitioners are recognizing that their spheres—which once seemed so separate—are intimately intertwined. It is not enough, though, for these fields to recognize each other. Rather, they both need to creatively integrate one another and navigate the complexities and possibilities inherent in the process.

Heritage is an important aspect of who we are, what we value, and what we want to preserve and create for the future. It is an anchor that can help ground us, but we must be sure that it is indeed grounding us and giving us room to explore and create rather than holding us in place. Ultimately, it should be a source of hope and a way to connect us and our lives not only with the past but also with the future.

39
National Park Service, "Portsmouth Homecoming," 2019, https://www.nps.gov/calo/planyourvisit/pvhomecoming.htm.

40
Elyse Zavar, "An Analysis of Floodplain Buyout Memorials: Four Examples from Central U.S. Floods of 1993–1998," GeoJournal 84, no. 1 (2019): 135–146, https://doi.org/10.1007/s10708-018-9855-6.

41
Tom Dawson, "Taking the Middle Path to the Coast: How Community Collaboration Can Help Save Threatened Sites," in The Future of Heritage as Climates Change: Loss, Adaptation and Creativity, ed. D. C. Harvey and J. Perry (New York: Routledge, 2015), 248–267.

42
Roberto Scopigno et al., "3D Models for Cultural Heritage: Beyond Plain Visualization," Computer 44, no. 7 (2011): 48–55, https://doi.org/10.1109/MC.2011.196; Alberto Guarnieri, Francesco Pirotti, and Antonio Vettore, "Cultural Heritage Interactive 3D Models on the Web: An Approach Using Open Source and Free Software," Journal of Cultural Heritage 11, no. 3 (2010): 350–353, https://doi.org/10.1016/j.culher.2009.11.011.

43
Helena Rua and Pedro Alvito, "Living the Past: 3D Models, Virtual Reality and Game Engines as Tools for Supporting Archaeology and the Reconstruction of Cultural Heritage— The Case-Study of the Roman Villa of Casal de Freiria," Journal of Archaeological Science 38, no. 12 (2011): 3296–3308, https://doi.org/10.1016/j.jas.2011.07.015.

44
See, e.g., National Park Service, "Producing HABS/HAER/HALS Measured Drawings from Laser Scans: The Pros and Cons of Using Laser Scanning for Heritage Documentation," n.d., https://www.nps.gov/hdp/standards/laser.htm.

New Residents, New Heritage, New Policy:
Planning for Climate Change Displacement, Migration,
and Emplacement into America's Cities

Victoria Herrmann

Confronting Adaptation and Relocation

Climate change and the extreme weather events it intensifies are (and will continue to be) the largest catalyst for migration worldwide and pose the biggest threat to displacing cultural communities—groups constituted by socially cohesive, communal identities.[1] The Internal Displacement Monitoring Center estimates that the number of new displacements associated with weather events in 2019 will ultimately amount to twenty-two million, making it the worst year for weather-related disaster displacement since records began.[2] The United States is not immune to climate-induced displacement of cultural communities. According to the 2019 "Global Report on Internal Displacement," "almost 10 per cent of all disaster-related displacement in 2018 occurred in the United States."[3] No matter what corner of this country one calls home, whether it be the coast, the mountains, the Great Lakes, or the Great Plains, climate change is already causing billions of dollars in damages and irreplaceable cultural loss. Ninety-six percent of Americans live in counties that have been hit by a climate change-induced major weather event in the last five years.[4] In 2017 Hurricane Harvey made landfall as a category 4 hurricane near Rockport, Texas, dumping more than 30 inches of rain on 6.9 million people.[5] This historic US rainfall displaced more than thirty thousand people and damaged more than two hundred thousand homes and businesses.[6] In 2018 California experienced its costliest, deadliest, and largest wildfires to date, costing $25.4 billion in damages and leading to thousands of displaced households.[7] And in 2019 historic Midwest inland flooding inundated millions of acres of agriculture, cities, and towns and caused widespread damage to infrastructure.

Sudden-onset disasters like wildfires and hurricanes, along with slow-onset events like erosion, subsidence, and desertification, are already causing displacement and urban migration across the United States and US territories. In the past three years, the United States has witnessed the displacement of more than three million people as a result of extreme weather events. Each of these affected towns, communities, neighborhoods, and individuals hold their own histories, traditions, landscapes, and cultural practices, which are at risk of climate impacts. While most research, planning, and discussion of migration attributable to climate change and storms focuses on displaced coastal communities and human security in the immediate aftermath of a storm, migration is a long, two-way street. As at-risk coastal and wildfire-country residents retreat inland for safety, families often migrate to nearby cities, with their concentrated resources and economic activity. In the aftermath of Hurricane Katrina in 2005, researchers found that families displaced by the hurricane moved to nearby major regional cities, including Baton Rouge, Atlanta, and Houston.[8] More recently, Hurricane Maria displaced tens of thousands of Puerto Ricans from their home island to the US mainland, with FEMA reporting that a total of 40,013 household members and 19,271 households have changed their mailing address after the hurricane to the US mainland since they first registered with FEMA.[9] Current research and capacity-building programs on climate-induced migration narrowly focus on residents and infrastructure at risk of being displaced, failing to engage the heritage and histories of urban communities that will receive large influxes of displaced coastal residents. In climate displacement,

1
A. Gutmann, "Multiculturalism and Identity Politics: Cultural Concerns," International Encyclopedia of the Social and Behavioral Sciences (2001), 10175–10179, https://doi.org/10.1016/B0-08-043076-7/04622-2.

2
"Mid-Year Figures Internal Displacement from January to June 2019," Internal Displacement Monitoring Center, September 2019, https://www.internal-displacement.org/sites/default/files/inline-files/2019-mid-year-figures_for%20website%20upload.pdf.

3
"Global Report on Internal Displacement 2019," Internal Displacement Monitoring Center, May 2019, https://www.internal-displacement.org/sites/default/files/publications/documents/2019-ID-MC-GRID.pdf.

4
"Extreme Weather Map," Environment America, 2015, https://environmentamerica.org/page/ame/extreme-weather-map.

5
Paola Rosa-Aquino, "One of the Biggest Climate Threats Is the Most Familiar: Rain," Grist.org, July 18, 2019, https://grist.org/article/rain-hurricane-barry-flooding-climate-change.

6
Doyle Rice, "Supercharged by Global Warming, Record Hot Seawater Fueled Hurricane Harvey," USA Today, May 14, 2018, https://www.usatoday.com/story/news/2018/05/14/hurricane-harvey-record-hot-seawater-global-warming/607715002.

7
Nic Querolo and Brian K. Sullivan, "California Fire Damage Estimated at $25.4 Billion," Bloomberg, October 28, 2019, https://www.bloomberg.com/news/articles/2019-10-28/california-fire-

damages-already-at-25-4-billion-and-counting.

8
William H. Frey and Audrey Singer, *Katrina and Rita Impacts on Gulf Coast Populations: First Census Findings* (Washington, DC: Brookings Institution, Metropolitan Policy Program, 2006), 11, https://www.research-gate.net/profile/Audrey_Singer/publication/252099478_Katrina_and_Rita_Impacts_on_Gulf_Coast_Populations_First_Census_Findings/links/54e619e50cf277664ff2c822.pdf.

9
Jennifer Hinojosa, Nashia Román, and Edwin Meléndez, "Puerto Rican Post-Maria Relocation by State," Center for Puerto Rican Studies, Hunter College, March 2018, https://centropr.hunter.cuny.edu/sites/default/files/PDF/Schoolenroll-v4-27-2018.pdf.

10
Brady R. Couvillion, John A. Barras, Gregory D. Steyer, William Sleavin, Michelle Fischer, Holly Beck, Nadine Trahan, Brad Griffin, and David Heckman, "Land Area Change in Coastal Louisiana from 1932 to 2010" (Reston, VA: US Geological Survey, 2011), https://pubs.usgs.gov/sim/3164/downloads/SIM3164_Pamphlet.pdf.

11
"USGS: Louisiana's Rate of Coastal Wetlands Loss Continues to Slow," US Geological Survey, July 12, 2017, https://www.usgs.gov/news/usgs-louisiana-s-rate-coastal-wetland-loss-continues-slow.

12
"Louisiana's Comprehensive Master Plan for a Sustainable Coast," State of Louisiana, 2017, http://coastal.la.gov/wp-content/uploads/2016/08/2017-MP-Book_2-page-spread_Combined_01.05.2017.pdf.

13
Mathew E. Hauer, Jason M. Evans, and Deepak R. Mishra, "Millions

migration, and emplacement into cities, there is a critical need to better understand whose heritage is privileged in the process and to ask how to facilitate proactive planning of the urban emplacement and empowerment of cultural heritage assets of displaced communities. In what ways can preservation policy be reformed to better promote a just and sustainable built environment for climate migrants?

▶ THE VELOCITIES OF DISASTER DISPLACEMENT

To plan effectively and equitably for the urban migration of individuals, households, and cultural communities displaced by environmental impacts, it is critical to first understand that climate change-induced migration occurs at two velocities: slow and sudden. Slow-onset hazards include land loss, drought, and other changes that do not emerge from a single, distinct event but rather emerge gradually over time and are often based on a confluence of different events. The Gulf Coast, the Chesapeake Bay, and the western coast of Alaska are three North American geographies facing coastal land loss, one form of slow-onset disaster attributable to the cumulative effects of sea level rise, unsustainable land use and human impact, subsidence, and storm surges. These forces, for example, and a disconnection of the Mississippi River from coastal marshes have all contributed to some of the most dramatic land loss in America over the past eighty years. Between 1932 and 2010, Louisiana's coast lost more than 1,800 square miles of land. From 2004 through 2008 alone, more than 300 square miles of marshland were lost to Hurricanes Katrina, Rita, Gustav, and Ike. [10] According to a 2017 analysis of Louisiana's changing coastal wetlands, "while land loss rate is not a constant, this equates to losing an average of an American football field's worth of coastal wetlands in 34 minutes when losses were rapid, or in 100 minutes at more recent rates."[11] This trend of land loss is poised only to worsen as greenhouse gas emissions exacerbate extreme weather events and accelerate sea level rise. If business-as-usual projections continue, Louisiana's Terrebonne and Lafourche Parishes will each lose 41 percent of their land areas over the next fifty years. [12] By the end of this century, at least 1.29 million coastal Louisianans will be at risk of displacement. [13]

Statewide plans like Louisiana's Strategic Adaptations for Future Environments (LASAFE), launched in 2019 to address these 1.29 million future displacements, are focused on a proactive, inclusive, and holistic approach to managing displacement, migration, and relocation. One of the plan's primary goals is to "establish a framework for preparing Louisiana's coastal areas to adapt to 50-year projections of land loss."[14] In planning for a slow-onset displacement, LASAFE's "envisioned outcome is a systems-based approach to community-led planning and group migration. It is a small-scale, targeted strategy for culturally sensitive, at-risk communities and special needs groups, including the disabled, the elderly, disaffected minority groups, and very low-income populations."[15] The LASAFE plan also aims to be culturally sensitive by acknowledging that cultural communities, and in particular Indigenous communities, require special recognition within a multicultural community that may take the form of rights of self-governance for the group. 16 Isle de Jean Charles, Louisiana, is one case study within LASAFE that endeavors to create a framework for wholesale community relocation—an adaptation strategy also pursued in Alaska as riverine and coastal Native villages are being forcibly displaced by erosion. Slow-onset disasters allow for the possibility of proactive relocation, although such relocation is all too often limited by governance issues of funding. 17

When a sudden-onset disaster occurs, governments at the local, state, and national level operate under a different set of limitations and parameters that are frequently driven by reactive decision-making. A sudden-onset disaster is one triggered by a hazardous event that occurs quickly and unexpectedly. 18 Flooding, wildfires, and extreme weather events like hurricanes are all examples of sudden-onset disasters being made more frequent and intense by a warming world. Sudden climate-related disasters displace residents quickly, and oftentimes decisions are made to evacuate and move temporarily to a safer location at the individual or the household level. It is these displacements, both temporary and permanent, that comprise the majority of climate migrants in the United States and US territories. Flooding of the Missouri and the Mississippi Rivers from March to July 2019, wildfires in California in 2018, and the combination of Hurricanes Maria, Harvey, and Irma in the Caribbean and on the Gulf Coast in 2017 have been the primary drivers of displacement in the United States over the past five years.

Nonetheless, slow-onset and sudden-onset events do not exist independently of one another. Slow and sudden disasters can intersect and amplify each other and contribute to the risk of displacement in four key ways, as outlined by Andrej Přívara and Magdaléna Přívarová:

(1) through diminished ecosystem services, including access to basic human needs such as fresh water, food, energy production, shelter, and those that are necessary for human beings. The lack of vital resources may cause the severe turmoil of livelihoods. In case this turmoil of livelihoods crushes the community's capability to handle the hazards, the situation becomes a disaster and displacement risks become more serious. Slow-onset hazards may, for instance, in combination with other factors, cause critical food insecurity as their effects on food production affect naturally based livelihoods, because they are based on agriculture, fisheries, hunter gathering, pastoralism, or horticulture livelihoods. When communities are not able to handle severe food insecurity, they can be displaced to survive in other locations that suggest food security; (2) by becoming a disaster provoked by the sudden-onset event. Numerous slow-onset events are in fact sudden-onset events. For instance, when the sea level rises quickly and this turns into flooding, desertification becomes a wildfire, or temperature rises turn into heat waves. In these cases, sudden-onset events may exacerbate the risk of displacement; (3) by deteriorating community's and ecosystem's readiness to resist the impacts of sudden- and slow-onset events if caused by a cascade of hazards, provoking displacement. If livelihoods do not recover after a disaster, either prompted by a slow or a sudden-onset event,

Projected to Be at Risk from Sea-Level Rise in the Continental United States," *Nature Climate Change* 6, no. 7 (2016): 691–695.

14 "Louisiana's Comprehensive Master Plan for a Sustainable Coast."

15 "Louisiana's Comprehensive Master Plan for a Sustainable Coast."

16 Gutmann, "Multiculturalism and Identity Politics."

17 Adapt Alaska, "Relocation Challenges across Alaska," 2020, https://adaptalaska. org/case-study/ relocation-challenges-across-alaska.

18 UN Office for Disaster Risk Reduction, "Terminology: Disaster," 2020, https://www. undrr.org/terminology/ disaster.

19
Andrej Přívara and Magdaléna Přívarová, "Nexus between Climate Change, Displacement, and Conflict: Afghanistan Case," *Sustainability* 11, no. 20 (October 2019): 5586.

20
Minority Rights Group International, "No Escape from Discrimination: Minorities, Indigenous Peoples, and the Crisis of Displacement," 2017, https://reliefweb. int/sites/reliefweb. int/files/resources/ MRG_Displacement_ Report_Dec17.pdf.

21
United Nations, "2018 Revision of World Urbanization Prospects," 2018, https://www. population.un.org/wup.

22
United Nations, "2018 Revision of World Urbanization Prospects."

even if less stressful, this can push households into a situation of critical humanitarian need; (4) furthermore, slow-onset events are frequently a hidden provoking factor in many contexts, operating as a hazard multiplier for other determinants of crisis such as economic, social, political, and cultural factors.[19]

When the next large-scale extreme storm, flood, or fire hits, at-risk US residents will be forced to move. While a handful of communities will be able to accrue adequate resources and time for a fully planned, community-managed retreat, most will be displaced without knowing where their next home will be. And as families face the physical, mental, and spiritual health challenges of dislocation and seek new homes on safer ground, they are often forced to leave culturally important places, landscapes, traditions, and histories behind. These stressors hold the very real potential to exacerbate economic and racial tensions in receiving communities, resulting in discrimination and potential violence. "Climate-change-induced migration frequently exacerbates existing patterns of discrimination," argues Minority Rights Group International, and "most migrants displaced by environmental crises move to areas where there are already well- established communities, which in turn can expose them to discrimination and lead to conflict."[20] Preserving, empowering, and including cultural heritage as a keystone of resilience in sudden-onset disaster migration and resettlement is an important yet underresearched component of climate migration planning for American cities.

▶ PLANNING FOR MIGRATION OF CULTURAL COMMUNITIES INTO CITIES

Urbanization has been a dominant global demographic trend of the twentieth century and continues to guide migration routes in the twenty-first. More than half of the world's population lives in a city, and the world will continue to urbanize, with global urban population reaching 60 percent by 2030 and 75 percent by 2050.[21] In the United States, more than 80 percent of residents are urbanites, a number that is projected to peak at 89 percent in 2045.[22] As areas of concentrated economic activity, cities are where job creation has increased the most. Urban standards of living are comparatively better than rural ones, given that urban areas offer multiple and more readily available forms of public services. In addition, local governments can provide services to the urban population at a relatively lower cost than to the rural population thanks to economies of scale, centralized resources, shared networks, and relatively shorter distances for distribution.

Current data on displacement and migration from hurricanes and other extreme weather events is vital to planning for climate migration, but it is important to acknowledge that current research provides an incomplete picture. Save for ad hoc studies from specific storms, there does not yet exist a comprehensive geographic dataset for the United States concerning internally displaced residents who migrate to urban areas following sudden-onset events like extreme weather. In projecting future movement, most modeling focuses on impacts of sea level rise rather than nonlinear displacement catalyzed by sudden-onset disasters, both along and beyond America's coastlines. Improved data collection, analysis of current internal migrations, and modeling of future movement would help to facilitate proactive planning of the urban emplacement and empowerment of cultural heritage assets of displaced communities.

Nonetheless, even without a precise mapping of migration routes, evidence shows that residents displaced by sudden-onset disasters are more likely to temporarily or permanently migrate to a nearby regional urban area with lower unemployment and higher wages, or to cities where they have a relational connection through family, friends, or cultural community. [23] Depending on the severity of the event, a displacement may impact an individual household, a neighborhood, or an entire county. And although sudden-onset migrants might originate as disaster evacuees, many will become permanent residents as the recovery process extends into months or years and displaced families find employment, education, and other opportunities in new home cities. According to a study conducted by the Urban Institute, "most movers after California's 2015 and 2017 fires had moved to the neighboring counties and were still living there a year after. In contrast, though, a large portion of Puerto Rican migrants following Hurricane Maria were living farther away in Florida."[24] In Texas, one year after Hurricane Harvey, a survey led by the Kaiser Family Foundation and the Episcopal Health Foundation found that 8 percent of displaced Texans had still not returned home, and 15 percent of homes damaged or destroyed in the storm were still uninhabitable. [25] In modeling future US displacement and migration from climate impacts, a time series-based migration model predicts that "inland areas immediately adjacent to the coast, and urban areas in the southeast US will observe the largest effects from SLR [sea level rise] driven migration."[26]

In each of these cases of current and future climate migrations, a myriad of policies must be made to address the basic needs and services migrants require to thrive in a new home city. To promote a just and sustainable built environment for climate migrants in cities, integrated policy and planning adjustments must be made to housing, health services, employment support, and public infrastructure like utilities, water and sanitation, waste, transportation, education, and safety and security.

In parallel to addressing infrastructure and service fundamentals for new residents, migrant community culture, cohesion, and traditions must simultaneously be supported and uplifted. The loss of and damage to cultural heritage that comes from severing a community's attachment to a place-based identity is both emotionally demoralizing in the short term and hinders long-term community recovery and resilience. Severing social cohesion, dislocating local knowledge on how to absorb shock events, and weakening cultural practices like food, faith, and music that play a vital role in building friendships in new hometowns all erode the adaptability of individuals and the social safety net of communities. And climate change is not race, gender, or income neutral. Its impacts disproportionately affect low-income communities, communities of color, and women. [27] Centuries of economic, social, and environmental injustices have made it difficult to secure resources to prepare for and recover from disastrous events.

23
Christopher Wolsko and Elizabeth Marino, "Disasters, Migrations, and the Unintended Consequences of Urbanization: What's the Harm in Getting out of Harm's Way?" Population and Environment 37, no. 4 (2016): 411–428; Jonathan Eyer, Robert Dinterman, Noah Miller, and Adam Rose, "The Effect of Disasters on Migration Destinations: Evidence from Hurricane Katrina," Economics of Disasters and Climate Change 2, no. 1 (2018): 91–106, https://ideas.repec.org/a/spr/ediscc/v2y2018i1d10.1007_s41885-017-0020-3.html.

24
Carlos Martin, "Who Are America's 'Climate Migrants' and Where Will They Go?" Urban Institute, October 22, 2019, https://www.urban.org/urban-wire/who-are-americas-climate-migrants-and-where-will-they-go.

25
Brandon Formby, "Nearly 10 Percent of Texans Displaced by Harvey Still Haven't Gone Home, Survey Says," Texas Tribune, August 23, 2018, https://www.texastribune.org/2018/08/23/fema-and-texas-dont-know-how-many-people-hurricane-harvey-displaced.

26
Caleb Robinson, Bistra Dilkina, and Juan Moreno-Cruz, "Modeling Migration Patterns in the USA under Sea Level Rise," PLoS ONE 15, no. 1 (2020): e0227436.

27
Kimberly Thomas, R. Dean Hardy, Heather Lazrus, Michael Mendez, Ben Orlove, Isabel RiveraCollazo, J. Timmons Roberts, Marcy Rockman, Benjamin P. Warner, and Robert Winthrop, "Explaining Differential Vulnerability to Climate Change: A Social Science Review," Wiley Interdisciplinary Reviews: Climate Change 10, no. 2 (2019): e565.

28
United Nations,
"Approaches to Address
Loss and Damage
Associated with Climate
Change Impacts in
Developing Countries,"
Framework Convention
on Climate Change,
2020, https://unfccc.int/
topics/adaptation-and-
resilience/workstreams/
approaches-to-
address-loss-and-
damage-associated-
with-climate-change-
impacts-in-developing-
countries#eq-2.

In order to facilitate resilient migration, displaced communities' cultural heritage must be empowered at every step of the migration journey. Beginning with the occurrence of the sudden-onset disaster and ending with the emplacement into cities, there are three phases in the displacement cycle paramount to buttressing migrant heritage. These include (1) documentation of cultural heritage damaged or destroyed by the sudden-onset disaster; (2) facilitation of dialogue and bridge building between receiving communities and migrant communities; and (3) funding for physical space to build community, practice traditions, and retain cohesion in urban America. Combined, these three target areas for policy intervention can build community resilience to future shock events to bounce back together as a cultural community.

Documentation of Loss

Climate change loss and damage are traditionally discussed in relation to developing and least-developed nations through international climate negotiations, first codified in the Warsaw International Mechanism for Loss and Damage (2013) and later in the Paris Agreement (2015). Damage occurs when coping or adaptation measures are not effective enough; when the costs of measures are not regained; when measures are helpful in the short term but have adverse long-term consequences; or when no measures are possible to safeguard life, livelihoods, ecosystems, or cultural heritage from climate impacts. The Warsaw Mechanism, though not applicable to communities within the United States as a developed country, offers a foundation upon which cities can plan. In this framework, noneconomic losses include losses that are "additional to the loss of property, assets, infrastructure, agricultural production, and/or revenue that can result from the adverse effects of climate change. It covers loss and damage that are not easily quantifiable in economic terms, such as loss of life, degraded health, losses induced by human mobility, as well as loss or degradation of territory, cultural heritage, indigenous knowledge, societal/cultural identity biodiversity, and ecosystem services."[28]

To date, no US city's climate change plan includes the allocation of resources for noneconomic loss and damage of climate migrants moving to urban areas. But in every corner of the United States, communities are making difficult decisions on what will be lost, adapted, and relocated as climate change impacts trigger displacement, migration, and emplacement into cities. City climate change policies can allocate resources to document with dignity the historic sites, traditions, and cultural assets damaged or left behind by newly arrived climate migrants. This can take the form of small to medium grants to displaced neighborhood and community museums, nonprofit groups, universities, and art centers in cities for the documentation of cultural assets.

City and state governments receiving climate migrants could support documentation of loss and damage by funding programs within their own budgets and government offices, or fund nongovernmental programs that are already focused on cultural heritage documentation and rescue. Furthermore, city-to-city or state-to-state funds that include both states experiencing climate displacement and states receiving climate migrants could augment these programs and hold the potential to leverage federal funding. If pursuing the former, city governments could empower cultural heritage, cultural affairs, and historic preservation offices to provide such support at the state and local level through specific climate documentation grant schemes for new residents. If pursuing the latter option, local governments could partner with nongovernmental programs like the Smithsonian Cultural Rescue Initiative to support disaster recovery of cultural heritage. The Smithsonian Institution, in partnership with the Federal Emergency Management Agency and forty-two national service organizations, runs the Heritage Emergency National Task Force, which responds to natural disasters to protect cultural heritage in US states, territories, and local communities, and on tribal lands. [29] With either option—relying on internal capacity within the receiving city or state, or relying on external capability beyond the receiving geography—such a low-cost migrant heritage grant program embedded within climate change policy creates a number of co-benefits beyond the preservation of important cultural practices and assets of migrants. The creation of oral histories, exhibits, and other forms of documentation can simultaneously educate on climate change, build social connections between city institutions and migrants, and foster a sense of inclusivity and belonging in migrants' new homes.

Dialogue and Bridge Building between Communities

Effective migration and urban emplacement require a participatory planning process inclusive of both displaced and receiving communities. As residents at risk of or already impacted by extreme storms, flooding, wildfires, and land loss retreat to safer cities, there exists a wide variation in both migrants' perception of their new home cities and receiving residents' perceptions of migrants. For example, community survey research on displacement and urban emplacement from Hurricane Katrina in Louisiana and neighboring states in 2005 reveals that some displaced families found comfort in their new hometowns: "The evidence suggests that those who moved may be better off in terms of neighborhood satisfaction than those who stayed. Survey respondents who had moved were significantly more likely to report being very satisfied with their new neighborhood, compared with those who had stayed where they were in 2005."[30] Cities receiving displaced households have, at first, appeared warm and welcoming to migrating communities; this is particularly true in the immediate aftermath of a sudden-onset disaster like Hurricane Katrina or Hurricane Maria, when mayors and governors provided communities with the tools needed for recovery and relocation.[31] Nonetheless, receiving climate migrants is a complex sociocultural process that does not exist in a vacuum. Racism and discrimination, sometimes deeply rooted in violent histories, are a very tangible feature of community displacement, migration, and relocation into cities. One study of Hurricane Katrina evacuees from New Orleans to Houston showed hostility and racism toward people displaced by the storm. Five years after the hurricane, former Houston mayor Annise Parker reflected on the stress of accommodating thousands of new residents, which forced overcrowding in schools and a feeling among impoverished communities in Houston that evacuees "cut in line," recalling that "there was a perception of an increase in crime

29
"Heritage Emergency National Task Force," Smithsonian Institution, https://culturalrescue.si.edu/hentf.

30
Jennifer Turnham, Kimberly Burnett, Carlos Martin, Tom McCall, Randall Juras, and Jonathan Spader, "Housing Recovery on the Gulf Coast, Phase II: Results of Property Owner Survey in Louisiana, Mississippi, and Texas" (Washington, DC: US Department of Housing and Urban Development, Office of Policy Development and Research, 2011), https://docplayer.net/11753012-On-the-gulf-coast-phase-ii.html.

31
Bill White, "Mayor Welcomes Katrina Survivors," *Houston Chronicle*, September 7, 2005, https://www.chron.com/news/hurricanes/article/Mayor-welcomes-Katrina-survivors-1938718.php; Monivette Cordeiro, "Rick Scott Opens Relief Centers for Puerto Rico Evacuees as Democrats Push Further Action," *Orlando Weekly*, October 3, 2017, https://www.orlandoweekly.com/Blogs/archives/2017/10/03/rick-scott-opens-relief-centers-for-puerto-rico-evacuees-as-democrats-push-further-action.

32
White, "Mayor Welcomes Katrina Survivors."

33
Elizabeth Fussell,
Narayan Sastry, and
Mark VanLandingham,
"Race, Socioeconomic
Status, and Return
Migration to New
Orleans after Hurricane
Katrina," *Population
and Environment* 31,
no. 1–3 (2010): 20–42;
Lynn Weber and Lori A.
Peek, *Displaced: Life
in the Katrina Diaspora*
(Austin: University of
Texas Press, 2012).

34
Sophie Kasakove, "This
Is How the Climate
Crisis Wipes an
American Community
off the Map," *Vice*,
November 14, 2019,
https://www.vice.com/
en_us/article/mbmdzb/
this-is-how-the-climate-
crisis-wipes-an-
american-community-
off-the-map.

35
Carolina Scaramutti,
Christopher P. Salas-
Wright, Saskia R. Vos,
and Seth J. Schwartz,
"The Mental Health
Impact of Hurricane
Maria on Puerto
Ricans in Puerto Rico
and Florida," *Disaster
Medicine and Public
Health Preparedness*
13, no. 1 (2019): 24–27.

36
Weber and Peek,
Displaced.

37
Susan Sterett, *Disaster
and Sociolegal Studies*
(New Orleans: Quid Pro
Books, 2013).

38
Sterett, *Disaster and
Sociolegal Studies*, 33.

and a big increase in homicides among evacuees."[32] Displaced residents who had moved to Houston and other regional cities faced racial slurs, discrimination from private citizens offering assistance, and a higher rate of refusal by leasing agents to accept federal funding for recovery. [33]

Receiving cities, even those within the same state or region, have different economic, social, and demographic characteristics than displaced communities, which are oftentimes more coastal and rural. The community of Pecan Acres in Louisiana, a state where nearly two million coastal residents are threatened by land loss, offers a microcosm of these tensions between displaced and receiving communities. In 2018 residents of Pecan Acres, a predominantly low-income, elderly, and historically Black community that has endured severe repeat flooding, experienced pushback from white neighbors over a relocation site closer to the majority white neighborhood. The forty-home community, informally named "Flood City," received relief after years of loss and rebuilding in 2017 with an announced community buyout by the US Department of Agriculture's Natural Resources Conservation Service. At the end of 2019, Pecan Acres residents were still struggling to relocate to safer homes—a struggle attributable in part to racial and economic anxieties. As noted in a news interview with a Pecan Acres resident, "We basically felt that they didn't want us there. They felt as though, yeah we may have needed help, but we weren't good enough to be there." Other residents cited white city council members in New Roads—"who saw the demographic shift resulting from the relocation as a threat to their reelection bids"—as challengers to the relocation of households. [34]

Even in receiving cities that report an initial warm response to displacement, a welcoming immediate recovery can give way to long-term underpreparation and difficulty in establishing long-term resilience on the part of the receiving cities. A 2018 University of Miami study of Puerto Rican residents displaced to Florida after Hurricane Maria found that survey participants in central Florida cities like Orlando had a harder time finding jobs, housing, and transportation and felt less welcome than those who moved to Miami and surrounding areas. [35] This is perhaps, in part, because sudden-onset disasters are perceived as temporary phenomena wherein a receiving community expects the displaced to integrate or to move back home quickly. In the year following Hurricane Katrina, residents of receiving communities assumed it would not take long for displaced households to recover and either return to New Orleans or become self-sufficient. When this did not happen, the receiving community's compassion for those displaced dissipated. [36] Though disaster evacuees may have initially been perceived as victims worthy of assistance, as temporary migrants become long-term, permanent residents, migrants are then perceived as outside competitors for jobs, social services, and housing and an unwelcome force of racial, cultural, and economic change in the receiving community. [37]

It is a foreseeable challenge that "environmental displacement increases the demand for services, infrastructure, and resources in the host community, which leads to resentment and hostility against displaced populations."[38] Therefore, for potential receiving cities to effectively plan for climate change and climate-induced migration, it is essential that policies and city budgets not only bolster available housing, social services, and utility resources but also address potential resentment of and hostility to displaced populations. A series of resilience dialogues can bring together displaced and receiving city government officials, local urban civil society leaders, neighborhood champions, and coastal or fire-country community leaders. In doing so, dialogues can build bridges to mitigate suspicions around migrants and help determine shared goals and potential collaborative projects that enhance the resilience of inter-dependent systems, including systems that protect the health, safety, and well-being of city residents.

The establishment of committed predisaster forums like dedicated climate town halls to discuss displacement, migration, and emplacement for city neighborhood leaders and displaced community leaders is a straight-forward first step in bolstering resilient climate migration. Partnering with already proven dialogue frameworks like the federal US Global Change Research Program's "Resilience Dialogues" to pilot conversations in cities within regions of high climate displacement vulnerabilities—namely, California; Louisiana, Texas, and Georgia; Florida and the US Caribbean territories; and Alaska—is a low-cost option to jump-start the inclusion of climate migration and cultural heritage into city policy. 39 Using a partici-patory action approach, these pilot programs can help to define a replicable and scalable framework for a displaced-receiving community migration dialogue that is effective, co-community designed, and guided by nonpar-tisan moderators. The engagement of community stakeholders; adaptation, planning, and disaster management practitioners; and researchers from the natural, social, and health sciences is key to the success of this project. Climate- and disaster-induced migration is a cross-sectoral challenge. A successful dialogue between displaced and receiving communities requires engaged participants from a diverse array of disciplines, communities, and professions in order to ensure the safe, empathetic, and successful retreat of coastal residents to inland towns and cities.

Such climate migration-specific dialogue programs can borrow from already existing immigration civil society actors who have already-established place-based integration strategies, and such programs may include migrant organizations and communities, charities, foundations, and NGOs operating in this area. 40 One example is Welcoming America, a national nonprofit organization that works with local leaders to create more inclusive communities for immigrants. Their series "Building Cohesive Communities in an Era of Migration and Change" addresses the importance of cultivating a sense of belonging and connection among residents by building trust as well as people-to-people connections. Welcoming America highlights the benefits of building bridges through structured, funded dialogue events:

> Convening people from different walks of life who share an interest in advancing a living wage, securing good childcare, improving local schools, or tackling an environmental problem provides an opportunity to work together in common cause… Well-designed dialogues and contact-building activities that bring people together across race, ethnicity, and immigration background continue to hold

39
"Resilience Dialogues," US Global Change Program, http://www. resiliencedialogues.org.

40
Organization for Economic Cooperation and Development (OECD), "Block 2. Time and Space: Keys for Migrants and Host Communities to Live Together," in Working Together for Local Integration of Migrants and Refugees (Paris: OECD Publishing, 2018), https://doi.org/10.1787/9789264085350-9-en.

41
Susan Downs-Karkos and Rachel Peric, "Building Cohesive Communities in an Era of Migration and Change," Welcoming America, February 2019, https://www.welcomingamerica.org/wp-content/uploads/2021/06/Building-Cohesive-Communities_FINAL.pdf.

42
"Building Meaningful Contact: A How-To Guide," Welcoming America and Welcoming Michigan, May 8, 2018, https://www.welcomingamerica.org/wp-content/uploads/2021/01/ContactGuide_FINAL_web.pdf.

43
OECD, "Time and Space."

44
Danielle Baussan, "Social Cohesion: The Secret Weapon in the Fight for Equitable Climate Resilience," Center for American Progress, May 2015, https://cdn.americanprogress.org/wp-content/uploads/2015/05/Social Cohesion-report-summary.pdf.

45
OECD, "Time and Space."

promise, though making sure these groups truly reflect the diversity of the community takes serious intentionality and extra time. 41

The tool kits offered by social cohesion dialogues, found in documents like "Building Meaningful Contact: A How-To Guide," which Welcoming America and Welcoming Michigan used in Macomb County, Michigan, offer tested methodologies that can be adapted to climate migration dialogues. 42

Creation of Physical Space for Cultural Heritage

As migrants adopt new home neighborhoods in receiving cities, it is critical to simultaneously build connections to new neighbors through resilient integration and strengthen social ties within their displaced community. In addition to targeting socioeconomic and racial discrimination, receiving urban areas must also find ways to uplift and preserve the cultural heritage, identity, and living traditions of climate migrants. Current national policies and programs like those administered by FEMA that support disaster displacements and hazard-induced buyouts do not aim to maintain the social and economic cohesion of communities. The focus on individual household and business support from the federal government leaves a policy opening for city and municipal governments to invest politically and financially in communities and their social cohesion—defined by Danielle Baussan as "the capacity of a society to ensure the well-being of all its members by creating a sense of belonging, promoting trust, working to eliminate disparities and promote equity, and avoiding exclusion and marginalization, fostering opportunity for all."43 Social cohesion has been identified as a critical component of resilient emplacement and recovery from displacement in postdisaster studies of Hurricane Sandy, Hurricane Katrina, and California wildfires like the 2018 Camp Fire. A 2015 white paper published by the Center for American Progress noted that social cohesion was "the secret weapon in the fight for equitable climate resilience."44

One pathway to supporting social resilience is to invest in access to indoor and outdoor public spaces. The spatial dimension of climate emplacement into new cities is multidimensional and includes connections to both a new place-based identity and retention of an existing community. As such:

> Active participation of migrants is sought not only through labor inclusion but also by expanding the spaces for their contribution to local public life. In this sense municipalities create partnerships with civil society, migrant associations, and the third-sector to organize spaces (public libraries, schools and preschools, theaters, squares, recreational centers, etc.) and activities (festival, cultural events, awards, etc.) for developing common interests, engaging in local causes, exchanging skills, and building social networks. Fostering collective experiences and social mixing, combined with local leaders' communication around integration, influence the perception of host and migrant communities and helps knock down trust barriers. 45

Having affordable and easily accessible physical space to practice traditions as a group and to sustain the social cohesion of a displaced community is essential for resilient emplacement. Ensuring climate migrants have space to dance, garden, sing, play music, weave, or offer youth culture camps to teach traditions is critical to the resilience of displaced populations. Rooms, centers, or parks designated for the continuation of community cultural practices sustain social cohesion from displaced neighborhoods, towns, and villages. These networks are critical for migrants in times of shock—climate-induced disaster or otherwise—for health, social, and economic support. Unlike the documentation of cultural loss and damage that may frame culture as static, communities and their heritage are constantly changing. Creating or opening already existing public space to the practice and sharing of cultural traditions complements documentation of lost heritage by supporting dynamic, living heritage.

Supporting migrant access and feelings of co-ownership over public space engages many departments and agencies within a city government, including but not limited to the department of planning, the department of parks and recreation, the department of transportation, the department of cultural affairs, and the public library, among others. Similar to their functions for refugees and recent immigrants, public spaces offer those displaced by climate emergencies "a source of stability and social interaction... where healing and connection often happen."[46] Here, too, city leadership can take advantage of already tested approaches using public space to support climate migrants and build social resilience. In Amsterdam, the city government converted an empty prison into a creative cultural hub, Lola Lik, which offers community space for art studios, offices, language schools, and start-ups. As a prerequisite for renting a spot at Lola Lik, applicants must demonstrate the contribution they will make to refugees in the surrounding neighborhood to cultivate social cohesion.[47] The Little Haiti garden in Miami is another example of elevating public space for use and ownership by migrant communities. In a communal plot of land, Miami's Haitian community practices traditional farming techniques for plants like callaloos and calabaza while simultaneously improving food security.[48]

▶ CONCLUSION

The proposed approaches outlined here are not blue-sky projects. They are tangible and targeted options for overcoming the challenges of climate-induced migration to US cities and for offering a culturally empowered, resilient pathway forward in an era of large demographic shifts. These recommendations require a proactive, whole-community approach that necessitates the buy-in of many city departments and agencies. But they also provide an opportunity to expand the pool of those considered important in climate migration decision-making. Beyond local elected officials, other actors, such as faith leaders, librarians, grassroots leaders, and civic associations engaged in social cohesion, inclusive placemaking, and cultural practice, all need seats at the table if cities are to successfully document loss, foster dialogue, and create space for migrant heritage.

46
Project for Public Spaces, "What Can Public Spaces Offer to the Globally Displaced?," April 2, 2018, https://www.pps.org/article/refugees-and-public-space.

47
Selina Cheah, "At Prison Turned Cultural Hub in Amsterdam, Refugees Are Welcome," Curbed.com, February 10, 2017, https://www.curbed.com/2017/2/10/14576182/amsterdam-lola-lik-refugees.

48
Brooke Saias, "Searching for Little Haiti," Culture-ist, March 22, 2018, https://www.thecultureist.com/2018/03/22/searching-little-haiti.

49
Project for Public Spaces, "What Can Public Spaces Offer?"

When analyzing what public spaces can offer to the globally displaced, the Project for Public Spaces notes that "a successful place not only
integrates refugees into the ever-changing fabric of the community; it
empowers them to take the lead on improving public spaces and services
for themselves, and for other new residents… It connects them with new
neighbors, gives them a way to explore their new home, and provides
space and opportunity for holding on to cultural traditions while building new community bonds."[49] In a rapidly warming world, a successful
urban receiving "place" is essential to community resilience. As temperature records continue to be broken each year, the next climate-induced
community displacement is never far off. The next hurricane or wildfire
season holds the immense potential for sudden-onset disasters to upend
close-knit communities from Alaska to Alabama. When the next large-
scale extreme storm or fire hits, rural residents across the country will
be displaced, forced to migrate to safer settlements. While a handful of
communities will be able to accrue adequate resources and time for a
fully planned, wholesale managed retreat, most will be displaced without
having the needed cultural mitigation measures in place to lessen the
resulting stress on both the receiving city and migration communities.
Support mechanisms like grants for cultural documentation lost to climate impacts, investment in inclusive dialogue, and guaranteed access to
physical spaces to share and practice traditions can make the difference
for climate migrants finding new homes in America's great cities.

Community-Led Relocation:
Protecting Culture with the Rising Tides

Robin Bronen

Confronting Adaptation and Relocation

The climate crisis will cause the relocation of millions of people from disappearing coastlines, causing erosion, sea level rise, and repeated extreme weather events that will permanently submerge land. The scale and the geographic scope of climate-forced population displacement is the greatest human rights challenge of our time. In the United States, roughly 40 percent of the population lives near the coast. Worldwide, more than 600 million people (roughly 10 percent of the global population) live within 10 meters of sea level. [1] The concentration of people in low-elevation coastal zones threatens millions of people's lives, homes, and livelihoods.

Many of the people and communities that are now on the front lines of losing their homes are those that have done the least to cause this crisis and often bear the brunt of institutional and structural racism, the ongoing legacies of slavery and colonization. What does cultural heritage preservation mean when vulnerability to sea level rise cannot be disentangled from the United States' role in the cultural genocide of Indigenous peoples and the enslavement of Africans, ripping them away from their homes and cultures? To answer this question, this essay focuses on the climate-forced relocation of Alaska Native communities and the human right to self-determination that must adhere when Indigenous communities are forcibly displaced. The right to self-determination is essential in protecting the cultural rights of Indigenous communities and beginning to decolonize the systems that have caused their vulnerability to accelerating environmental change. In addition, self-determination means that Indigenous communities should lead any research involving their communities so that they are creating the narratives that protect their cultural heritage.

► CLIMATE CRISIS

Our failure to reduce greenhouse gas emissions is causing air and ocean temperatures to increase, frozen regions of the world to melt, and sea levels to rise. The US National Oceanic and Atmospheric Administration (NOAA) proclaimed 2019 the second-hottest year in its 140-year record, and the decade between 2010 and 2019 the hottest. [2] East Coast cities in the United States, such as Miami and Charleston, are regularly inundated with "sunny day" flooding caused by high tides, not storm surges. Recently, NOAA documented an increase in this type of flooding, whose disruptive effects and damage encompass "1) access to homes and important transportation links due to flooding and erosion of roadways, 2) flooding of homes…, 3) the cost of replacing antiquated combined storm and wastewater systems being impacted by rising seas and groundwater tables, 4) the health effects of such combined systems, and 5) the negative pressure on real estate values." [3]

In Alaska, the only Arctic state in the United States, temperatures have already far surpassed the aspirational limit of a 1.5°C temperature increase of the United Nations Framework Convention on Climate Change (UNFCCC) Paris Agreement, with winter temperatures now approximately 3.5°C (7°F) above normal. In March 2019 average temperatures

1
P. R. Thompson, M. A. Merrifield, E. Leuliette, W. Sweet, D. P. Chambers, B. D. Hamlington, S. Jevrejeva, J. J. Marra, G. T. Mitchum, R. S. Nerem, and M. J. Widlansky, "Sea Level Variability and Change," in State of the Climate in 2017, ed. J. Blunden, D. S. Arndt, and G. Hartfield, Bulletin of the American Meteorological Society 99, no. 8 (2018): S84–S87; Scott A. Kulp and Benjamin H. Strauss, "New Elevation Data Triple Estimates of Global Vulnerability to Sea-Level Rise and Coastal Flooding," Nature Communications 10, no. 1 (2019), https://doi.org/10.1038/s41467-019-12808-z.

2
"2019 was the 2nd hottest year on record for Earth, say NOAA, NASA," National Oceanic and Atmospheric Administration, January 15, 2020, https://www.noaa.gov/news/2019-was-2nd-hottest-year-on-record-for-earth-say-noaa-nasa.

3
William Sweet, Gregory Dusek, Greg Carbin, John Marra, Doug Marcy, and Steven Simon, "2019 State of US High Tide Flooding with a 2020 Outlook," NOAA Technical Report NOS CO-OPS 092, National Oceanic and Atmospheric Administration, July 2020, https://tidesandcurrents.noaa.gov/publications/Techrpt_092_2019_State_of_US_High_Tide_Flooding_with_a_2020_Outlook_30June2020.pdf.

4
National Oceanic and Atmospheric Administration, "Arctic Report Card: Update for 2019," https://arctic.noaa.gov/Report-Card/Report-Card-2019.

5
Jianbin Huang, Xiangdong Zhang, Qiyi Zhang, Yanluan Lin, Mingju Hao, Yong Luo, Zongci Zhao, et al., "Recently Amplified Arctic Warming Has Contributed to a Continual Global Warming Trend," Nature

Climate Change 7
(2017): 875–879.

6
Zhanpei Fang, Patrick T.
Freeman, Christopher
B. Field, and Katharine
J. Mach, "Reduced Sea
Ice Protection Period
Increases Storm
Exposure in Kivalina,
Alaska," Arctic Science
4 (2018): 525–537.

7
Robin Bronen, Olin
Annauk, Jacqueline
Overbeck, DeAnne
Stevens, Susan Natali,
and Chris Maio, "Usteq:
Integrating Indigenous
Knowledge and
Social and Physical
Sciences to Coproduce
Knowledge and Support
Community-Based
Adaptation," Polar
Geography 43, no. 2–3
(2020): 188–205, https://
doi.org/10.1080/10889
37X.2019.1679271.

8
US Government
Accountability Office,
Alaska Native Villages:
Limited Progress
Has Been Made on
Relocating Villages
Threatened by Flooding
and Erosion, GAO-09-
551 (Washington, DC,
2009), https://www.
gao.gov/new.items/
d09551.pdf; Division
of Homeland Security
and Emergency
Management (DHSEM),
Alaska Department of
Military and Veterans
Affairs, "State of Alaska
Hazard Mitigation Plan,"
2018.

9
US Government
Accountability Office,
Alaska Native Villages:
Most Are Affected by
Flooding and Erosion,
but Few Qualify for
Federal Assistance,
GAO-04-142
(Washington, DC, 2003),
https://www.gao.gov/
assets/250/240810.
pdf; US Government
Accountability Office,
Alaska Native Villages:
Limited Progress.

10
University of Alaska
Fairbanks (UAF)
Institute of Northern
Engineering and
US Army Corps of
Engineers, "Statewide
Threat Assessment:
Identification of Threats
from Erosion, Flooding,
Thawing Permafrost,
and Usteq in Remote
Alaska Communities,"
2019, http://ine.uaf.edu/

were 11°C (20°F–30°F) above normal, shattering previous records. [4] Increased land and ocean temperatures are causing an unprecedented environmental transition in the Arctic. [5] The extent and duration of sea ice is rapidly decreasing, leaving Alaska Native coastal communities vulnerable to powerful storm surges. Arctic sea ice is now 40 percent of what it was in 1979, when satellites began capturing this data. [6] The diminishing of the Arctic sea ice that protects coastal communities, extreme erosion magnified by storm flooding, and thawing permafrost combine to threaten the lives and livelihoods of Alaska Native communities. [7] Permafrost, which is permanently frozen ground and which comprises the glue that keeps the land intact and habitable, is critical to the structural integrity of infrastructure. This combination of erosion, flooding, and thawing permafrost leads to catastrophic land collapse—known as *usteq*, a Yup'ik word adopted by Alaska's State Hazard Mitigation Plan. [8]

Numerous reports have documented the environmental hazards threatening public health and safety in Alaska Native communities. [9] In 2009 the US Government Accountability Office (GAO) found that thirty-one Alaska Native communities were imminently threatened by flooding and erosion, and twelve of these communities decided to relocate because of these environmental hazards. In 2019 the Denali Commission, a federal agency designed to provide utilities, infrastructure, and economic support throughout Alaska, updated the 2009 GAO report and published a statewide environmental threat assessment highlighting the most environmentally vulnerable communities in Alaska but did not identify the communities seeking to relocate. [10]

Shishmaref, Kivalina, and Newtok are three of the imperiled communities identified in these reports. Each community decided decades ago that relocation was the best long-term adaptation strategy to protect community residents from accelerating rates of erosion. [11] Yet while federal and state government agencies agree, relocation has not yet occurred, as of 2020, because of the quagmire of statutory barriers as well as the lack of a government agency that has the mandate and the funding for the relocations. As a result, the communities that decide that relocation is their best long-term adaptation strategy must work with several different federal and state government agencies (such as FEMA, HUD, and the Army Corps of Engineers) to acquire the funding needed. Community relocation is a multiyear planning process that requires not only the building of infrastructure but also the movement of people, whose livelihoods must be sustained, and, most importantly, the maintaining of cultural and kinship connections. [12] There is no one term that is recognized globally by community residents, local and national governments, and academics to describe the process of moving people and infrastructure away from environmental hazards—"managed retreat," "resettlement," and "relocation" are often used interchangeably. [13] In Alaska, the term "relocation" is used to describe moving an entire community's infrastructure and people to another location, while the term "managed retreat" is used to describe the movement of some infrastructure away from environmental hazards.

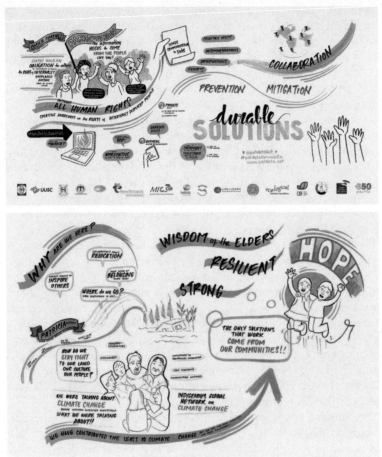

FIG. 1: *Diagrams from the First People's Convening on Climate-Forced Displacement, Girdwood, Alaska, October 2018.*

projects/
statewide-threat-
assessment.

11
Robin Bronen and
F. Stuart Chapin III,
"Adaptive Governance
and Institutional
Strategies for Climate-
Induced Community
Relocations in Alaska,"
*Proceedings of the
National Academy of
Sciences* 110, no. 23
(June 2013): 9320–9325,
https://doi.org/10.1073/
pnas.1210508110.

12
Abhas K. Jha, *Safer
Homes, Stronger
Communities:
A Handbook for
Reconstructing after
Natural Disasters*
(Washington, DC: World
Bank, 2010).

13
Jha, *Safer Homes,
Stronger Communities.*

14
*Relocation Report:
Newtok to Mertarvik*
(Anchorage: Alaska
Department of
Commerce, Community,
and Economic
Development, Division
of Community and
Regional Affairs, 2011).

Only one community, Newtok, is actively in a relocation process. In October 2019 one-third of the community relocated to Mertarvik, the tribe's chosen relocation site, 12 kilometers across the Ninglick River from the community's current location. [14] Due to funding constraints, there is no time frame for the relocation of the remaining two-thirds of the community.

The policy and the practical challenges of relocation are enormous. Currently, no governance framework exists in the United States to evaluate climate-change impacts and determine when people can no longer be protected in place and need to relocate. Recognizing this institutional gap and the complex challenges of climate-induced population displacement, the Bicameral Task Force on Climate Change issued a report, *Implementing the President's Climate Action Plan: US Department of the Interior*, in December 2013. This report recommended that:

the Administration devote special attention to the problems of communities that decide they have little choice but to relocate in

15
US Congress, Bicameral
Task Force on Climate
Change, *Implementing
the President's
Climate Action Plan:
US Department of the
Interior. Actions the
Department of the
Interior Should Take
to Address Climate
Change*, December
19, 2013, https://www.
whitehouse.senate.
gov/imo/media/
doc/2013-12-19%20
BTF%20DOI%20
White%20Paper.pdf.

16
*President's State,
Local and Tribal
Leaders Task Force on
Climate Preparedness
and Resilience:
Recommendations
to the President*
(Washington, DC:
White House, 2014),
https://obama
whitehouse.archives.
gov/sites/default/
files/docs/task_
force_report_0.pdf

17
House Select
Committee on the
Climate Crisis, *Solving
the Climate Crisis: The
Congressional Action
Plan for a Clean Energy
Economy and a Healthy,
Resilient, and Just
America*, 116th Cong.,
June 2020, 388,
https://climatecrisis.
house.gov/sites/
climatecrisis.house.
gov/files/Climate%20
Crisis%20Action%20
Plan.pdf

18
Bronen et al., "Usteq."

the face of the impacts of climate change. Because the relocation of entire communities due to climate change is such an unprecedented need, there is no institutional framework within the US to relocate communities, and agencies lack technical, organizational, and financial means to do so. 15

President Obama's Task Force on Climate Preparedness and Resilience (the Task Force) echoed this recommendation in November 2014 and affirmed that the federal government should take a lead role in establishing a relocation institutional framework that could respond to the complex challenges of climate-related population displacement. 16 Most recently, the US House Select Committee reaffirmed this recommendation:

> Congress should direct the MitFLG [Mitigation Framework Leadership Group] to create a federal relocation framework in collaboration with tribes, Indigenous communities, and Insular Areas that provides for the planned transition for communities seeking relocation assistance and protects access to traditional lands and waters for tribes and Indigenous communities, as well as rights to culture, health, safe drinking water, food, and adequate housing. 17

Despite recognition of the need for a federal relocation framework, no steps have been taken to begin this process.

Yet a new governance framework must be created—one that can provide guidelines for institutions to shift their efforts from protecting people in the places where they live to creating a relocation process when environmental and social thresholds are surpassed and harm the health and well-being of community residents. Complex governance issues must be resolved in order to facilitate relocation, including the process to determine when protection in place is no longer possible and community relocation is required. Determining which communities are most likely to encounter displacement requires a sophisticated assessment of the vulnerability of a community's ecosystem to climate change, as well as the vulnerability of its social, economic, and political structures. 18 Human rights principles must be embedded in any relocation governance framework because severe economic, social, and environmental consequences can occur in the relocation process. Human rights principles are also a critical underpinning of any relocation governance framework to ensure that current racial and economic inequities, the legacies of colonization and slavery, are addressed when responding to climate-forced displacement.

► THE RIGHT TO SELF-DETERMINATION

The right to self-determination is the most important human right to protect in order to decolonize the systems that have subjugated Indigenous communities. In the United States, settler colonialism created the legal and institutional structures that forcibly removed and relocated Indigenous populations from their traditional lands to locations vulnerable to accelerating environmental change and recast Indigenous peoples' land as property and as a resource. 19 These government-mandated relocations have been uniformly disastrous for the Indigenous peoples displaced, weakening their institutions and social networks, disrupting subsistence and economic systems, and impacting the cultural identity and traditional kinship ties within communities.

In Alaska, during World War II, the federal government forcibly relocated the Unangan people thousands of miles away from their home on the Aleutian Islands. Ten percent of the population died. 20 In 1971, unlike the reservation system in the majority of states within the United States, the Alaska Native Claims Settlement Act created a corporate structure to land title, transferring millions of acres to Alaska Native regional and village corporations with corporate ownership by Alaska Native shareholders. As a consequence, tribal governments have no governing authority over the land on which tribal community members reside. This action of separating tribal governments from the territory upon which tribal members dwell and harvest foods is another colonist imposition to fracture tribal sovereignty and culture. For Indigenous communities, land, culture, and government are inseparable. 21

The federal government also forced Alaska Native communities to become sedentary. The ancestors of the current residents of Kivalina, Shishmaref, and Newtok moved seasonally among coastal and inland hunting and fishing camps. This migratory lifestyle changed during the late nineteenth and early twentieth centuries primarily because the US Department of the Interior's Bureau of Education forced the Alaska Native population to participate in the newly developed formal educational system. 22 The construction of schools along the western coast of Alaska and the requirement that Alaska Native children attend school caused the population to consolidate and settle. Barge accessibility to transport construction materials determined the location of the schools. 23 The building of permanent schools, housing, and infrastructure for sewage, water, and electricity led to a change from seasonal migration to establishment of permanent communities at the school sites selected by the federal government. 24 This US government-mandated disruption of the traditional migratory settlements of Alaska Native communities has made it more difficult for these communities to flexibly and effectively respond to environmental changes and has also made these communities more reliant on extensive federal technical assistance and funding to relocate these communities.

In order to ensure that these government-mandated relocations and settlements are not repeated as Indigenous communities are forcibly displaced by accelerating environmental change, the right to self-determination is an essential cornerstone of the human rights that need to guide climate-forced community relocations, and is also an essential principle of decolonization. Indigenous communities in the United States were autonomous self-governing peoples living on the land, long before the current manifestation of the United States of America and its constitutional democracy as it stands today. Decolonization is the restoration of cultural practices and values that were taken away or abandoned through colonization and that are now important and/or necessary for survival, well-being, and subsistence lifestyles. Decolonization advances and

19
Eve Tuck and K. Wayne Yang, "Decolonization Is Not a Metaphor," Decolonization: Indigeneity, Education & Society 1, no. 1 (2012): 1–40; Kyle Whyte, "Settler Colonialism, Ecology, and Environmental Injustice," Environment and Society: Advances in Research 9, no. 1 (2018): 125–144.

20
Charles M. Mobley, World War II Aleut Relocation Camps in Southeast Alaska (Anchorage: National Park Service, Alaska Region, 2012).

21
Gerald Taiaiake Alfred, Peace, Power, Righteousness: An Indigenous Manifesto, 2nd ed. (Don Mills, Canada: Oxford University Press, 2009).

22
Bronen and Chapin, "Adaptive Governance and Institutional Strategies."

23
Robin Bronen, "Climate-Induced Community Relocations: Creating an Adaptive Governance Framework Based in Human Rights Doctrine," New York University Review of Law and Social Change 35, no. 2 (2011): 356–406.

24
Bronen and Chapin, "Adaptive Governance and Institutional Strategies."

25
Whyte, "Settler Colonialism, Ecology, and Environmental Injustice."

26
International Covenant on Economic, Social and Cultural Rights, December 16, 1966, UN Treaty Series, vol. 993, http://refworld.org/docid/3ae6b36c0.html, 5; International Covenant on Civil and Political Rights, December 16, 1966, UN Treaty Series, vol. 999, http://refworld.org/docid/3ae6b3aa0.html, 173.

27
General Assembly Resolution 61/295,

UN Declaration on the Rights of Indigenous Peoples, A/RES/61/295 (September 13, 2007), articles 18–19, http://undocs.org/A/RES/61/295.

28
Else Grete Broderstad and Jens Dahl, "Political Systems," in *Arctic Human Development Report*, ed. Niels Einarsson, Joan Nymand Larsen, Annika Nilsson, and Oran R. Young (Akureyri, Iceland: Stefansson Arctic Institute, 2004), 85–100; Office of the UN High Commissioner for Human Rights, *Fact Sheet No. 16 (Rev. 1)* (Geneva: United Nations, 1991), ohchr.org/Documents/Publications/FactSheet16rev.1en.pdf, section 4.

29
Broderstad and Dahl, "Political Systems."

30
Both treaties use the word "peoples," signifying that the right to self-determination is a collective right. Through the realization of the collective right to self-determination, an individual can also enjoy the right to self-determination. Office of the UN High Commissioner for Human Rights, *Fact Sheet No. 15 (Rev. 1)* (Geneva: United Nations, 2005), http://ohchr.org/Documents/Publications/FactSheet15rev.1en.pdf; UN Development Group, *Guidelines on Indigenous Peoples' Issues*, HR/P/PT/16 (Geneva: United Nations, 2009), http://un.org/esa/socdev/unpfii/documents/UNDG_guidelines_EN.pdf.

31
UN General Assembly, United Nations Declaration on the Rights of Indigenous Peoples, October 2, 2007, A/RES/61/295, https://www.refworld.org/docid/471355a82.html, articles 9 and 33.

32
UN General Assembly, United Nations Declaration on the Rights of Indigenous Peoples, articles 5 and 7.

empowers Indigenous peoples and stops perpetuating their subjugation and exploitation. [25] In the context of climate-forced relocation, the right to self-determination means that communities make the decision of whether, when, and how relocation will occur. For Indigenous peoples, this initial decision to relocate is arguably the most important step in the relocation process because of their cultural and spiritual connection to their lands.

International law supports the importance of self-determination. Both the International Covenant on Economic, Social, and Cultural Rights and the International Covenant on Civil and Political Rights establish that "all peoples have the right to self-determination," by virtue of which "they freely determine their political status and freely pursue their economic, social, and cultural development."[26] The UN Declaration on the Rights of Indigenous Peoples includes similar provisions. Article 18 states that "Indigenous peoples have the right to participate in decision-making processes which would affect their rights, through representatives chosen by themselves in accordance with their own procedures, as well as to maintain and develop their own Indigenous decision-making institutions," while Article 19 declares that "states shall consult and cooperate in good faith with the Indigenous peoples concerned through their own representative institutions in order to obtain their free, prior, and informed consent before adopting and implementing legislative or administrative measures that may affect them."[27] The inclusion of the right to self-determination in these documents indicates that it is intrinsic to all political, civil, economic, social, and cultural rights and specifically critical to Indigenous peoples. Since the creation of the United Nations in 1945, when the concept of self-determination was initially interpreted to apply to a nation-state's right to independence, noninterference, and democracy in relation to other nation-state governments, its interpretation has evolved. [28] Now, the concept of self-determination also includes the development of self-government institutions in Indigenous communities. [29]

International human rights law also affirms the collective human rights of Indigenous communities, including the right to self-determination. [30] For example, the UN Declaration on the Rights of Indigenous Peoples states that Indigenous peoples possess collective rights, indispensable for their existence and well-being, including the right to collective self-determination and the collective right to the lands, territories, and natural resources they have traditionally occupied and used. The collective right to self-determination ensures that Indigenous communities can determine their own identities, belong to "an indigenous community or nation, in accordance with the traditions and customs of the community or nation concerned," and make decisions about internal and local affairs. [31] The Declaration also provides that Indigenous peoples have the right to freely define and pursue their economic, social, and cultural development. These rights seek to protect the collective right of Indigenous peoples to live as "distinct peoples" and "maintain and strengthen their distinct political, legal, economic, social and cultural institutions."[32]

The United Nations, in its Convention for the Safeguarding of the Intangible Cultural Heritage, also affirms the collective rights of communities to safeguard and respect "intangible cultural heritage," which it defines as any practice, expression, or skill—including all objects and cultural places—that communities recognize as part of their cultural heritage. Further, "intangible cultural heritage" means the practices, representations, expressions, knowledge, and skills—as well as the instruments, objects, artifacts, and cultural spaces associated with them—that communities, groups, and, in some cases, individuals recognize as part of their cultural heritage. "This intangible cultural heritage, transmitted from generation to generation, is constantly recreated by communities and groups in response to their environment, their interaction with nature and their history, and provides them with a sense of identity and continuity, thus promoting respect for cultural diversity and human creativity."[33] Although the United States is not a signatory to this convention, it establishes the importance of collective human rights. Collective self-determination is essential for the relocation process, as it ensures that communities are empowered to make the critical decisions affecting their relocation, including whether, when, and how to relocate. All of these decisions are critical to protecting intangible and tangible cultural heritage when an Indigenous community is forced to relocate.

33
"Convention for the Safeguarding of the Intangible Cultural Heritage," *Treaty Series: Treaties and International Agreements Registered or Filed and Recorded with the Secretariat of the United Nations* 2368 (2003): 35–48.

In addition, in the United States, the federal National Historic Preservation Act (NHPA) and Alaska's preservation laws do not ensure the protection of cultural heritage if an Indigenous community is forced to relocate, because these laws fundamentally define heritage as tangible, place-based cultural resources and lands (with the exception of "traditional cultural properties"). The NHPA provides for the creation of Tribal Historic Preservation Offices to assume the responsibilities of State Historic Preservation Offices on tribal lands—allowing them to define heritage in more autonomous ways—but only for tribes that are federally recognized. These laws undermine the right to self-determination because the criteria for determining cultural heritage were not established by Indigenous communities, and as a consequence they limit participation to tribal communities within the United States that are federally recognized while also limiting the definition of cultural heritage by not recognizing intangible heritage. Moreover, the laws do not ensure that Indigenous communities forced to relocate can maintain access to their traditional lands and waters, which are critical to their cultural heritage and subsistence lifeways.

The Newtok tribal government highlighted the importance of the right to self-determination and protection of their cultural heritage when they created guiding principles for their relocation effort:

- Remain a distinct, unique community—our own community.
- Stay focused on our vision by taking small steps forward each day.
- Make decisions openly and as a community and look to elders for guidance.
- Build a healthy future for our youth.
- Our voice comes first—we have first and final say in making decisions and defining priorities, by implementing nation-building principles and working with our partners.
- Share with and learn from our partners.
- No matter how long it takes, we will work together to provide support to our people in both Mertarvik [the relocation site] and Newtok.

34
*Relocation Report:
Newtok to Mertarvik.*

35
Henry P. Huntington,
Mark Carey, Charlene
Apok, Bruce C. Forbes,
Shari Fox, Lene K. Holm,
Aitalina Ivanova, et al.,
"Climate Change in
Context: Putting People
First in the Arctic,"
*Regional Environmental
Change* 19 (2019):
1217–1223.

36
Melanie Bahnke,
Vivian Korthuis,
Amos Philemonoff,
and Mellisa Johnson
to Navigating the
New Arctic Program,
National Science
Foundation, March 19,
2020, https://www.
arctictoday.com/
wp-content/uploads/
2021/02/2020-03-19-
NNA-Letter-Final-1.pdf.

- Development should:
  — Reflect our cultural traditions.
  — Nurture our spiritual and physical well-being.
  — Respect and enhance the environment.
  — Be designed with local input from start to finish.
  — Be affordable for our people.
  — Hire community members first.
  — Use what we have first and use available funds wisely.
- Look for projects that build on our talents and strengthen our economy. [34]

These are the essential principles that need to be included in any relocation process to ensure that the right to self-determination is protected and promoted.

Similarly, self-determination and decolonization also mean that communities control the narrative about how the climate crisis impacts them. Colonization continues when scholars who are non-Indigenous write narratives about "vanishing cultures."[35] Scholars also continue the colonization of Indigenous communities when they are not represented in the research about their communities. Four Alaska Native organizations, representing northwestern and southwestern regions in Alaska, recently wrote a letter to the National Science Foundation highlighting the importance of Indigenous scholarship and voices leading any research projects involving their communities:

> We have unparalleled first-hand experience living in and with and knowing the Arctic environment. As such, we have many of our own research questions that are practical and address our biological, ecological, social, and economic interests and concerns from the perspective of our own worldviews and cosmologies. We have concerns about outside academics defining food security, well-being, resilience, prosperity, and adaption for us, without our explicit knowledge and active participation in the process. The potential outcomes of such research are dangerous and may perpetuate erroneous and damaging conclusions that become the dominant narratives about our communities and Indigenous Peoples in the Arctic in general. [36]

Both the Newtok tribal government's guiding principles and the letter to the National Science Foundation highlight the importance of decolonizing the structural and institutional systems that continue to subjugate Indigenous communities so that Alaska Native communities can protect their culture and lifeways. This is critical as accelerating environmental change threatens the places Alaska Native communities call home. Protecting the right to self-determination is essential to protecting cultural heritage when tribes are forcibly displaced and relocated. Communities forced to make the awful decision to leave their ancestral lands must be able to define every aspect of how they want to create long-term adaptation strategies to respond to the accelerating climate crisis. They are being forced to make these decisions when they have done the least to contribute to the crisis. Decolonization is a path forward that will ensure they define their future in a climate-altered world.

Avoiding Carbon: Mitigating Climate Change
through Preservation and Reuse

James B. Lindberg

Reorienting toward Climate and Justice

For a movement organized to protect the past, historic preservation has an impressive record of envisioning the future, even when others can't see it yet. During the oil crisis of the 1970s, for example, few paid much attention when preservationists pointed out that old buildings contained valuable "embodied energy" that should not be wasted. A 1979 report from the Advisory Council on Historic Preservation even provided a methodology for measuring the energy saved when buildings are rehabilitated rather than replaced. [1]

More than forty years later, the preservation message may finally be breaking through. A recent article about climate change in the *Guardian* asked: "What if every existing building had to be preserved, adapted, and reused, and new buildings could only use what materials were already available?"[2] A new report from the World Green Building Council recommends "increasing utilization of existing assets through renovation or reuse" as one of its top strategies to reduce carbon emissions. [3] The winners of the 2021 Pritzker Architecture Prize, French architects Anne Lacaton and Jean-Philippe Vassal, are known for their motto: "Never demolish, never remove or replace, always add, transform, and reuse!"[4]

After years of making the environmental case for saving old buildings, historic preservationists are no longer alone in calling for action. A consensus is emerging among architects, researchers, green building advocates, and climate policy makers that building reuse is an effective way to decrease carbon emissions—right away, when reductions are most important. Preservationists have a unique role to play in this effort. While many agencies, organizations, and businesses are working to reduce CO_2 emissions through low-carbon construction techniques and more efficient building operations, few have our knowledge of how to conserve, maintain, and adaptively reuse older buildings. Are preservation advocacy organizations, local commissions, state preservation offices, and other members of the preservation community ready to step into more prominent roles as part of climate action? Are we prepared to join new allies in a global campaign to mitigate the impacts of climate change through building conservation and material reuse?

To answer these questions, the key issue we must address is scale. Every building we save, rehabilitate, and reuse eliminates the need to construct a new building that serves the same purpose. Reuse avoids the carbon emissions incurred when the materials for a new building are mined, manufactured, transported, and assembled. Research conducted by the National Trust's Preservation Green Lab found that it can take between ten and eighty years to overcome the carbon debt that is incurred when an existing structure is replaced, even if the new building is highly energy efficient. [5] *FIG. 1* But to have a significant impact on global climate change, the decision to reuse rather than demolish cannot be an exception to common practice. Reuse must become routine, not just for exceptional buildings that are determined eligible for historic designation, but also for ordinary buildings of all ages and types.

Can the practice of preservation evolve to help lead this paradigm shift within the building sector? Are we prepared to broaden our scope to include older buildings generally, not just those that are designated as historic? If so, what changes to our current system are needed to achieve

1
Advisory Council on Historic Preservation, *Assessing the Energy Conservation Benefits of Historic Preservation: Methods and Examples* (Washington, DC: Advisory Council on Historic Preservation, 1979).

2
Oliver Wainwright, "The Case for... Never Demolishing Another Building," *Guardian*, January 13, 2020, https://www.theguardian.com/cities/2020/jan/13/the-case-for-never-demolishing-another-building.

3
World Green Building Council, *Bringing Embodied Carbon Upfront*, September 2019.

4
Kriston Capps, "Can America Learn from France's Award-Winning Public Housing Architects?" *Bloomberg CityLab*, March 17, 2021, https://www.bloomberg.com/news/articles/2021-03-17/pritzker-prize-honors-public-housing-architecture.

5
Preservation Green Lab, *The Greenest Building: Quantifying the Environmental Value of Building Reuse*, National Trust for Historic Preservation, 2011, ix.

6
Conference of the
Parties, Adoption of
the Paris Agreement,
U.N. Doc. FCCC/
CP/2015/L.9/Rev/1,
December 12, 2015,
https://unfccc.int/
resource/docs/2015/
cop21/eng/l09r01.pdf.

7
Intergovernmental
Panel on Climate
Change (IPCC),
*Special Report on
Global Warming
of 1.5°C* (Geneva:
Intergovernmental
Panel on Climate
Change, 2018), https://
www.ipcc.ch/sr15.

FIG. 1: *Preservation Green Lab report,* The Greenest Building: Quantifying the Environmental Value of Building Reuse (2011). *Preservation Green Lab report. Research across multiple building types and climate zones found that it takes between ten and eighty years to recover the carbon debt that is incurred when an existing structure is replaced, even if the new building is highly energy efficient. Courtesy of the National Trust for Historic Preservation.*

this expansion? How can new policies, incentives, and partnerships extend our reach beyond designated properties? How can we reduce the carbon emissions from our own work to rehabilitate and maintain historic buildings?

This essay offers five policy strategies for how preservation practitioners, agencies, and advocacy organizations can assume larger roles in mitigating the impacts of climate change through building conservation and reuse: (1) expand preservation and zoning tools; (2) create more building reuse incentives; (3) prioritize materials conservation in rehabilitation; (4) strengthen demolition review policies; and (5) add deconstruction to the preservation policy toolbox. Before discussing these policy ideas, however, it is important to understand why the decisions we make about the future of older buildings are so important to the wider effort to reduce carbon emissions from our built environment.

▶ BUILDINGS AND CLIMATE CHANGE

The 2015 Paris Agreement calls for dramatic reductions in carbon emissions from buildings and all other sectors, with the goal of "holding the increase in the global average temperature to well below 2°C above pre-industrial levels and pursuing efforts to limit the temperature increase to 1.5°C above pre-industrial levels."[6] A 2018 report from the United Nations Intergovernmental Panel on Climate Change (IPCC) underlines the critical importance of not exceeding the lower end of this range. The IPCC report warns that allowing temperatures to rise beyond 1.5°C risks triggering irreversible changes—melted ice sheets, thawed permafrost, warmed oceans—that could lead to a cascading economic and humanitarian crisis.[7]

To limit temperature increases to no more than 1.5°C, net carbon emissions from building construction and operations must decline to zero by 2050, if not sooner. This rapid decarbonization of the building sector will require dramatic transformations over the next three decades, including conversion of the power grid from fossil fuels to renewables, electrification of all building systems, sharp reductions in the energy needed to operate buildings, and implementation of carbon-neutral construction practices.

According to current estimates, buildings generate 39 percent of annual carbon emissions worldwide—28 percent from the operation of existing buildings and 11 percent from construction of new buildings. [8] Recent efforts to curb carbon emissions from building operations are showing positive results. From 2005 to 2019, despite an increase in total floor area, carbon emissions from building operations in the United States declined by 21 percent. [9] Much of this decline is due to progress in converting the electric grid to renewable power sources.

While the recent downward trend of operating emissions is hopeful, efforts to shrink the total carbon footprint of buildings must also address embodied carbon. Embodied carbon emissions occur when fossil fuel energy is used to extract, harvest, manufacture, transport, and assemble the materials needed for new buildings. Some have described embodied carbon as the "blind spot" of the building industry because these processes occur in disparate locations and are largely invisible to end users. [10] In a recent report entitled *Bringing Embodied Carbon Upfront*, the World Green Building Council notes, "Embodied carbon and the tools and methods needed to calculate it are relatively complex and new to many and the methods for addressing it are generally not well understood."[11] A lack of consensus on how to measure embodied carbon in buildings has made it difficult to assemble comprehensive data. [12] While energy and carbon emissions statistics related to building operations are readily available, no government agency is currently tracking embodied carbon emissions from the building sector.

Recognition of the importance of embodied carbon is growing, however, for two key reasons. The first is that as building operations become more efficient, the proportion of total life cycle CO2 emissions due to embodied carbon increases. [13] Perhaps the most compelling reason to address embodied carbon is that a significant proportion of these emissions occur upfront, at the beginning of the building life cycle. As the New Buildings Institute observes, the embodied carbon impacts from new construction are immediate and irreversible: "Owners can address carbon from building operations on a periodic basis by upgrading lighting, mechanical systems and other equipment, but once a concrete floor is poured or ceiling tiles are installed, the carbon emitted during the manufacture and transport of those materials can never be recovered."[14]

▶ "THE TIME VALUE OF CARBON"

Because every ton of carbon that we emit stays in the atmosphere for hundreds of years, the effects of emissions are cumulative. Our goal cannot be to merely reduce annual carbon emissions to a lower level. At

8
International Energy Agency, *2018 Global Status Report: Towards a Zero Emission, Efficient and Resilient Buildings and Construction Sector* (Nairobi: United Nations Environment Programme, 2018).

9
Architecture 2030, "Unprecedented: A Way Forward," https://architecture2030.org/unprecedented-a-way-forward.

10
Anthony Pak, "Embodied Carbon: The Blind Spot of the Building Industry," *Canadian Architect*, July 3, 2019, 26–29.

11
World Green Building Council, *Bringing Embodied Carbon Upfront*, 35.

12
Manish K. Dixit, "Life Cycle Recurrent Embodied Energy Calculation in Buildings: A Review," *Journal of Cleaner Production* (March 2018): 732.

13
Preservationists forecast this future as well. In a 1981 National Trust publication, energy consultant William Whiddon predicted, "As new and existing buildings are made increasingly efficient in the ways they use energy, embodied energy becomes an even more significant fraction of the energy investment required in the use of buildings." William I. Whiddon, "The Concept of Embodied Energy," in *New Energy from Old Buildings* (Washington, DC: Preservation Press, 1981), 113.

14
Amy Cortese, "The Embodied Carbon Conundrum: Solving for all Emission Sources from the Built Environment," New Buildings Institute, February 26, 2020, https://newbuildings.org/embodied-carbon-conundrum-solving-for-all-emission-sources-from-the-built-environment.

15
IPCC, *Special Report on Global Warming of 1.5°C.*

16
Larry Strain, "The Time Value of Carbon," research paper developed for the Carbon Leadership Forum, 2017, http://www.siegelstrain.com/wp-content/uploads/2017/09/Time-Value-of-Carbon-170530.pdf.

17
Architecture 2030, "Why the Building Sector," https://architecture2030.org/why-the-building-sector.

18
US Energy Information Agency, *Commercial Buildings Energy Consumption Survey (CBECS)* (Washington, DC: US Energy Information Agency, 2012); *Residential Energy Consumption Survey (RECS)* (Washington, DC: US Energy Information Agency, 2015).

19
Frederick Eggers and Fouad Moumen, "American Housing Survey Components of Inventory Change: 2015–2017" (US Department of Housing and Urban Development, June 2020), https://www.huduser.gov/portal/datasets/cinch/cinch15/National-Report.pdf.

some point, we must stop generating emissions altogether. According to international scientific consensus, if we hope to have a 67 percent chance of limiting global warming to no more than 1.5°C, our remaining carbon emissions budget is about 340 gtCO2. [15] At current global emission rates, we will exceed that budget in less than ten years. The only way to buy more time is to reduce annual emissions sharply and quickly. Architect Larry Strain uses the phrase "the time value of carbon" to underscore this urgency. In an influential research paper, he writes: "When we evaluate emission reduction strategies, there are two things to keep in mind: the amount of reduction, and when it happens. Because emissions are cumulative and because we have a limited amount of time to reduce them, carbon reductions now have more value than carbon reductions in the future."[16]

The time value of carbon multiplies the importance of reducing "upfront" embodied carbon emissions. Architecture 2030, a research and advocacy group, estimates that embodied carbon will be responsible for 74 percent of the total carbon emissions from new construction in the next ten years. [17] What can be done to quickly curtail embodied carbon emissions? One option is to construct new buildings out of materials produced in ways that emit less carbon. The building industry is already shifting in this direction. Environmental product declarations (EPDs) quantify the embodied carbon content of a widening spectrum of building materials. New software programs allow architects to calculate the impacts of material choices and specify lower-carbon alternatives when available. Low-carbon (and even negative-carbon) wood construction techniques are becoming more viable. Experimental techniques to lower carbon emissions from concrete and steel production are showing promise. Local and state governments are starting to specify low-carbon materials for new building projects.

The problem with this supply-side approach is that it will take years to fully implement. Carbon-free construction is all but impossible without zero-emission mining operations, manufacturing plants, transportation infrastructure, and construction equipment. We need strategies that will reduce carbon emissions in the next few years, not decades from now. When the time value of carbon is included in calculations of how best to reduce carbon emissions from the building sector, the result is clear: we must conserve and reuse as many existing buildings as possible.

▶ TAKING PRESERVATION AND REUSE TO SCALE

The urgency of reducing embodied carbon emissions inverts common perceptions about older buildings and climate change. Rather than being seen as outdated structures that we hope to replace, older buildings should be valued as climate assets that we cannot afford to waste. There are approximately 125 million existing buildings across the country. About 39 percent of these structures—nearly fifty million buildings— are at least fifty years old. [18] FIGS. 2, 3 Although comprehensive data is not available, the Census Bureau estimates that approximately 162,000 housing units are lost each year due to demolition and natural disasters. [19] More alarming in terms of embodied carbon impact is the number of

FIG. 2: *An older neighborhood in Brooklyn, New York City, 2010. In New York and many older cities, more than 80 percent of existing buildings are more than fifty years old. Analysis by the National Trust found that local landmark programs protect an average of just 4 percent of existing buildings in major cities across the country. Photograph by the author.*

FIG. 3: *Sign for new, replacement home in Denver, Colorado, 2007. Building conservation and reuse avoid the carbon emissions that occur when new, replacement structures are built. Photograph by the author.*

20
Paul Emrath, "New NAHB Estimate: 58,600 Single-Family Tear-Down Starts in 2017," March 8, 2018, National Association of Home Builders, http://eyeonhousing. org/2018/03/new-nahb-estimate-58600-single-family-tear-down-starts-in-2017.

21
"NYC Construction Dashboard," https:// www1.nyc.gov/assets/ buildings/html/ dob-development-report-2019.html.

22
"Demolitions Tracker," Chicago Cityscape, https://www. chicagocityscape. com/demolitions.php; "Demolition Watch," Curbed Philadelphia, https://philly.curbed. com/demolition-watch.

existing homes that are demolished simply to make way for new ones. The National Association of Home Builders reports that nearly 225,000 of the new houses constructed between 2014 and 2017 involved the "teardown" of an existing home. 20 Data from the municipal level paints a more detailed picture. In New York City, for example, more than two thousand demolition permits were approved in each of the past five years. 21 In Philadelphia and Chicago during the same period, demolition claimed about one thousand buildings annually in each city. Websites that track demolished buildings in these cities show page after page of solid-looking houses, commercial blocks, schools, and churches—most constructed of brick and almost all built before World War II. 22

How can municipal-level preservation policy slow the pace of demolitions? Although more than two thousand communities have adopted

23
The Atlas of
ReUrbanism,
"Philadelphia Fact
Sheet," https://forum.
savingplaces.org/act/
research-policy-lab/
atlas/atlas-factsheet.

24
Preservation Green
Lab, The Atlas
of ReUrbanism:
Summary Report,
National Trust for
Historic Preservation,
2016, https://forum.
savingplaces.org/act/
research-policy-lab/
atlas.

25
National Park Service,
Federal Tax Incentives
for Rehabilitating
Historic Buildings,
annual reports for 2015–
2019, https://www.nps.
gov/tps/tax-incentives/
reports.htm.

26
Elevate Energy,
Segmenting Chicago
Multifamily Housing
to Improve Energy
Efficiency Programs,
January 2017, https://
www.elevatenp.org/
wp-content/uploads/
Chicago-Multifamily-
Segmentation.pdf.

27
Chas Sirrage, "Newly
Approved Demolition
Fee Pilot Program Is a
Positive Step to Stem
the Loss of 2 to 4 Flats,"
Chicago CityScape,
March 24, 2021, https://
www.chicagocityscape.
com/blog/newly-
approved-demolition-
fee-pilot-program-is-a-
positive-step-to-stem-
the-loss-of-2-to-4-flats-
dd627da5e5.

ordinances to designate and protect historic buildings, their current impact is limited. In Philadelphia, for example, more than 90 percent of the city's nearly five hundred thousand buildings are at least fifty years old. Two-thirds were constructed before World War II. [23] These older, smaller buildings—row houses, corner stores, apartments, warehouses—define the character of the city's highly prized walkable and mixed-use neighborhoods. Yet only 2 percent of Philadelphia's built fabric—a mere twelve thousand buildings—is protected by the city's landmark ordinance. Data gathered by the National Trust for more than fifty major US cities shows a similar pattern; on average, just over 4 percent of existing buildings in these cities are designated and protected through local landmark laws. [24] The reach of building rehabilitation incentives is similarly limited. Across the country, developers complete about one thousand rehabilitation projects each year using the federal historic tax credits. [25]

For the preservation movement to become a more powerful force in the fight to mitigate climate change, we need to move beyond the "4 percent solution" offered by our current system. Two shifts in preservation practice could expand our impact. One is to collaborate more fully and intentionally with allied organizations and interests. Some of today's most urgent policy dialogues, including those about affordable housing and climate change, offer opportunities to partner around a shared goal of building conservation.

In Chicago, for example, local housing, community development, and energy efficiency advocates are developing "preservation" strategies aimed at saving and retrofitting the city's vast inventory of small apartment buildings. Nearly 60 percent of the 445,000 unsubsidized affordable housing units in Chicago are found in modest "two-flats" and "four-flats" that characterize many of the city's older neighborhoods. [26] Although more than 90 percent of these structures were built before 1942, few are protected within local historic districts, and thousands have been abandoned or demolished in recent years. At the urging of affordable housing and preservation advocates, the Chicago city council recently approved a sharp increase in demolition fees to help stem the loss of these small apartments in two pilot neighborhoods. [27] As cities across the country wrestle with similar issues, local preservation staff and advocates will have opportunities to join and shape sweeping initiatives aimed at the existing building stock. To be most effective as partners in these efforts, preservationists will be challenged to bring relevant data and nuanced policy approaches to the table.

These partnership opportunities point to the need for a second key shift: our preservation policy toolbox must expand to include a broader spectrum of designation, protection, and financial assistance options. The British system of graded designation levels offers one potential model. Several local preservation programs in the United States are beginning to experiment along these lines, adding new designation categories such as cultural districts and neighborhood conservation overlays, along with tailored approaches to design review. The following sections discuss five specific policy approaches to extend the reach and impact of historic preservation at a time of urgent need for climate action. By no means comprehensive, these ideas are offered to spur discussion, debate, and innovation.

Expand preservation and zoning tools

With local preservation ordinances protecting an average of fewer than one in twenty existing buildings across major US cities, new tools are needed to reduce demolition and conserve carbon. One approach is to expand the menu of designation and protection options offered through local preservation programs. Several cities have moved beyond the one-size-fits-all approach where all designated buildings receive the same level of protection and design review. In New Orleans, for example, the Historic Districts Landmark Commission has full design review authority for properties located in the ribbonlike St. Charles Avenue Historic District, while only demolitions are reviewed in the adjacent and much larger Uptown Historic District. Adding less restrictive alternatives to full design review can make historic district designation more politically viable, reduce staff time required, and extend protections to more areas of the city.

Conservation districts are another alternative to traditional landmark designation that can add protections to more buildings. First implemented in the 1970s, conservation districts provide more fine-grained development regulations than base zoning but are less restrictive than historic districts. Administration may be through a local historic preservation program, planning department, or specific conservation district commissions. Including demolition review as a standard element of conservation overlays would ensure that these districts conserve carbon as well as neighborhood character.

Zoning codes strongly influence whether existing buildings will stand for decades or fall to the wrecking ball. Three common zoning situations can shorten building life spans: (1) outdated zoning that includes parking minimums, setback requirements, and other provisions that make adaptive use difficult; (2) permissive zoning that invites speculative demolition and replacement; and (3) restrictive zoning that prohibits alternative uses for existing buildings and limits infill construction. While "Goldilocks zoning" for building reuse may remain elusive, preservationists can help shape this powerful land use tool by getting involved in zoning updates and rewrites.

Many communities are adopting new form-based codes (FBCs) that more closely regulate the physical characteristics of development while allowing a greater mix of uses. The best FBCs start with analysis of historic development patterns. This informs the creation of new zone districts that better fit the shape and scale of existing buildings and blocks and allow a greater range of building uses. Shrinking the differential between the size of existing development and what zoning allows can reduce pressure for replacement, while still making room for more uses and higher densities.

When comprehensive zoning reform is not feasible, targeted zoning code changes can remove key barriers that prevent or delay rehabilitation projects. Between 2012 and 2016, the National Trust worked with the Urban Land Institute, local preservation organizations, community development groups, and city leaders in five cities to identify common impediments to building reuse, including regulations. Parking minimums ranked high on the list, along with setback and open space requirements, use restrictions, and minimum unit sizes. A report on the project promotes adaptive reuse ordinances (AROs) as a strategy to quickly overcome these

28
Preservation Green Lab, *Untapped Potential: Strategies for Revitalization and Reuse,* National Trust for Historic Preservation, 2017, https://forum.savingplaces.org/viewdocument/untapped-potential-strategies-for.

29
Mike Powe, "From Vacancy to Vitality in Little Havana," National Trust for Historic Preservation, August 15, 2019, https://forum.savingplaces.org/blogs/mike-powe/2019/08/15/from-vacancy-to-vitality-in-little-havana.

30
Angie Schmitt, "How Philadelphia Fixed Parking Craters Using Tax Policy," *Streetsblog USA,* October 30, 2017, https://usa.streetsblog.org/2017/10/30/how-philadelphia-fixed-parking-craters-using-tax-policy; City of Oakland, "Vacant Property Tax," https://www.oaklandca.gov/topics/vacantpropertytax; Vancouver, British Columbia, "Empty Homes Tax," https://vancouver.ca/home-property-development/empty-homes-tax.aspx.

31
National Park Service, *Federal Tax Incentives for Rehabilitating Historic Buildings, Annual Report for Fiscal Year 2019,* https://www.nps.gov/tps/tax-incentives/taxdocs/tax-incentives-2019annual.pdf.

32
House Select Committee on the Climate Crisis, *Solving the Climate Crisis: The Congressional Action Plan for a Clean Energy Economy and Healthy, Resilient, and Just America,* majority staff report, June 2020, https://climatecrisis.house.gov/report, 161.

33
S. 2615, "Historic Tax Credit Growth and Opportunity Act of 2019," introduced October 10, 2019, https://www.congress.

and other obstacles to reuse, highlighting the pioneering Los Angeles ARO as an example for other cities.[28] AROs provide a bridge between outdated zoning and more comprehensive zoning overhauls that can support building conservation and reuse at a citywide scale.

Zoning can also reduce the likelihood of demolition and replacement by directing new development toward vacant land and buildings that can be repurposed. Even our densest cities contain excess surface parking, vacant lots, and empty buildings. In Little Havana, one of Miami's most densely populated neighborhoods, a National Trust study found enough vacant space to add 550 new buildings and ten thousand new residents—all without demolishing a single structure.[29] Zoning can support this kind of incremental infill development by legalizing accessory dwelling units, removing parking requirements, reducing minimum lot sizes, and allowing more diversity and intensity of uses. Some cities have gone even further, using financial disincentives such as parking taxes and vacant building taxes to encourage development of underused properties.[30]

Create more building reuse incentives

Preservationists have built an effective system of local, state, and federal tax incentives to encourage building reuse. Since 1976 federal historic tax incentives have supported the rehabilitation of more than 45,000 buildings.[31] Parallel tax-credit programs in thirty-nine states as well as numerous local incentives have spurred additional investment in older buildings and neighborhoods. While the catalytic effects and community benefits of historic tax incentives are well documented, the scale of their impact remains modest in the context of 125 million existing buildings.

Two strategies could extend financial support to more building rehabilitation and reuse projects. One approach is to make current incentives available for a greater variety of undertakings, including work on undesignated buildings. There is precedent for this idea in preservation history. Begun as a simple demolition disincentive, by 1981 the federal historic tax incentive program offered three levels of support for building reuse: a 15 percent income tax credit for rehabilitation of nonresidential buildings at least thirty years old; a 20 percent credit for work on nonresidential buildings at least forty years old; and a 25 percent credit for rehabilitation of certified historic buildings. A series of tax reform bills pared back this robust system, and today only income-producing, certified historic structures are eligible for the 20 percent federal credit.

The time may be ripe to reinstate a tiered system of rehabilitation tax incentives. A recent congressional report on climate change highlights the carbon emission reductions that could be achieved by making rehabilitation credits available for more buildings: "Re-expansion of the tax credit could help incentivize further building reuse beyond certified historic buildings and could be used to specifically incentivize reduction of embodied emissions associated with building construction if the non-historic credit provisions were tied to this goal."[32] Two current legislative proposals move in this direction: one would deepen the federal historic tax credits for smaller projects, and another would create a new federal tax credit for the rehabilitation of nonhistoric buildings.[33] In addition, several states have developed innovative tax incentives for reuse, such as

South Carolina's program for vacant textile mills, which applies to any textile mill abandoned for at least five years. [34]

Future carbon-tax programs may offer an even larger opportunity to expand incentives for building reuse. Most climate policy makers believe that we need carbon pricing to spur the economic and technological transformations necessary to eliminate CO2 emissions by 2050. Preservationists could join with climate advocates to position the rehabilitation of older and historic buildings as eligible beneficiaries of new funds created through carbon taxes. For example, some local governments may begin assessing fees on new development projects that exceed embodied carbon emission thresholds. A portion of these fees could be reallocated to building reuse projects. Alternatively, low-carbon developments, such as adaptive reuse projects, could receive carbon-tax rebates.

Sweeping new state or federal carbon-tax policies could provide additional support for building reuse and retrofitting. Carbon cap-and-trade programs may be more politically viable than across-the-board carbon taxes. Already in place in California and nine northeastern states, cap-and-trade programs require large carbon emitters to purchase permits, in the form of tradeable certificates, to emit beyond certain limits, which ratchet down over time. Perhaps the carbon savings achieved through the rehabilitation and long-term preservation of an existing building could be quantified and purchased as a tradable certificate. Easements or covenants could be required to prevent future demolition and replacement. Taken together, new local, state, and federal carbon policies could transform the building industry and tip development practices toward greater reuse. To maximize the benefits from these policies, however, preservation and climate advocates must offer clear and affordable methodologies to quantify the carbon savings achieved when new construction is avoided through building reuse and rehabilitation.

Prioritize materials conservation in rehabilitation

Measurement and tracking of carbon emissions from all aspects of construction—including rehabilitation and maintenance—will become increasingly important as new carbon-tax programs, zero-carbon building codes, and other climate policies are adopted in coming years. For preservationists, it will not be enough to simply say that reusing an older building avoids the carbon emissions that would have occurred during the production of materials for a new replacement structure. The process of adapting and rehabilitating an older building inevitably requires new materials as well. A key finding from the *Greenest Building* report is that the carbon savings achieved through reuse are erased if too many new materials are added. [35] Seemingly small decisions such as adding ceiling panels, constructing partition walls, installing wall-to-wall carpet, or paving a parking lot can undo much of the carbon reduction benefit from a building reuse project.

As we seek to reduce embodied carbon emissions from the building sector, it is important to keep in mind that embodied carbon is released in three stages during a building's life cycle: *initial* embodied carbon emissions when a building is constructed; *recurrent* embodied carbon emissions from periodic building maintenance and rehabilitation; and

gov/116/bills/s2615/ BILLS-116s2615is.pdf; H.R. 6175, "Revitalizing Economies, Housing, and Businesses Act of 2020," introduced March 10, 2020, https://www.congress.gov/bill/116th-congress/house-bill/6175/text.

34 "South Carolina Textiles Communities Revitalization Act," effective June 12, 2008, South Carolina Code of Laws Unannotated, Title 12, Chapter 65, https://www.scstatehouse.gov/code/t12c065.php.

35 Preservation Green Lab, *Greenest Building*, 87.

36
Dixit, "Life Cycle
Recurrent Embodied
Energy Calculation in
Buildings," 739.

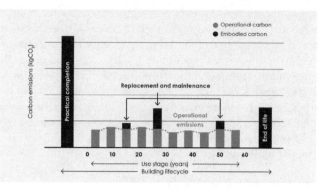

FIG. 4: Emissions across the life cycle of a building. From the London Energy Transformation Initiative, LETI Embodied Carbon Primer, January 2020.

demolition embodied carbon emissions at the end of a building's life. *FIG. 4* Recent research has found that recurring embodied carbon emissions may account for as much as 60 percent of total life cycle embodied carbon emissions over a hundred-year building life span. [36] Methods to assess and minimize recurrent carbon emissions should be integrated into design guidance for rehabilitation projects.

Developed during the 1970s in tandem with new federal grant programs and tax incentives for preservation, the Secretary of the Interior's Standards for the Treatment of Historic Properties (the "Standards") provide guidance to designers and review bodies at the local, state, and national level. The Standards articulate strong material conservation principles and commonsense practices. Ideas such as "repair rather than replace" and "reversibility" resonate anew in an era of concern about carbon emissions. As with other preservation policies, however, the Standards currently impact a relatively small set of designated historic buildings.

To increase the relevance and influence of the Standards, a new "reuse" treatment for older buildings could join the current list of four approaches (preservation, rehabilitation, restoration, reconstruction) for historic properties. A more flexible reuse treatment might fit well with new tax incentives aimed at the reuse and retrofitting of older, undesignated "nonhistoric" buildings. Local preservation commissions and planning departments could apply a reuse treatment in regulating changes to properties in conservation districts as well as noncontributing buildings in historic districts. This treatment could also respond to the growing need to retrofit mid- and late twentieth-century buildings that are now "coming of age" by the millions. Some argue that many buildings from this era are poorly built, waste energy, and need replacement. A reuse treatment could prioritize retention of structural elements and other high-carbon materials, while allowing a greater range of alterations to improve energy performance.

To become even more responsive to the climate crisis, additional guidance for applying the Standards could more explicitly support materials conservation. For example, the Standards could recommend the use of low-carbon or carbon-sequestering materials (such as wood or other organic materials), allow replacement of damaged or missing elements with salvaged materials when none are available on-site, and offer guidance on how to responsibly deconstruct unneeded building elements. Building on the concept of reversibility, the Standards might also allow the use of modular, temporary elements that can be easily disassembled, removed, and reused elsewhere as needs change. Guidance could recommend the use of mechanical fasteners instead of adhesives ("screws, not glues") and exposing connections and systems where possible to facilitate future changes without requiring demolition and waste of materials. [37] Finally, to ensure carbon accountability and measure savings, the Standards could recommend full life-cycle carbon assessment for all treatments.

37
These and more ideas to reduce the carbon impacts of rehabilitation are found in *Buildings That Last: Design for Adaptability, Deconstruction, and Reuse* (Washington, DC: American Institute of Architects, 2020), http://content.aia.org/sites/default/files/2020-03/ADR-Guide-final_0.pdf.

Strengthen demolition review policies

In many communities, including almost all major cities, local landmark ordinances include the power to deny the proposed demolition of a listed or contributing historic structure. Demolitions are rare in local historic districts. But as noted earlier, landmark ordinances protect only a small fraction of properties, leaving the vast majority of existing buildings undesignated and vulnerable to demolition. Some municipalities have enacted demolition review ordinances for undesignated properties. Triggered when a demolition permit is requested, these ordinances typically include a delay provision ranging from thirty days to six months to allow for consideration of alternatives to demolition, including designation.

In practice, demolition review ordinances cast a very coarse net, catching only those properties that are significant enough to attract the attention of local preservation advocates. Outside of a handful of high-profile cases, most demolitions move forward without delay. For example, Denver's demolition review policy resulted in fewer than a dozen "saves" between 2014 and 2019. Meanwhile, more than two thousand structures were demolished over the same period. FIG. 5

Current demolition review policies presume that permits will be approved, except in unusual circumstances. With the urgent need to limit carbon emissions from construction activity, perhaps it is time to flip this

FIG. 5: *Teardown in Denver, Colorado, 2007. Salvageable building materials, as well as history, are lost when older buildings are mechanically demolished. Photograph by the author.*

38
A version of this
approach is described
by Tom Mayes in
"Changing the Paradigm
from Demolition to
Reuse — Building
Reuse Ordinances,"
in *Bending the Future:
50 Ideas for the Next
50 Years of Historic
Preservation in the
United States*, ed. Max
Page and Marla Miller
(Amherst: University of
Massachusetts Press,
2016), 162–165.

39
Health Impact
Assessments (HIAs)
offer a precedent
for applying public
benefit evaluation
criteria to proposed
construction projects;
see *A Review of Health
Impact Assessments
in the US: Current
State-of-Science, Best
Practices, and Areas
for Improvement*,
Environmental
Protection Agency,
December 2013,
https://www.epa.gov/
sites/production/files/
2015-03/documents/
review-hia.pdf.

40
City of Portland, Oregon,
"Deconstruction
Requirements," https://
www.portland.gov/bps/
decon/deconstruction-
requirements.

41
City of Milwaukee,
Wisconsin,
"Deconstruction
Ordinance," enacted
January 1, 2018, https://
city.milwaukee.gov/
DNS/Inspections_
Sections/Decon.

model around. What if our policies presume that demolition requests will *not* be approved unless certain criteria can be met? And what if those criteria expand beyond historic, architectural, and cultural significance to include environmental impacts, including embodied carbon emissions? [38]

This approach could bring preservationists together with climate activists who are also seeking ways to reduce carbon emissions. In the future, demolition permits could require a "carbon impact assessment" for proposals over a certain size threshold. [39] Applicants would be asked to document how a proposed demolition and replacement would result in fewer carbon emissions than a scenario that includes retention and reuse of the existing building. Other ideas for strengthening demolition review include requiring approval of plans for new construction before demolition permits are issued (to avoid speculative demolition) and requiring deconstruction when demolition permits are approved.

Add deconstruction to the preservation policy toolbox

Instinctively, many preservation advocates are uncomfortable with the idea of building deconstruction. Although careful disassembly, salvaging, and repurposing of building materials save valuable resources, the building itself is lost. If deconstruction is seen as an acceptable path, will whole-building preservation and reuse become less common? Could a growing market for salvaged materials create an incentive to demolish more buildings?

Portland, Oregon, offers the most complete test case for deconstruction ordinances in the United States. In 2016 the city enacted an ordinance requiring deconstruction for houses and duplexes built prior to 1916. Restore Oregon, the statewide preservation advocacy organization, helped shape the Portland deconstruction program, in part to slow demolitions in a state where property rights law limits the protections available through local landmarking. Data through 2019 shows that approximately one-third of permitted demolitions in Portland required deconstruction as opposed to mechanical demolition, diverting an estimated 2.4 million pounds of construction materials from the landfill. Meanwhile, demolition applications dropped by nearly 50 percent, from more than 350 in 2016 to 185 in 2019. Following this success, the Portland city council voted to extend deconstruction requirements to houses and duplexes constructed in 1940 or earlier, a change that is expected to double the percentage of demolition permits requiring deconstruction citywide. [40]

Portland's example is inspiring other cities to enact similar programs. In late 2017 the Milwaukee city council passed an ordinance requiring deconstruction rather than demolition for homes and small apartments built before 1929. In addition to creating jobs and diverting materials from the landfill, the ordinance is intended to "reduce carbon emissions associated with demolition activity by preserving the embodied carbon and energy of existing building materials and avoiding the creation of greenhouse gasses associated with producing new materials." [41] Additional municipal and nonprofit deconstruction programs are underway in cities such as Baltimore, Cleveland, Detroit, Pittsburgh, and Seattle. The San Antonio Office of Historic Preservation launched a deconstruction and salvage initiative in 2017 to help meet the city's climate action and adaptation plan goals. San Antonio's example puts deconstruction firmly in the preservation toolbox, adding it to a spectrum of carbon-saving strategies for older buildings.

Although the use of "spolia" from ruined buildings has a long history, the modern building materials reuse industry is relatively young. Many questions remain, including whether the market for reclaimed materials could become too strong. In Vancouver, British Columbia, which instituted deconstruction requirements in 2015, demand for old-growth timber from deconstructed homes may be accelerating demolition rates.[42] Cautionary tales like this underscore the need to combine deconstruction requirements with other policies, such as demolition review, carbon-impact assessments, and building-reuse incentives.

▶ CONCLUSION: TAKING PRESERVATION
   TO A MATERIAL LEVEL

A greater focus on building materials may become one of the hallmarks of preservation practice, and construction generally, in the era of climate action. Armed with data on the embodied carbon content of steel I beams, concrete floor slabs, and glass curtain walls, preservation advocates in the coming years may have more success in making a case for the conservation and reuse of large buildings—or at least for the retention of their structural systems. Additive design solutions, weaving together old and new elements, may become more common. At the same time, the growing availability of high-efficiency, low embodied carbon replacement products may challenge the decision criteria and guidance of landmark commissions and other preservation review bodies. Local preservation departments may choose to add materials conservation and deconstruction experts to their staff. Preservationists at all levels will need to understand the embodied carbon content of common building materials as well as they know the difference between Italianate and Greek Revival architectural styles.

As we realize that every building contains a unique combination of materials, each with a history, our definition of stewardship will grow as well.[43] Consider a wood rafter in an old attic: observing its dense grain, we learn that years ago, a tree absorbed carbon through photosynthesis and grew for decades to create a sturdy trunk and limbs that were harvested, cut into logs, trucked to a mill, sawn into lumber, dried in a kiln, trucked again to a building site, and finally nailed into place to hold up the roof above us. We understand how using that rafter thoughtfully, in this house today and perhaps in another building years from now, not only avoids the need to harvest more wood but also prevents the release of carbon that occurs when lumber is left to decompose, wasted, in a landfill. In the story of an ordinary rafter, abstract concepts of "sequestering" carbon in buildings and material "life cycles" become real. Enlightened, we look again at a block of old houses and think: that's a lot of carbon.

42
Susan Ross, "Re-Evaluating Heritage Waste: Sustaining Material Values through Deconstruction and Reuse," *The Historic Environment: Policy and Practice* 11, no. 2–3, February 2020, 15–16.

43
The Delta Institute in Chicago developed the "StoryWood" tool kit to foster greater awareness, documentation, and reuse of salvaged wood; see https://delta-institute.org/project/storywood.

Balancing Sustainable Growth, Preservation,
and Equity: Lessons from California

An Interview with Louise Bedsworth and Ken Bernstein

Reorienting toward Climate and Justice

ERICA AVRAMI

While policies governing the built environment and community preser-
vation exist across various scales, most power is invested at the local level
across the United States. However, California has a history of challenging
and working across traditional state versus local divides in creative ways,
both top-down and bottom-up. From your respective points of view—Ken
as director of the Office of Historic Resources in Los Angeles and Louise as
executive director of the California Strategic Growth Council—could you
explain how these local/state dynamics play out in your work?

KEN BERNSTEIN

I bring the perspective of a historic preservation and planning practitioner at the municipal level, working for the nation's second-largest city and one of the most diverse cities in the world. In many ways, our work is intensely local and at the grassroots neighborhood level, but because it's Los Angeles, it feels at times like it's a miniregion or even a state unto itself. Los Angeles is a city of about 470 square miles and four million people, a diverse city with about 225 languages spoken in the home. So it is local work, but perhaps at a grand scale. The Office of Historic Resources works closely with individual neighborhoods, with community organizations, even at the block level, but that work is very much shaped by the framework of citywide policy and the relationship between local government and the state.

California has long led the way on a variety of policy issues. Whether on environmental protection or air quality, or on questions of immigration and diversity, California has been well ahead of many other states in the nation. We've also been at the forefront of dealing with how taxes and fiscal issues have influenced land use. This dates back to Proposition 13 in the 1970s, which dramatically changed the incentive structure for land use and development in California. By severely limiting property taxes, Proposition 13 incentivized revenue-generating uses such as sales taxes and, in many cases, disincentivized the development of housing. California's tradition of innovation and that long-standing interaction between larger state policies and local planning has significantly shaped our work at the local level.

Recently, that relationship has been very much defined by an increasingly assertive state role in the development of housing to address the California housing crisis.

LOUISE BEDSWORTH

It's within that historic context that the Strategic Growth Council (SGC) was established just over ten years ago to support sustainable community development in California by bringing together relevant state agencies to coordinate our actions. We have seven cabinet-level members that represent six state agencies, the Governor's Office of Planning and Research, and three public members. We do our work through direct investment in communities. We also do a lot of collaborative policy work, trying to work across state agencies to align different policy initiatives.

However, as we think about how we support communities in achieving sustainability and equity goals, it's critically important that it's not a top-down process but one that is led by the vision and goals of local communities. One thing we do in our program design and implementation is provide technical assistance and capacity building in support of community partnership, collaboration, and visioning. Enabling access to funding programs by building partnerships and community collaboration has become central to all of our programmatic work.

We also work within the context of specific programs or with given communities to say, "What are you looking to accomplish? And how can we help with that?" The council has received a continuous appropriation of funding from the Greenhouse Gas Reduction Fund, which comes from revenues from the state's Cap-and-Trade Program. Reducing greenhouse gas emissions is a top priority for the State of California, and we consider our work supporting community-led collaborations that advance equity a part of that context. We put this funding into a program called Affordable Housing and Sustainable Communities. It takes an integrated approach to investing in affordable housing in infill areas that is integrated with transit that provides urban greening and programming for residents. That integrated approach has become a model for how we do our work. Another of our large programs is called Transformative Climate Communities, where we work at a neighborhood scale and invest in a set of integrated projects. Within that program, we require a collaborative stakeholder structure and extensive partnerships across the community. We provide technical assistance, both in accessing the funds and in implementing the programs. The idea is that we're investing in a set of projects and programs that have been identified by a community or a neighborhood as priority needs.

Much of our work supports disadvantaged communities. These are places with high rates of pollution and other environmental burdens, and areas of concentrated poverty. That classification has been a way for the state to prioritize investment through our climate programs. When we're investing in these places, we want to ensure that the people who live and work there benefit. So when I first thought about preservation in the context of our work, it was actually around antidisplacement, focusing on how we might build in systems to support communities. This is a challenge working across levels of governance, but it ensures that when we make those investments, it is not going to spur displacement of current residents or businesses, while at the same time providing much-needed housing and infrastructure.

KB   Balancing housing needs with local neighborhood preservation can be complicated. Los Angeles County alone has as many as sixty thousand people without homes and has been experiencing a proliferation of homeless encampments throughout the city. This crisis extends well beyond downtown Los Angeles, which traditionally had the highest concentration of homeless individuals within its Skid Row neighborhood. Ninety-two percent of the homes sold in Los Angeles are now unaffordable to those earning the median household income.

That has generated calls for action at the local and state levels, and we've seen a new type of advocate emerge locally and throughout California to combat some of the obstacles that had been thrown in the way of developing new housing. As a countermeasure to the NIMBY, or "not in my back yard," mentality, we've seen a new type of advocate called YIMBYs saying, "yes, in my back yard"—arguing that we need more housing supply at all levels and in all locations to address the disconnect between housing supply and housing demand. That has in turn generated a series of state bills, a number of which have become law, that have dramatically changed how we review proposed housing at the local level and the ways in which we can administer our existing historic preservation protections. In Los Angeles, and in most cities in California, there has been a strong tradition of local control of land use. Increasingly this new framework of new housing laws has changed what it is that we can do at the local level.

Two of these recently approved new laws are amendments to the state's Housing Accountability Act and Senate Bill 330. Together, these laws now significantly tie our hands at the local level, preventing us from rejecting the designs of new housing developments or reducing the number of units (or even the size of units). In Los Angeles we have thirty-five Historic Preservation Overlay Zones (HPOZs), or local historic districts, covering about twenty-one thousand separate parcels in the city. Each of those has its own tailored design guidelines meant to preserve significant historic architecture in those communities and ensure that new development is complementary to and respectful of its historic context. In the past, as we reviewed proposed housing projects using the design guidelines, we might have recommended modest reductions in scale to achieve more compatibility with the design of the district. While some shifting of a building's massing may still be permitted, local governments can no longer reduce a project's overall scale or housing capacity.

The new state laws further limit the ability of local governments to apply existing design guidelines. We can now apply only guidelines that are considered objective or quantifiable, that have numeric values associated with them such as size, or that do not involve any subjective judgment on the part of decision makers or city staff. SB 330 additionally prohibited local governments for the next five years from adopting any new "nonobjective" guidelines or standards and applying them to the review of housing. This provision will have the unintended consequences of preventing the City of Los Angeles from refreshing, enhancing, or streamlining our existing guidelines in local historic districts.

All of this is a real sea change in how we address historic preservation, moving from a system that traditionally has involved a level of judgment and flexibility to one where review is very limited and based upon only objective or quantifiable measures.

Historically, spatial arrangements are embedded in landscapes, whether through restrictive covenants, legacy codes, or how land use guidelines are applied. California has a rich and multicultural history, but like most cities in the United States, it also has a history of social and spatial exclusion. How are those conditions informing your work? How is the current amplification of structural racism compelling new ways of thinking and operating?

LB   About two years ago, the Strategic Growth Council, in partnership with the Public Health Institute, launched a racial equity training program for state employees. It was a pilot program with the Government Alliance on Race and Equity (GARE), involving about fifteen agencies and departments in its first learning cohort. As a result of our participation in that training, in April 2019 we became the first state agency to publicly adopt a racial equity action plan, which is now posted on SGC's website. Part of what we've done through that work is look at how we embed racial equity into our workforce, into our operations, into our programs, and into how we do our technical assistance and capacity building. We've also been focusing on how we operationalize that racial equity work. What does that look like? How do we measure that? How are we accountable for making those changes? And then how do we do that at a statewide enterprise level, not just internally?

Translating that work into projects, we think about how state goals work at a very local level. For example, we have state priorities and goals for energy efficiency, renewable energy installations, affordable housing, transit, or active transportation, but ultimately what we end up investing in is a project that reflects those goals, but in a manner that aligns with community needs and priorities. The idea is that we have a suite of programs that are within the framework of our statewide commitments around climate change, but that also ensure that we're being resilient in the face of changing climate conditions. Ultimately, in a Transformative Climate Communities (TCC) project, what that looks like is driven by the community. The community establishes this collaborative stakeholder structure that brings all the partners together with the local government and others, becoming an oversight mechanism. Our role is to enable the community to see that work through, and then, of course, we're there as the funder and as a form of top-down oversight.

For example, we did a whole suite of awards in June 2020 and gave one to a project in East Oakland, which had one of the highest incidences of COVID-19 in the Bay Area. The East Bay has a largely Latinx and African American population. The project team started working and planning before COVID-19 was being talked about anywhere. They had identified the needs of their community, one of which was a community health clinic. One of the funded projects in their application and in their ultimate award was an affordable housing development with a community garden and a number of other pieces, alongside a health clinic on the ground floor. It goes to show how you can marry different needs in a single project. The community identified housing as a critical need, but they also knew that they needed a health resource in their community, in a way that we would never know. When they design that project, we're able to bring those things together.

KB   Los Angeles is a city of tremendous ethnic, cultural, and socioeconomic diversity, and we have always tried to put these issues of inclusion and cultural significance front and center in our historic preservation program. In many ways, Los Angeles was at the leading edge of some of that thinking. Since 1962, when Los Angeles became one of the first large cities in the United States to pass a local landmarks ordinance, our designated local landmarks have been called Historic-Cultural Monuments, putting culture on an equal footing with architecture in terms of contemplating what is significant for historic designation in our communities. Through our citywide historic resources survey program, SurveyLA, we did our very best to ensure that the identification of historic resources in Los Angeles was informed by a deep understanding of the multiple layers of cultural significance in our communities and by a commitment to identify places that are significant to all of the diverse communities in Los Angeles.

For SurveyLA's citywide historic context statement, we developed context themes reflecting the major ethnic and cultural communities in the city—to begin to tell less-told stories in each of those communities, and to identify the extant places that reflect each of those histories. We did the first LGBTQ historic context statement of major cities in the country, as well as similar contexts with our Latinx communities, five of our Asian American communities, the African American community, and a pioneering context statement on women's rights, from the suffrage movement to the feminist movement of the 1970s.

More recent events have led our city and communities across the country to take a deeper look at our historic preservation practices, asking whether the roots of historic preservation and some of our specific policies and practices may be contributing to systemic racism and racial inequity in our communities. And this is very important work for our city to undertake. The Office of Historic Resources is part of the larger LA City Planning Department, which issued a statement in June 2020 acknowledging that planning has played a significant role in contributing to structural racism in our communities. The department further pledged to take a number of steps, now being led by our department's first racial equity officer, to develop an action plan to address those policies and practices. The issues here are very complex because, as in most cities, planning practices have contributed to racial and socioeconomic inequities in many different ways through a history of exclusionary zoning, redlining practices in lending, and the legacies of racially restrictive covenants. In addition, planning resources have not always been allocated equitably to address the deeper needs of communities of color.

As the City of Los Angeles actively reexamines its planning and preservation practices through an antiracist lens, it is also important for the Los Angeles preservation story to recognize and celebrate the key role that many Angelenos played in combating structural racism and exclusion. For example, SurveyLA highlighted that Los Angeles communities played an important leadership role in breaking down racially restrictive covenants. Take, for instance, the Sugar Hill neighborhood in West Adams, which was a predominantly African American community, home to some prominent Hollywood celebrities at the time, such as Hattie McDaniel. Sugar Hill residents broke down the racially restrictive covenants that had prevailed for decades and pursued legal challenges that ultimately led to the US Supreme Court taking up this issue in the 1940s. FIG. 1 These are communities that now have historic and cultural significance, both architecturally and for the role that they played in bringing about important social change, locally and nationally. FIGS. 2, 3 Los Angeles also has communities of color that see historic preservation and our existing historic preservation protections not as a legacy of exclusion but as a way of protecting unique cultural heritage and preventing further gentrification, displacement, or cultural dislocation.

FIG. 1: *The Hattie McDaniel residence in the Sugar Hill neighborhood of Los Angeles's West Adams, once owned by the actress who won an Oscar for her role in* Gone with the Wind, *is significant for its association with the legal struggle to end deed restrictions that reinforced racial segregation. Photograph by Stephen Schafer.*

It's interesting that at this moment when we are examining our thirty-five Historic Preservation Overlay Zones to evaluate whether they are contributing to racial inequities, the highest concentration of communities that are eager for new HPOZs are communities that are majority people of color. Several predominantly and historically Black communities in our city are impatient with us for not moving quickly enough to designate their neighborhoods as historic districts. It is interesting that twenty-one of our existing thirty-five HPOZs in Los Angeles have a higher percentage of residents of color than the citywide average. Our Los Angeles historic districts have tremendous ethnic and socioeconomic diversity. Many of these districts have sought historic designation not only to protect and enhance their neighborhood's architecture but also as a way of preventing erasure of their community's unique cultural identity. So these are very nuanced and multilayered conversations that we're beginning to have as we embark on this deeper examination of structural racism and historic preservation in our communities.

One of the interesting things about HPOZs in Los Angeles is the way in which they involve neighborhood representatives. Can you discuss how they empower community members to self-determine their environments, and what dynamics arise?

KB   In Los Angeles, our system is somewhat unique in that we don't have a single municipal preservation commission. We do have our citywide Cultural Heritage Commission, but we also have individual local HPOZ boards associated with each of our thirty-five HPOZs. As the program has grown, the HPOZ ordinance now allows multiple HPOZs to share a single board, so we've reduced the number of separate boards from thirty-five to twenty-one. Nevertheless, we have a well-established system of community-level design review and neighborhood involvement with our historic preservation program.

In part that decentralized system is dictated by the size of Los Angeles. Many residents who live ten, twenty, or thirty miles from downtown feel very disconnected from City Hall. It is also a way of bringing the historic preservation program down to the grassroots level, to the community, with evening meetings in the neighborhood itself, and a way of providing a human face to the program. Board appointees from the community are made by the city council member and the mayor, as well as the Cultural Heritage Commission, so that power is diffuse.

Having community members directly involved in the program, as well as helping to craft our preservation plans and design guidelines

FIGS. 2, 3: *The Mafundi Building/Watts Happening Cultural Center, established in 1969, became an important hub for African American artists, musicians, and writers in the years following the 1965 civil unrest in Watts; the building included the Watts Coffee House, a longtime Black-owned business. Photographs by Stephen Schafer.*

before those HPOZs are adopted, is a way of enhancing local buy-in and ensuring that neighborhood voices are heard in how historic preservation regulations or guidelines get adopted. That said, it's very important that the HPOZ boards reflect the diversity of viewpoints and backgrounds within each of the communities. We try to work very closely with all of the appointing entities to ensure that there is a good balance on the boards. It's also very important that board members are well trained and knowledgeable, both in historic preservation and in techniques to work productively and positively with local communities, because it is very possible when you have a multiplicity of local boards that they could, if not appropriately managed, verge into parochialism or arbitrary decision-making.

As an Office of Historic Resources, we do regular training with our board members. Right now, we are doing a series of training sessions on the changes in state housing law that I've already referred to so that they better understand the new dynamics of local decision-making and what their purview is under this new relationship. It's very important, as we continue this discussion about racial equity and structural racism, that we also look at our HPOZ boards and our practices. We need to make our processes as accessible, clear, and consistent as possible, especially for property owners or stakeholders who have limited resources to prepare detailed architectural plans or to hire consultants to navigate the city process. We are carefully examining all of these processes to make certain that they are not creating unintended inequities and are beginning to develop new strategies to provide more helpful guidance, as well as pro bono technical assistance, where needed, to make everything as accessible and workable as possible.

Historically, advocates for sustainable growth and for preservation have often been at odds over the issue of density. Given the housing crisis in California and its climate change-related risks, and the ways in which equity is central to both, how are questions of density being redefined, and how are you finding common ground?

LB   We often think about density in the context of big cities, like you need to live in Los Angeles or New York or Oakland or San Francisco. The fact is, you can get the benefits of a more dense development pattern in all kinds of places. The state has a number of programs that try to incentivize development in areas that have lower vehicle miles traveled. The fact is you see those kinds of places all over the state. That does not mean you need to live in San Francisco—you can find a more rural or smaller town where you're going to be able to drive less.

Density needs to be thought of in a much more contextual way. It's about accessibility. It's about social networks, cohesion, and connection. It's not about packing people in. It's about building in the right way. Now more than ever, given the context of COVID-19, it's critically important that we're able to talk about that in a better way. I don't know if we have either the programs or the language right now, but I think it's a challenge. The real risk is coming out of the pandemic, and all of a sudden we feel like we shouldn't be living next to people. That is not the answer, but I think it's the knee-jerk reaction.

When we look at the communities that have been most affected by the pandemic in California, we're seeing much higher rates of COVID-19 in our Latinx and in our Black and Brown communities, just like we see most other burdens—a lot of which can be traced to overcrowding and housing. And that directly ties back to the issues of housing affordability and housing production in California, not to density. Crowding and density need to be talked through. Density is people and dwelling units, but it's also what that enables in terms of access to services, to resources, to social networks, and to other people who can help you. We've seen tremendous benefits in the pandemic coming from the fact that you can shop for your elderly neighbor who shouldn't be going out, who is just right there, and you can be helping. It's a complex question. I do think that crowding is an important point of focus and that it results from a lack of affordable and accessible housing.

KB   I agree completely with Louise. Early on, during the COVID-19 crisis, there was an unfortunate conflation of the term "density" with the idea of overcrowding.

Los Angeles does have a historic level of density that surprises many, and that carries over as well to our HPOZs, our historic districts, which have a level of residential density that is 50 percent higher than the residential density in the rest of the city. FIG. 4 One writer termed Los Angeles's level of density "dense sprawl" because it is a more widespread and consistent level of density across the region, whereas New York has Manhattan and some of its central boroughs and then very large lot single-family housing out in the suburbs.

Los Angeles has been going through a significant transition that Louise's agency has been fostering to help create transit-oriented communities in our city, accelerating our gradual shift from an auto-oriented metropolis to a transit-oriented metropolis. Our citywide plans continue to call for focusing additional growth and density and activity near transit stops and continuing to invest significantly in transit, which we've done through significant sales tax measures and other measures. We think about it as trying to build upon what we have in Los Angeles, recognizing that some of our historic districts have this level of livability, walkability, and density, but allowing focused growth. Our region has suffered some setbacks this year in that regard, losing transit ridership from discretionary riders, although those who rely upon transit as essential workers have not decreased their use of our transit system. We've certainly seen the public discourse around the term "density" begin to affect the public conversation around land use debates at the local level in recent months. The current crisis highlights some opportunities to consider models of increased density that would have a beneficial effect, both from a public health standpoint and as a broader strategy to address planning and affordable housing priorities.

One of those is the accessory dwelling unit (ADU), or granny flat, as a way of introducing modest levels of additional housing opportunity into single-family neighborhoods. This is another area where we've seen significant new state mandates that have dramatically reduced the

FIG. 4: LA's historic districts often feature livable density and eclectic housing options: this block within the Lincoln Heights Historic Preservation Overlay Zone includes a hipped-roof cottage, a Spanish Colonial Revival triplex, and a Prairie/Craftsman-style apartment building. Photograph by Stephen Schafer.

barriers to creating new ADUs in our communities. These have included a requirement that local governments approve new ADUs without any type of discretionary review processes—essentially through an over-the-counter objective approval. ADUs are a way of introducing a certain degree of density to single-family neighborhoods that need not undermine the historic integrity of local historic districts. The new state laws allow for three dwelling units on any single-family lot in California—any owner of a single-family property can now build a new detached unit on their property and can also create a small "junior ADU" within the existing residence, creating three separate units. I think it's important to point out that ADUs, by virtue of being small and not requiring additional land acquisition, can provide new housing opportunities at a much lower price point. They can also provide for flexibility within an extended family to allow for a place to live independently or semi-independently, or to socially distance in the case of a pandemic, like COVID-19.

While our hands have been more tied by state government in reviewing ADUs at the local level, we have not seen negative outcomes in terms of impacts to our local historic districts, even though we cannot apply all of our usual design guidelines to the review of new detached ADUs. Some of the other housing laws have been more problematic in creating unintended consequences and precluding any real design review or adjustments of design that might reduce the size of even a single unit within a complex. However, the state's intervention on ADUs has had positive impacts in addressing the housing crisis on a large scale and providing a sensible level of density that can provide community benefits, as highlighted by the recent health crisis.

LB   One thing I have been contemplating quite a bit is how we could be thinking in a much more useful and creative way about density. We want to see dense housing. Projects score better under the SGC's program if they have more units per acre, but at the same time we want those units to be near different uses. Should we be thinking about density in that project area? Not just the development itself, but in the larger area, trying to capture more of the diversity of uses in the community? And this is linked to the question of accessibility. We look a lot at proximity to transit, but those transit centers also have a lot to do with how we sustain vibrant local economies and local businesses—which we now know, in light of COVID-19, are critically important. Are there ways that we could be expanding our ideas about density that get at more of those characteristics that make up a complete, vibrant community? Could we build more of that in, and could that be used to think about local economic development, opportunity for residents, and opportunity for businesses?

I worked with an intern this summer to research case studies that worked with these types of concepts, and there is an interesting set of options and ideas that we can start playing around with and possibly integrate into more helpful measures of density. Thinking in the long term is important, too, for social resilience and social networks. Having everybody move out of the middle of cities is not what we want for a variety of reasons, greenhouse gas emissions being just one.

This is why ADUs are so critically important, particularly in older cities with a more traditional development pattern. It is a way to put density into those areas in a pretty unobtrusive way. Can you then bring in a few other higher-density options without radically changing the character?

In California, at the moment we're speaking, you've got fires raging across northern parts of the state and moving south. The long coastline means that you are going to be contending with sea level rise in ways that some states can't even imagine. How do you see climate change complicating the way in which you balance sustainable growth, equity, preservation, and resilience?

LB We have to be thinking much more proactively about this. The Bay Area has three major airports: San Francisco, Oakland, and San Jose. Given current sea level rise projections, they will all be underwater. Some already experience periodic flooding. That's massive infrastructure and a huge economic impact. We have to come up with a more proactive plan. I don't even know at what scale we do that; is it a network of regional plans? It's an incredible challenge.

One approach is to be more thoughtful about structures and buildings. But another is about natural and working lands, which in many cases have a cultural or historic significance—cultural landscapes—and the role that they can play in climate mediation. We have recently funded a grant through our climate change research program to a group in Southern California, at UC Riverside, working across all of Southern California down to San Diego with eighteen tribal nations as partners to understand how ecological restoration can protect cultural resources and support resilience. This will provide an example of how to bring traditional ecological knowledge into programs and policies.

KB As Louise said, this is a large question, and, by way of background, I would say in Los Angeles we're really just beginning to become more engaged with this intersection of climate action and cultural heritage. We are now active participants in the international Climate Heritage Network, and our mayor, Eric Garcetti, has been very active on climate issues as the current chair of the C40 Cities. Several years ago, the mayor put forward a "Sustainable City pLAn" that proposed bold steps for climate action and that's now been reissued as a Los Angeles "Green New Deal" plan. There are a number of important substantive and numerical commitments as part of that planning, but we're still very early in our work in making the connection between that climate action and our cultural heritage work—both in how cultural heritage can contribute to positive outcomes in carbon reduction and in preparing ourselves through adaptation to protect significant cultural resources.

I am pleased that we're looking at a number of steps to address the mitigation role that our historic buildings can play by becoming more energy efficient and making a positive contribution to our fight against climate change. But we're just beginning to address the complexity of these issues of adaptation, who gets assistance, and what we're going to prioritize. Communities are still not fully facing up to the realities that are before them in terms of the impacts of climate change.

One of the areas where these considerations come into play most compellingly in Los Angeles is Venice, as a coastal community where a number of key policy priorities and challenges come into conflict. We are in the process of updating a community plan and preparing a local coastal plan for the Venice community. Venice has a legacy of bohemian culture and artistic creativity that made it a distinctive and unconventional community within Los Angeles for many decades. It is also a community that has a historically African American neighborhood, the Oakwood community, that has gone through a great deal of displacement and gentrification in recent decades. As we've seen the demolition of many smaller homes for new multifamily development or newer, larger single-family homes in that community, it has raised concerns about cultural assets and cultural preservation and how we capture the more intangible heritage that defines that Oakwood community or the unique businesses or cultural institutions that made Venice in the first place.

On top of these development pressures and cultural complexities, you now have projections for significant sea level rise that may put most of these Venice neighborhoods underwater just a few decades from now. In the public engagement that our department has done in Venice, most of the neighborhood leaders are still more focused on the immediate challenges and the immediate questions before them. Questions of density versus preservation, property rights for individual property owners, or concerns about immediate gentrification or displacement within the community of Oakwood still dominate. So how do we also think about adaptation in the Venice community when we have a number of identified potential historic districts that are likely to be lost altogether due to sea level rise? And how do we address those threats amid the ongoing challenges of equity, displacement, or cultural dislocation? These issues are very nuanced and challenging, and we don't have all the answers yet, but we're beginning these conversations.

Viewing Sustainable Preservation through an Energy Justice Lens

Amanda L. Webb
David Moore

Reorienting toward Climate and Justice

1
Carl Elefante, "The Greenest Building Is... One That's Already Built," Forum Journal 21, no. 4 (2007): 26–38.

2
Baird M. Smith and Carl Elefante, "Sustainable Design in Historic Buildings: Foundations and the Future," APT Bulletin: The Journal of Preservation Technology 40, no. 3/4 (2009): 19–26, https://www.jstor.org/stable/40284500.

3
Giovanni Carbonara, "Energy Efficiency as a Protection Tool," special issue: Historic, Historical and Existing Buildings: Designing the Retrofit, Energy and Buildings 95 (May 15, 2015): 9–12, https://doi.org/10.1016/j.enbuild.2014.12.052.

4
Erica Avrami, "Making Historic Preservation Sustainable," Journal of the American Planning Association 82, no. 2 (April 2, 2016): 105, https://doi.org/10.1080/01944363.2015.1126196.

5
Kirsten Jenkins, Darren McCauley, Raphael Heffron, Hannes Stephan, and Robert Rehner, "Energy Justice: A Conceptual Review," Energy Research & Social Science 11 (January 1, 2016): 174–182, https://doi.org/10.1016/j.erss.2015.10.004.

6
Jenkins et al., "Energy Justice."

► SUSTAINABLE PRESERVATION
AND THE NEED FOR ENERGY JUSTICE

Historic preservation has long been seen as a strategy to address broader societal concerns about sustainability. In part, this view is attributable to the inherently conservative nature of preservation itself, which provides an alternative to unsustainable resource consumption and is summarized in the maxim "the greenest building is the one that is already built."[1] But this view is also a result of four decades of touting the inherent energy-efficient features of older buildings (e.g., operable windows, overhangs, low window-to-wall ratio) and incorporating energy efficiency and sustainable design solutions into preservation practice.[2] These solutions can provide a range of benefits in retrofitted buildings, including reduced energy consumption and carbon emissions, reduced utility bills, improved thermal comfort, and increased rental and sales prices. When added to an older building, these desirable characteristics can serve as a protective tool, helping to preserve the building by keeping it in use.[3] The result is a series of compounding benefits, a virtuous cycle in which energy retrofits make an older building more desirable, desirability is more likely to preserve the building by keeping it in use, and keeping it in use is a sustainable act.

The appeal of this narrative and the compounding nature of these benefits highlights the need to understand whether they are, in fact, being realized, as well as who benefits when they are. If these benefits are real, then those who live in historic buildings and neighborhoods—particularly those that have undergone energy retrofits—are distinctly advantaged. A recent review of work in this area finds that while some progress has been made in learning about the environmental and economic benefits of sustainable preservation, "society does not preserve a place simply because it makes money or saves energy," and understanding the social impacts of sustainable preservation remains critical to ensuring its success.[4]

The concept of energy justice provides a useful lens for understanding both the environmental and the social impacts of sustainable preservation. Closely linked to concepts of social and environmental justice, energy justice applies justice principles to issues of energy production, consumption, policy, security, and activism.[5] It is founded on three primary tenets: (1) distributional justice, which posits that energy-related benefits and burdens should be distributed fairly; (2) recognition justice, which acknowledges the rights and needs of marginalized and misrepresented groups; and (3) procedural justice, which requires fairness in decision-making processes.

Together, the tenets of energy justice can serve as a framework to better guide historic preservation toward sustainable ends. Adopting such a framework would have two major consequences for preservation research and practice. First, it would provide a new, cross-disciplinary agenda. It would facilitate the identification of sites where injustices occur, the creation of better processes to prevent and remediate such injustices, and the recognition of previously marginalized groups; these steps provide a means to develop both evaluative claims and normative solutions.[6] An energy justice framework would therefore not only enable

7
Benjamin K. Sovacool,
"What Are We Doing
Here? Analyzing
Fifteen Years of Energy
Scholarship and
Proposing a Social
Science Research
Agenda," *Energy
Research & Social
Science* 1 (March 1,
2014): 15, https://
doi.org/10.1016/
j.erss.2014.02.003.

8
Jamal Lewis, Diana
Hernández, and Arline
T. Geronimus, "Energy
Efficiency as Energy
Justice: Addressing
Racial Inequities
through Investments
in People and Places,"
Energy Efficiency,
November 6, 2019,
https://doi.org/10.1007/
s12053-019-09820-z.

our assessment of injustices but also compel us to resolve them. Second, it would propagate the view that energy and its related material benefits are a basic human necessity. Energy justice is a framework that "recognizes that energy needs to be included within the list of things we prize"[7] and that stands in contrast to the prevailing view, which considers energy efficiency a luxury.[8]

The intent of this essay is to highlight how an energy justice framework can help make sustainable preservation more equitable and, conversely, can identify ways in which sustainable preservation might serve as a mechanism that furthers energy justice. While energy justice addresses a broad range of energy systems, its discussion here is necessarily limited to buildings, as these are the primary focus of historic preservation. Each section of this essay is organized around one of the three tenets of energy justice, providing additional insight into the tenet and describing relevant existing work within the preservation or building energy fields. *FIG. 1*

It is important to note that the terms "older" and "historic," which are both used here, are overlapping but distinct. "Older" refers simply to the broad segment of the building stock that is advanced in age (usually fifty years or older), while "historic" refers to the subset of older buildings that are designated as historic (or eligible for such designation). The literature on sustainable preservation often blurs this distinction, partly under the

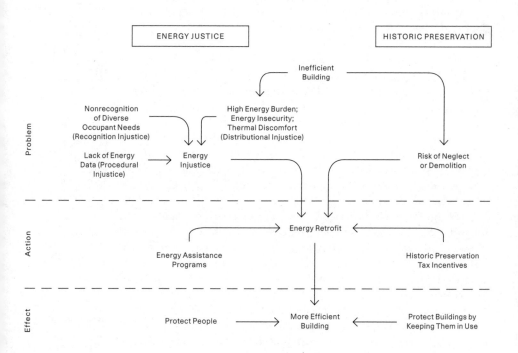

FIG. 1: This diagram depicts the frameworks of energy justice (left) and historic preservation (right) and serves as a visual outline of the essay. It illustrates the connection points between these frameworks: both regard inefficient buildings as a problem and view energy retrofits as a protective tool. Acting simultaneously, these frameworks can provide simultaneous benefits to buildings and occupants.

assumption that older and historic buildings—with their traditional construction methods and inherent energy-efficient features—have similar energy-related characteristics. However, the distinction between these two terms is important in a policy context because historic preservation policy generally applies only to historic buildings, and historic buildings (but not older ones) are treated differently in energy codes (and are often exempt from them). This essay uses each term very deliberately depending on the context.

▶ DISTRIBUTIONAL JUSTICE AND ENERGY RETROFITS

Distributional justice calls for the even distribution of both benefits and burdens on all members of a society regardless of socioeconomic or demographic differences. 9 It encompasses the distribution of both physical resources and environmental conditions across society and space. 10 The idea of equal distribution is strongly associated with intuitive notions of justice and may be the most tangible tenet of energy justice. Distributional justice is especially important in a building energy context because energy inefficiency can create a cumulative burden on households, including physical hardship (e.g., the trade-off between buying food or staying warm) and housing instability (e.g., utility shutoffs and displacement). 11

One metric used to compute distributional injustice is energy burden. Energy burden refers to the proportion of a household's income that is spent on utilities. It is related to the concept of energy poverty (also referred to as fuel poverty), a binary indicator of whether a household's energy burden is too high, and to energy insecurity, which encompasses economic strain and physical deficiencies as well as the coping and decision-making strategies associated with energy burden. 12 Data on energy burden in the United States shows an uneven distribution, with low-income and African American households experiencing a median energy burden of 7.2 percent and 5.4 percent respectively, compared to only 3.5 percent for all households. 13 As it disproportionately affects low-income and minority households, high energy burden exacerbates already existing inequities.

Energy burden is the result of three main drivers: household income, the cost of fuel, and housing energy efficiency. 14 Household income is an important driver because it determines the amount of money a household has to spend on utilities. For two households of equal energy use and housing condition but different incomes, the lower-income household will experience higher energy burden. The cost of energy varies by location and by fuel type, which puts some households at a greater risk of energy burden simply because of higher fuel prices. Finally, the energy efficiency of housing also influences utility costs and consequently energy burden. While raising household income and controlling the cost of fuel cannot be easily implemented, energy efficiency can be improved simply through alterations to the building fabric and systems.

Since building energy efficiency is a particularly crucial component of energy burden, it is necessary to understand how energy efficiency is distributed across the building stock and who is suffering the effects

9
Jenkins et al., "Energy Justice."

10
Lewis, Hernández, and Geronimus, "Energy Efficiency as Energy Justice."

11
Lewis, Hernández, and Geronimus, "Energy Efficiency as Energy Justice."

12
Diana Hernández and Douglas Phillips, "Benefit or Burden? Perceptions of Energy Efficiency Efforts among Low-Income Housing Residents in New York City," Energy Research & Social Science 8 (July 1, 2015): 52–59, https://doi.org/10.1016/j.erss.2015.04.010.

13
Ariel Drehobl and Lauren Ross, "Lifting the High Energy Burden in America's Largest Cities: How Energy Efficiency Can Improve Low-Income and Underserved Communities" (American Council for an Energy-Efficient Economy [ACEEE], April 2016), https://www.aceee.org/research-report/u1602.

14
Gordon Walker and Rosie Day, "Fuel Poverty as Injustice: Integrating Distribution, Recognition, and Procedure in the Struggle for Affordable Warmth," special section: Fuel Poverty Comes of Age: Commemorating 21 Years of Research and Policy, Energy Policy 49 (October 2012): 69–75, https://doi.org/10.1016/j.enpol.2012.01.044.

15
Tony Gerard Reames, "Targeting Energy Justice: Exploring Spatial, Racial/Ethnic and Socioeconomic Disparities in Urban Residential Heating Energy Efficiency," Energy Policy 97 (October 2016): 549–558, https://doi.org/10.1016/j.enpol.2016.07.048.

16
Jonathan L. Bradshaw,
Elie Bou-Zeid, and
Robert H. Harris,
"Comparing the
Effectiveness of
Weatherization
Treatments for Low-
Income, American,
Urban Housing Stocks
in Different Climates,"
Energy and Buildings
69 (February 2014):
535–543, https://
doi.org/10.1016/j.
enbuild.2013.11.035.

17
Drehobl and Ross,
"Lifting the High Energy
Burden."

18
Constantine E.
Kontokosta, Vincent
J. Reina, and Bartosz
Bonczak, "Energy
Cost Burdens for Low-
Income and Minority
Households," Journal of
the American Planning
Association 86, no. 1
(January 2, 2020):
89–105, https://doi.org/
10.1080/01944363.201
9.1647446.

19
US Department of
Energy, "Weatherization
Assistance Program—
National Evaluations:
Summary of Results,"
August 2015, https://
www.energy.gov/sites/
prod/files/2015/08/
f25/WAP_National
Evaluation_WxWorks_
v14_blue_8%205%
2015.pdf.

20
Bradshaw, Bou-Zeid,
and Harris, "Comparing
the Effectiveness
of Weatherization
Treatments."

21
Dominic J. Bednar
and Tony G. Reames,
"Recognition of and
Response to Energy
Poverty in the United
States," Nature Energy,
March 23, 2020, 1–8,
https://doi.org/10.1038/
s41560-020-0582-0.

22
Anne E. Grimmer et al.,
The Secretary of the
Interior's Standards
for Rehabilitation and
Illustrated Guidelines
on Sustainability for
Rehabilitating Historic
Buildings (Washington,
DC: Technical
Preservation Services,
National Park Service,
US Department of the
Interior, 2011).

of inefficiency. Research has shown that low-income, less educated, and minority populations disproportionately live in areas with higher energy use per square foot, an indicator of less efficient housing stock. [15] Low-income households in particular are 20 percent more energy intensive on average compared to higher-income households. [16] Building energy inefficiency is caused by many factors, including poor insulation, air leakage, and heating system inefficiency, which are more prevalent in unretrofitted older buildings, constructed before the advent of energy codes in the 1970s.

Energy retrofits, which are measures taken to improve the energy efficiency of a building, can serve as a mechanism to create a more equitable housing stock while advancing the practice of sustainable preservation. Retrofits can range from simple measures, such as installing energy-efficient light bulbs, to more costly measures, including replacing heating and cooling systems. Improving the energy efficiency of low-income and minority households to the level of the median household efficiency value would significantly reduce excess energy burden for those populations. [17] Through the installation of low-cost energy retrofits, low-income households could save up to $1,500 on energy costs per year. [18] However, many of these households are unable to afford energy retrofits, and renters must rely on landlords, who have little incentive to make such improvements to the property since tenants typically pay utility bills. The ability to distribute retrofits to those who need them therefore requires effective policy.

One such policy, the Weatherization Assistance Program, is a federally funded initiative that currently provides energy retrofits to eligible households based on criteria such as income and age of householder. According to the Department of Energy's national summary of the program, weatherization resulted in an average annual cost savings of $283 for single-family homes in 2008. [19] Additional research has shown that weatherization is especially effective in colder climates where greater savings potential can be realized. [20] Although there is consensus that weatherization does improve energy efficiency and therefore reduces utility bills, studies suggest that existing programs such as the Weatherization Assistance Program are underfunded or not easily accessible. [21] There is also concern from the preservation perspective that certain weatherization retrofits, such as additional insulation or window replacement, can negatively impact heritage values of existing buildings. For example, the Secretary of the Interior's Standards for the Treatment of Historic Properties discourages weatherization treatments such as the replacement of windows or the application of wall insulation. [22] More broadly, a study in Sweden found that buildings with facade insulation retrofits had lower levels of heritage designation. [23]

Rehabilitation tax credit programs are another policy tool for implementing energy retrofits into historic buildings. These programs are designed to retain residents, encourage the renovation of existing homes, and aid in neighborhood revitalization. Evidence has shown that the federal rehabilitation tax credit does, in fact, spur significant investment and results in more housing options. [24] However, one issue surrounding many tax credit programs is the apparent distributional inequity of tax incentives. Richard Swaim's examination of the Maryland Heritage

Preservation Tax Credit, for example, notes the high cost of the program and the fact that equity was not addressed. Swaim goes on to say that "tax expenditures are often cited as [a] classic example of good politics but bad policy: easily enacted, largely hidden from view, seldom cut back, transferring billions of dollars to powerful but undeserving constituencies."[25] A further implication of tax incentives is the reduced funding of government services and public schools, which can result in additional distributional inequity.

▶ RECOGNITION JUSTICE AND UNDERSTANDING OCCUPANTS

Recognition justice "refers to the acknowledgement of, and respect for, the complex circumstances and vulnerabilities of individuals and social groups in patterns of cultural value."[26] It asks us to examine which segments of the population are overlooked. In the absence of recognition, the distinct needs of vulnerable and marginalized groups remain hidden, unable to be addressed through policy.[27] Lack of recognition can also perpetuate harmful misrepresentations, such as when the energy poor are seen as inefficient users, uninformed or unwilling to live a more energy-efficient lifestyle.[28] These distortions rationalize ongoing material deprivation by portraying the energy poor as unworthy of aid, and they act as a barrier to effective interventions.[29]

Examples of recognition injustice related to building energy efficiency include a variety of marginalized groups, as observed in a number of key texts relating to energy justice. Kirsten Jenkins et al. cite the United Kingdom's policy on fuel poverty, which had long failed to recognize the need of elderly and chronically ill individuals to maintain above average space temperatures.[30] Gordon Walker and Rosie Day likewise link older individuals' physiological need for higher temperatures to recurring excess winter deaths, most of which happen to older people.[31] In addition to the elderly, the authors also mention the chronically ill, the disabled, and families with young children as groups that may have differential space temperature needs and may spend more time at home, resulting in a higher energy burden. In the United States, Jamal Lewis, Diana Hernández, and Arline T. Geronimus classify the disproportionately high rates of energy burden and energy insecurity experienced by African Americans as an example of recognition injustice, since the long history of racist housing policies and disinvestment in racially segregated neighborhoods that has produced this condition continues to go largely unacknowledged in policy.[32]

Sustainable preservation, too, fails to recognize the distinct energy-related needs of all people who live in older and historic buildings and districts. Consider interventions like replacing original single-pane windows or adding wall insulation, which improve thermal comfort and save energy but are discouraged in official preservation guidance.[33] These are obvious solutions to improving a poor thermal envelope, thermal discomfort, and high energy costs, and finding adequate alternatives can require specialized technical expertise and additional capital; these obstacles may keep sustainable preservation beyond the reach of the

23
Martin Tunefalk, Mattias Legner, and Gustaf Leijonhufvud, "Long-Term Effects of Additional Insulation of Building Facades in Sweden: Towards a Holistic Approach," International Journal of Building Pathology and Adaptation 38, no. 2 (January 1, 2019): 374–385, https://doi.org/10.1108/IJBPA-02-2019-0020.

24
Stephanie Ryberg-Webster and Kelly L. Kinahan, "Historic Preservation in Declining City Neighbourhoods: Analysing Rehabilitation Tax Credit Investments in Six US Cities," Urban Studies 54, no. 7 (May 1, 2017): 1673–1691, https://doi.org/10.1177/00420980 16629313.

25
Richard Swaim, "Politics and Policymaking: Tax Credits and Historic Preservation," Journal of Arts Management, Law, and Society 33, no. 1 (January 1, 2003): 32–39, https://doi.org/10.1080/10632920309597339; quotation from p. 38.

26
Lewis, Hernández, and Geronimus, "Energy Efficiency as Energy Justice," 425.

27
Walker and Day, "Fuel Poverty as Injustice."

28
Jenkins et al., "Energy Justice."

29
Walker and Day, "Fuel Poverty as Injustice."

30
Jenkins et al., "Energy Justice."

31
Walker and Day, "Fuel Poverty as Injustice."

32
Lewis, Hernández, and Geronimus, "Energy Efficiency as Energy Justice."

33
Grimmer et al., Secretary of the Interior's Standards for Rehabilitation.

34
Binyamin Appelbaum,
"When Historic
Preservation Hurts
Cities," New York Times,
January 26, 2020,
https://www.nytimes.
com/2020/01/26/
opinion/historic-
preservation-solar-
panels.html.

35
Laurajane Smith, Uses
of Heritage (London:
Routledge, 2006), 11.

36
Theodora Koukou
and Kalliopi Fouseki,
"Heritage Values and
Thermal Comfort
in Neoclassical
Residential Buildings of
Athens, Greece: Tension
or Co-Existence?,"
in Proceedings of
the 3rd International
Conference on
Energy Efficiency in
Historic Buildings
(Visby, Sweden, 2018),
463–471.

37 Kalliopi Fouseki and
Yekatherina Bobrova,
"Understanding the
Change of Heritage
Values over Time
and Its Impact on
Energy Efficiency
Decision-Making at
Residential Historic
Buildings through
System Dynamics,"
in Proceedings of
the 3rd International
Conference on Energy
Efficiency in Historic
Buildings (Visby,
Sweden, 2018), 11–21.

38
Annette Henning,
"Solar Collectors in
a Roof Landscape:
Balancing Change
and Preservation in a
World Heritage Site,"
in Postprints from the
Conference Energy
Efficiency in Historic
Buildings, ed. Tor
Broström and Lisa
Nilsen (Visby, Sweden:
Gotland University
Press, 2011), 151–163,
https://uu.diva-
portal.org/smash/
get/diva2:507200/
COVER02.pdf.

average homeowner. This rigidity toward energy retrofits also percolates into the public perception of historic preservation as protecting only the lifestyle of the affluent. [34]

This failure to recognize is a consequence of what Laurajane Smith calls the "authorized heritage discourse," which defines heritage as a specific set of material objects and places to be protected and admired. It forms the official philosophies and practices of preservation. It relies heavily on the knowledge claims of technical experts and becomes established as a dominant set of values and practices through state agencies. This authorized heritage discourse serves to reinforce existing divisions of nation, class, and technical expertise—privileging chiefly the values of elite social classes and preservation experts—and in doing so also acts as a mechanism of nonrecognition, discounting the perspectives of those outside of this discourse. As Smith writes, "One of the consequences of this discourse is to actively obscure the power relations that give rise to it and to make opaque the cultural and social work that 'heritage' does."[35]

Recognizing potential conflicts between authorized heritage discourse and the experiences of building occupants, recent work on energy retrofits in historic buildings has examined and elevated nonexpert perspectives. Theodora Koukou and Kalliopi Fouseki investigate how values assigned by residents in Athens, Greece, to their historic homes influence retrofit decisions. [36] Ultimately, functional values such as thermal and acoustic comfort were the highest priorities for most residents. The study also suggests that occupants, who have intimate knowledge of a building's indoor environment through their lived experience, are an underutilized but valuable source of information on a historic building's performance. In a similar vein, Fouseki and Yekatherina Bobrova have developed a model for how homeowner values change over time, with historic features valued highest at the time of purchase and declining in value with time as functional priorities such as thermal comfort and utility bill savings take precedence. [37] In Sweden, Annette Henning conducted interviews with both technical experts and homeowners in the UNESCO World Heritage site of Visby to understand perspectives on installing rooftop solar thermal panels on historic homes. [38] The results showed that the functionality of the homes and energy cost savings were priorities for the homeowners. The results also demonstrated the homeowners' obvious knowledge of and care for their historic homes, even when that care involves changing the house in ways that may seem undesirable to preservationists.

▶ PROCEDURAL JUSTICE AND ACCESS
TO ENERGY INFORMATION

Procedural justice addresses access, influence, and fairness in decision-making processes. It is closely tied to distributional justice, as a lack of procedural justice functions to produce and sustain distributional injustices. It is also closely linked to recognition justice, since acknowledgment and respect are prerequisites for influence in decision-making processes. Previous work illustrates this concept by identifying specific mechanisms of procedural justice. Walker and Day identify three pillars of procedural justice: access to information, meaningful participation in decision-making, and access to legal processes for redress. [39] Jenkins et al. similarly highlight mechanisms of inclusion: local knowledge mobilization, greater information disclosure, and better institutional representation. [40] These authors highlight information as a key mechanism and component of procedural justice.

In the context of building energy efficiency, greater access to and disclosure of energy data is a necessary prerequisite for redressing distributional injustice. Access to energy information is especially critical because energy, compared to other goods, is abstract and invisible to end users. Jacquelin Burgess and Michael Nye even describe energy as "doubly invisible," hidden first as an abstract concept consumed through invisible wires and second as a set of everyday behaviors, the impacts of which remain hidden. [41] Corinna Fischer notes that energy consumption is actually a collection of diverse activities that include both consumption (e.g., watching television, doing laundry) and purchasing (e.g., buying a TV set or a washing machine), making it challenging for end users to form a coherent picture of their energy consumption. [42] Energy information can operate on two scales to make energy more visible: first, data at the level of the building stock, which can inform policy and transform the market for energy-efficient buildings, and second, feedback at the level of an individual household, which can influence end users to adopt energy-efficient behaviors.

In the United States, one increasingly common use of information to inform policy and transform the market is municipal energy benchmarking and disclosure ordinances, with more than two dozen major cities enacting them to date. [43] These laws require buildings to report their energy consumption to the local municipality on an annual basis, and they typically have some provision for disclosing that information to the public through a report, an interactive website, or building energy labels. While they do not directly mandate energy efficiency improvements, these laws are intended to disclose information that is typically unavailable to actors in the real estate market (e.g., potential renters, buyers, and investors), enabling them to include energy costs in their decisions and moving the market toward greater efficiency over time. [44]

These laws are a particularly important mechanism for addressing the energy performance of historic buildings, which are generally exempt from energy codes, as well as older buildings in general. However, their scope is not well suited to provide sufficient coverage of the older and historic building stock. Since larger buildings use more energy than smaller ones, benchmarking ordinances have a size threshold (typically 50,000 square feet and up) making them applicable only to a city's largest commercial and multifamily residential buildings. [45] The focus on large buildings limits the impact of these policies on older and historic buildings, which tend to be smaller.

The limited scope of these disclosure laws leaves a market information gap for homeowners and renters in single-family or small multifamily buildings. This gap can be especially problematic for those in older or historic homes, as data from the US Energy Information Administration

39
Walker and Day, "Fuel Poverty as Injustice."

40
Jenkins et al., "Energy Justice."

41
Jacquelin Burgess and Michael Nye, "Re-Materialising Energy Use through Transparent Monitoring Systems," special issue: Foresight Sustainable Energy Management and the Built Environment Project, Energy Policy 36, no. 12 (December 1, 2008): 4454–4459, https://doi.org/10.1016/j.enpol.2008.09.039.

42
Corinna Fischer, "Feedback on Household Electricity Consumption: A Tool for Saving Energy?," Energy Efficiency 1, no. 1 (May 6, 2008): 79–104, https://doi.org/10.1007/s12053-008-9009-7.

43
Institute for Market Transformation, "Comparison of US Commercial Building Energy Benchmarking and Transparency Policies," February 2019, https://www.imt.org/resources/comparison-of-commercial-building-benchmarking-policies.

44
Karen Palmer and Margaret Walls, "Using Information to Close the Energy Efficiency Gap: A Review of Benchmarking and Disclosure Ordinances," Energy Efficiency 10, no. 3 (June 1, 2017): 673–691, https://doi.org/10.1007/s12053-016-9480-5.

45
Palmer and Walls, "Using Information to Close the Energy Efficiency Gap."

46
US Energy Information Administration, "Table CE1.1 Summary Annual Household Site Consumption and Expenditures in the US—Totals and Intensities, 2015," 2015, https://www.eia.gov/consumption/residential/data/2015/c&e/pdf/ce1.3.pdf.

47
Richard Faesy et al., "Populating the MLS with Energy Information—A Progress Report," in *ACEEE Summer Study on Energy Efficiency in Buildings* (Asilomar, CA, 2018).

48
Magali A. Delmas, Miriam Fischlein, and Omar I. Asensio, "Information Strategies and Energy Conservation Behavior: A Meta-Analysis of Experimental Studies from 1975 to 2012," *Energy Policy* 61 (October 1, 2013): 729–739, https://doi.org/10.1016/j.enpol.2013.05.109.

49
Fredrik Berg et al., "User-Driven Energy Efficiency in Historic Buildings: A Review," *Journal of Cultural Heritage* 28 (November 1, 2017): 188–195, https://doi.org/10.1016/j.culher.2017.05.009.

50
Tom Hargreaves, Michael Nye, and Jacquelin Burgess, "Keeping Energy Visible? Exploring How Householders Interact with Feedback from Smart Energy Monitors in the Longer Term," *Energy Policy* 52 (January 2013): 126–134, https://doi.org/10.1016/j.enpol.2012.03.027.

51
Lewis, Hernández, and Geronimus, "Energy Efficiency as Energy Justice."

suggests that households in older buildings use more energy on a per-square-foot basis than newer ones.[46] While energy information is provided to occupants post-occupancy based on utility bills, privacy laws typically protect this data from disclosure to anyone besides the current building occupant. This leaves prospective buyers or renters unaware of the true burden of energy costs. One strategy for addressing this issue is incorporating energy-related information into the Multiple Listing Service used by residential real estate consumers and brokers, but adoption is still a work in progress.[47]

Energy information can also be used to provide feedback to individual households for the purpose of encouraging more energy-efficient behaviors. Most households receive feedback on energy use only through a monthly utility bill, which provides no information on how various end uses and everyday behaviors impact energy costs. Enhanced feedback can take various forms, including peer comparisons, energy-saving tips, and real-time displays. Previous studies have shown average energy savings from feedback-based behavioral interventions to be around 7 percent.[48] Such user-driven energy savings are of particular interest in historic buildings, as they can reduce energy consumption with no physical impact on the historic character or fabric of the building.[49]

While feedback-induced behavioral changes can lead to real energy savings, the impacts of this feedback can differ considerably according to the context of each household and may even be detrimental to vulnerable populations. Tom Hargreaves, Michael Nye, and Jacquelin Burgess find that for low-income households or households with a member suffering from a medical condition that requires higher space temperatures, real-time energy feedback can highlight a household's lack of control over its energy behaviors and can create additional anxiety regarding high energy costs. They draw attention to the differential meaning of energy information, writing that "rather than being a neutral form of information provision, therefore, feedback on energy use acquires meaning through the discursive, interpretive lens of each household's cultural practices."[50] Informational feedback is also unlikely to result in energy savings for households that are low energy consumers and for those that are already exhibiting restriction behaviors (e.g., keeping temperatures very low to reduce energy costs), as is the case for many households with a high energy burden.

▶ RESTORATIVE JUSTICE:
TOWARD A MORE SUSTAINABLE PRESERVATION

Recent scholarship has added a fourth tenet of energy justice: restorative justice, which requires action that redresses observed injustices.[51] In the absence of restorative justice, injustices can be described and acknowledged, but they will still persist. Here, restorative justice provides a means to summarize the solutions discussed throughout this essay by explicitly asking, What can the preservation community do to promote energy justice? How can sustainable preservation be used as a tool to fix distributional, recognition, and procedural injustices?

Regarding distributional justice, the preservation community first needs to help identify the roles of older buildings and historic buildings in creating a high household energy burden, especially for low-income and minority households. More quantitative research is needed to better understand the interactions between building age, energy efficiency, and demographics. Second, preservationists need to view energy retrofits as a potential tool for restorative justice through energy efficiency. Households living in retrofitted historic buildings benefit from lower utility bills and improved thermal comfort, which protect them from secondary impacts of energy inefficiency, like poor health outcomes, housing insecurity, and the choice between buying food or paying for utilities. Current instruments like the federal rehabilitation tax credit, which are guided by aesthetic concerns for building fabric and character, are poorly suited to ensuring that historic building energy retrofits are directed to where they are most needed. New financial mechanisms and programs should be developed to achieve this end, and they will require creative collaboration between the historic preservation, sustainability, and energy justice communities. For example, existing energy efficiency programs (especially those at the municipal level) could be modified to include a track specifically to assist low-income residents living in older or historic homes.

Regarding recognition justice, the preservation community needs to challenge the "authorized heritage discourse" and recognize the value of occupant perspectives. Older and historic buildings house a diverse range of occupants with differing needs, capacities, and experiences. These experiences are a valuable and underutilized source of information that should inform the retrofit process. To better understand these experiences, ongoing research gathering nonexpert and occupant perspectives on historic building retrofits should be expanded. Sustainable preservation guidance should also be adapted to acknowledge the importance of user perspectives and the need for affordable and functional retrofit solutions. The European Standard EN 16883 provides an example in this regard, stating that the process of retrofitting a historic building should be done in close cooperation with the users. 52

Regarding procedural justice, the preservation community needs to promote greater access to and disclosure of energy information about older and historic buildings. Accurate, publicly available data can help identify distributional injustices and inform policy to remediate them. It can also make issues of energy burden and energy justice more widely known and can promote sustainable preservation as an important policy tool. Current benchmarking and disclosure policies provide one data collection mechanism, but additional strategies are needed to address the many older and historic buildings that lie beyond their scope.

Preservationists and, more recently, the building energy community take the view that older and historic buildings are "too valuable and leave too large an environmental footprint to be neglected or abandoned."53 Likewise, the occupants of these buildings are too valuable to be neglected or abandoned. While sustainable preservation has provided a tool to properly care for these buildings, it has neglected to properly care for the diversity of people who inhabit them. Adopting an energy justice framework ultimately enables the preservation community to recognize the impacts—both positive and negative—of sustainable preservation on people.

52
CEN, *EN 16883:2017, Conservation of Cultural Heritage—Guidelines for Improving the Energy Performance of Historic Buildings* (Brussels: European Committee for Standardization [CEN], 2017).

53
Thomas Phoenix, "Lessons Learned: ASHRAE's Approach in the Refurbishment of Historic and Existing Buildings," special issue: Historic, Historical and Existing Buildings: Designing the Retrofit, *Energy and Buildings* 95 (May 15, 2015): 13–14, https://doi.org/10.1016/j.enbuild.2015.02.034.

Housing Preservation, Health, and Sustainability

Stephanie Ryberg-Webster

Reorienting toward Climate and Justice

Cities across the United States have vast landscapes of housing, comprising the spaces of daily life for millions of city dwellers. Residential structures are a core part of the older and historic built environment, and houses are a defining element of neighborhood character regardless of whether they have historic designation. Older housing also presents contemporary challenges such as ongoing maintenance, repair, or replacement of aging materials to fulfill the demands of modern living. Population decline, common in the Rust Belt, results in an oversupply of buildings, making the preservation of older housing particularly difficult.

Ohio's three major cities, Cleveland, Cincinnati, and Columbus, offer insight into housing rehabilitation and preservation within the context of recent citywide sustainability and climate action planning, with a particular focus on public and nongovernmental policies, programs, and planning. These cities all have an aging housing stock that exists within differing economic and population conditions. Cleveland is a shrinking city with a high poverty rate and an older housing stock that suffers from decades of disinvestment. Cincinnati has had less severe population decline than Cleveland, resulting in a stronger market, some newer housing, and lower vacancy rates. Columbus has older neighborhoods but is growing, giving it a newer and more diverse housing stock. Three key research questions guide this exploratory analysis: What range of housing rehabilitation initiatives exist at the local level? How do housing programs originating in the preservation sector and those focused on lead abatement relate to the broader spectrum of housing strategies? And how do sustainability and climate action planning reveal ongoing disconnects between preservation and broader urban agendas, while also pushing preservationists to think differently about addressing housing rehabilitation?

Housing rehabilitation occurs through public, private, and nongovernmental action, with historic preservation-centered strategies comprising just a small fraction of this work. Moderate rehabilitation programs that emphasize basic maintenance and livability are undertaken by public and nongovernmental organizations that operate outside the historic preservation umbrella but serve an essential role in retaining overall urban fabric. Preservation-centered housing rehabilitation occurs mostly through the nongovernmental sector. In Ohio, the most prominent is the Heritage Home program of the Cleveland Restoration Society (CRS), which provides low-interest loans for owner-occupied housing across the city of Cleveland and its many surrounding suburbs. Additionally, many cities support lead-abatement initiatives to combat lead contamination in water, soil, and housing. Lead paint likely exists in buildings built before 1978, and its abatement or mitigation is an important environmental justice issue with clear ties to housing viability and safety, sustainability, and social justice. Viewed comprehensively, these efforts create a robust housing rehabilitation sector, although there are missed opportunities for collaborations and variation across municipalities.

Urban sustainability and climate action planning have grown in prominence in recent years, including in midwestern cities. The efforts undertaken in Cleveland, Cincinnati, and Columbus provide evidence of the ways in which housing rehabilitation is (or is not) intertwined with sustainability. All three cities have municipal sustainability offices and recently adopted climate action plans. The plans, to varying degrees, advocate for housing rehabilitation as one sustainability strategy. Yet there are almost no explicit connections to historic preservation, specifically. Dissecting the synergies and disconnections between the range of housing rehabilitation efforts and urban sustainability helps urban policy makers, including preservation professionals, develop more holistic and coordinated approaches.

Generally, preservation practitioners and advocates support housing rehabilitation and sustainability. Housing advocates support residential preservation and urban sustainability. Sustainability proponents support retaining existing housing, creating livable and vibrant neighborhoods, and reducing deadly contaminants such as lead. Despite these evident synergies, policies and programs designed to spur residential rehabilitation, lead abatement, and sustainability often take place in silos, suggesting a need for improved connections, dialogue, and partnerships.

▶ OHIO'S THREE CS

Despite their proximity and location within the same state, Cleveland, Cincinnati, and Columbus each has a unique history, political culture, preservation sector, and planning climate. The three cities also have divergent population and economic trajectories: Cleveland remains in a state of decline, Cincinnati is stable, and Columbus is growing. All have older residential housing common to aging midwestern cities.

These cities incorporated shortly after Ohio achieved statehood in 1803. Cincinnati, located in southwest Ohio, gained economic prominence from its location along the Ohio River. Cleveland, in northeast Ohio, boomed in the late 1800s and early 1900s as a powerhouse industrial center. For the first half of the twentieth century, Cleveland was Ohio's largest city, before suffering sustained population and economic decline. Centrally located Columbus is the state capital. Columbus has emerged as a center of insurance, finance, education, and health care and has grown in recent decades.

Cleveland has the oldest (median year built of 1939) and most disinvested housing, based on its vacancy rate (19 percent) and median value ($68,500). By contrast, Columbus has the newest and highest valued housing ($143,000) and the lowest vacancy rate (11 percent). These conditions reflect the dichotomy of Cleveland's postindustrial decline and Columbus's growth through annexation and new development. The majority of all three cities' housing was built before 1980.

▶ HOUSING REHABILITATION IN THE THREE CS

In all three of Ohio's major cities, there are public and nongovernmental programs to rehabilitate and maintain housing, particularly in low-income areas. These include general housing rehabilitation approaches, historic preservation-centered initiatives, and residential

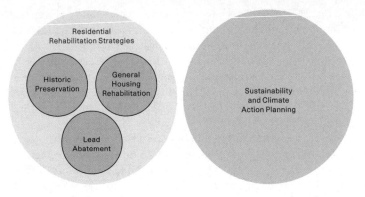

FIG. 1: *Demographic, economic, and housing conditions.*

1
Each city also has other housing-related programs including code enforcement, point-of-sale inspections, and building code reviews. They also often have other nongovernmental support, particularly from community development corporations and private-sector affordable housing developers. This essay intentionally focuses on the most prominent and citywide housing rehabilitation efforts in each city.

2
Jordan S. Yin, "The Community Development Industry System: A Case Study of Politics and Institutions in Cleveland, 1967–1997," *Journal of Urban Affairs* 20, no. 2 (1998): 137–157; Stephanie Ryberg-Webster, "Urban Preservation: A Community and Economic Development Perspective," in *Human-Centered Built Environment Heritage Preservation*, ed. Jeremy C. Wells and Barry L. Stiefel (New York: Routledge, 2018), 195–211.

3
Cleveland Housing Network, "Home," https://chnhousingpartners.org. Beginning in the 1970s, there were numerous home rehabilitation organizations in Cleveland including the Cleveland Action to Support Housing (CASH) and Neighborhood Housing Services (NHS). In 2014 CASH merged into NHS, which then merged into the Cleveland Housing Network in 2019.

4
Cuyahoga Land Bank, "About Us," http://cuyahogalandbank.org/aboutUs.php.

5
Jordyn Grzelewski, "After 10 Years and 8,000 Demolitions, Cuyahoga Land Bank Shifts Focus to Rehabs," Cleveland.com, June 24, 2019, https://www.cleveland.com/business/2019/06/

lead-abatement programs. The efforts described below capture the most prominent housing rehabilitation strategies and are intended to provide a picture of the range of programs, strategies, and initiatives that exist across these three cities. [1] FIG. 1

General housing rehabilitation

Public and nongovernmental housing rehabilitation programs typically serve low-income residents and support basic maintenance, essential repairs, and weatherization. Such initiatives respond to an aging housing stock that requires intervention to prevent deterioration. Of the three cities, Cleveland has the most robust housing rehabilitation programs, reflecting the city's more severe economic and population decline and its well-established nongovernmental community development sector. [2] Cincinnati, which is smaller, with moderate decline, also has a strong rehabilitation sector. Columbus, with the newest housing and the strongest current economic conditions, has only a few general rehabilitation programs.

Cleveland benefits from nongovernmental and public-sector rehabilitation programs, with the most prominent led by the Cleveland Housing Network (CHN), the City of Cleveland, and the Cuyahoga Land Bank. Established in 1981, CHN operates a lease-purchase program to assist low-income residents in purchasing and rehabilitating homes. It also develops affordable housing through new construction and rehabilitation and supports homeowners through energy and weatherization assistance. [3] The City of Cleveland's Division of Neighborhood Services, within the Department of Community Development, supports residential rehabilitation through the low-interest Repair-A-Home loan program and Senior Homeowner Assistance grants, which help low-income, elderly residents with basic maintenance and essential repairs. The Cuyahoga Land Bank, established in the wake of the 2008 housing crisis, initially emphasized demolition in response to high vacancy and foreclosure rates. [4] As financial assistance for demolition has waned, the Land Bank has shifted to housing rehabilitation. [5]

In Cincinnati, key efforts include People Working Cooperatively (PWC) and Rehab Across Cincinnati and Hamilton County (REACH). PWC after-10-years-and-143-billion-in-economic-impact-cuyahoga-land-bank-prepares-to-shift-gears.html.

6
People Working Cooperatively, "PWC Story," http://www.pwchomerepairs.org/about-pwc/pwc-story.aspx; City of Cincinnati, "Available Financial Assistance Programs," https://www.cincinnati-oh.gov/buildings/property-maintenance-code-enforcement/code-enforcement-quarterly-abatement-fee/home-repair-assistance-programs.

7
City of Columbus, "Rebuilding Together Central Ohio Tool Library," https://www.columbus.gov/development/housing-division/Rebuilding-Together-Central-Ohio-Tool-Library_M; City of Columbus, "Critical Home Repair Program," https://www.columbus.gov/development/housing-division/Critical-Home-Repair-Program; City of Columbus, "Emergency Repair Program," https://www.columbus.gov/development/housing-division/Emergency-Repair_M. For insight into housing rehabilitation and gentrification issues in Columbus, see the 2003 documentary *Flag Wars*, which portrays housing quality and restoration tensions in the city's Olde Towne East neighborhood.

8
The Cleveland Landmarks Commission was established in 1971. There are 389 historic buildings and 29 historic districts in Cleveland. For more information, see the Landmarks Commission website, http://www.city.cleveland.oh.us/CityofCleveland/Home/Government/CityAgencies/CityPlanningCommission/LandmarksCommission. Cincinnati's Historic Conservation Board was created in 1980. There are 46 designated buildings and 25 historic districts in Cincinnati. For more

is a nongovernmental program established in 1975 to help low-income homeowners—its typical client makes around $13,500/year—with rehabilitation. PWC offers emergency repair grants for things like heat, water, and indoor plumbing. Through a partnership with the City of Cincinnati, PWC also manages the Homeowner Assistance Repairs and Building Order Remission (HARBOR) grant program to help owners correct code violations. 6 REACH is a partnership between the Port Authority and the Hamilton County Landbank that focuses on transforming blighted and deteriorated housing into habitable homes and neighborhood assets.

Columbus's Housing Division, within the Department of Development, assists low-income homeowners, veterans, and the elderly through a tool-lending library and critical home repair and emergency repair programs. 7 The city does not have prominent nongovernmental housing rehabilitation programs, likely reflecting its strong economy and newer housing stock.

Historic preservation

All three cities have municipal historic preservation agencies that are responsible for designation and design review for historic districts and buildings. Ohio is a strong home-rule state, giving each city autonomy in the design, composition, and function of its preservation commission. 8 Each preservation commission is a regulatory agency with a small staff and a low budget. Aside from an occasional historic resource survey, the municipal preservation offices do not provide residential rehabilitation assistance such as local tax abatements for historic properties or homeowner grants.

In Cleveland and Columbus, nongovernmental organizations offer preservation-based housing rehabilitation initiatives. 9 The Cleveland Restoration Society's signature program is Heritage Home, launched in 1992 to provide low-interest rehabilitation loans through a linked deposit program in two Cleveland neighborhoods. In 2002 CRS made the program available to Cleveland wards (based on councilperson participation) and surrounding suburbs. Participating wards and communities pay CRS a program participation fee, which makes residents whose homes are more than fifty years old eligible for loans with interest as low as 1.4 percent. In 2020 CRS entered into an agreement with the city's Department of Community Development making the program available to all homeowners in Cleveland for the first time. Homeowners can use the program for interior and exterior projects ranging from kitchen remodels to exterior restorations. 10 In the program's early years, CRS held borrowers to strict preservation standards. For instance, if a house had vinyl siding and the owner wanted a loan for interior HVAC upgrades, CRS would require the removal of the vinyl siding. Recognizing the economic conditions and dire need for housing rehabilitation in northeast Ohio, CRS relaxed these rules. As of this writing, borrowers cannot use loans for historically inappropriate changes such as installing vinyl siding or replacement windows, but having these historically inaccurate materials already on a home does not preclude an owner from using the program for other renovations.

Columbus Landmarks initiated its Home Preservation Program (HPP) in 2014, modeled after CRS's Heritage Home. Columbus Landmarks provides free technical assistance, holds rehabilitation workshops, links owners with qualified contractors, and connects owners to low-interest loans. A key difference between the HPP and Heritage Home is that the HPP explicitly focuses on sustainability. The program operates through a linked-deposit system with participating banks, with an interest rate deduction through Ohio's Eco-Link Program. Borrowers must use at least half of their loan for sustainability improvements such as energy upgrades, while the remaining loan can support other improvements and renovations. 11

Lead abatement

Housing maintenance and rehabilitation is essential in cities' ongoing mitigation of lead poisoning. Lead contamination occurs in soil, pipes, and water supplies, and in older interior and exterior paint. The United States banned lead paint in 1978 due to the impact of lead poisoning. Since then, municipalities, states, and the federal government have addressed residential lead abatement to varying degrees. In recent years, the issue has gained renewed prominence in the wake of the water-related lead-poisoning crisis in Flint, Michigan. 12

Homes built before 1978 likely have lead paint, which can cause brain damage and developmental challenges, especially in children. 13 Proper maintenance can prevent peeling and chipping paint, reducing the probability of lead poisoning, while lead poisoning concerns rise in homes with deferred maintenance. Lead poisoning in young children is identified through blood tests, and elevated lead levels are a notifiable public health condition. This facilitates public assistance to individuals and tracking to identify clusters of high lead levels. 14

According to 2017 data from the Centers for Disease Control, Cuyahoga County (Cleveland) had the highest rate of elevated lead levels of these cities, at 9.5 percent of children tested. In Hamilton County (Cincinnati), 3.1 percent of tested children had elevated results, while in Franklin County (Columbus), the rate was 0.7 percent. 15 These varied outcomes likely reflect each city's age of housing, economic conditions, racial composition, and poverty rates, which can all contribute to higher levels of deferred maintenance and neglect.

All three cities have public-sector lead paint-abatement programs, although these are often disconnected from nongovernmental, public-sector, and historic preservation-centered residential rehabilitation. All offer small grants for lead-paint control, while Columbus also has a lead-safe registry with an online map of certified lead-safe homes.

Cleveland recently launched aggressive lead-abatement initiatives, stemming from the city's high rates of elevated lead in children and its vast stock of aging and deteriorating housing. In 2017 the city created the Healthy Homes Interdepartmental Initiative to coordinate efforts across the Building and Housing, Public Health, Community Development, and Law Departments, as well as the housing court and external partners. The city created a searchable database of homes that have known lead issues and capitalized on its existing rental registration process to hold landlords accountable for mitigating lead hazards. 16

In 2019 Lead Safe Cleveland (LSC) formed as a partnership between

information on the Historic Conservation Board, see https:// www.cincinnati-oh. gov/buildings/ historic-conservation/ historic-conservation-board. The Columbus Historic Preservation Office oversees 75 historic buildings and 18 districts. In Columbus, there are five commissions that review changes to designated historic resources. Four districts (German Village, Italian Village, Victorian Village, and the Brewery District) have their own commissions, while the Historic Resources Commission is responsible for all remaining historic districts and buildings. For more information on the Columbus Historic Preservation Office, see https://www.columbus. gov/planning/hpdra.

9
The Cincinnati Preservation Association (CPA), established in 1964, is the oldest nonprofit preservation advocacy organization in these three cities, but it does not provide home rehabilitation assistance. For more information, see http://cincinnati preservation.org.

10
Heritage Home Program, "Home," https://www.heritage homeprogram.org.

11
Columbus Landmarks, "Home Preservation Program," https://www. columbuslandmarks. org/home-preservation-program; Mark Ferenchik, "Program Gives Loans to Fix Up Old Homes," *Columbus Dispatch*, March 6, 2014, https://www.dispatch. com/content/stories/ local/2014/03/06/ program-gives-loans-to-fix-up-old-homes. html; Columbus Landmarks, "Home Preservation Funded for 2019!," https://www. columbuslandmarks. org/home-preservation-funded-for-2019. For more information on Ohio's Eco-Link program, see http:// treasurer.ohio.gov/ ECOLINK.

12
Victoria Morckel, "Why the Flint, Michigan, USA Water Crisis Is an Urban Planning Failure," *Cities* 62 (2017): 23–27.

13
Andrew Zaleski, "The Unequal Burden of Urban Lead," *Bloomberg CityLab*, January 2, 2020, https://www.citylab.com/environment/2020/01/lead-poisoning-toxic-paint-pipes-health-iq-crime-baltimore/604201; World Health Organization, "Lead Poisoning and Health," August 23, 2019, https://www.who.int/news-room/fact-sheets/detail/lead-poisoning-and-health.

14
Centers for Disease Control, "Childhood Lead Poisoning Prevention: Data and Statistics," https://www.cdc.gov/nceh/lead/data/index.htm.

15
County-level data on lead poisoning is available from the Centers for Disease Control at https://www.cdc.gov/nceh/lead/data/state/ohdata.htm. In 2017, 2,105 children had elevated lead levels in Cuyahoga County, with about 25 percent of children under the age of six tested. The next highest rate of elevated lead levels was in Crawford County, where 13 percent of children were tested, and 24 of them (6.7 percent) had high lead levels.

16
City of Cleveland, "City of Cleveland Announces Healthy Homes Interdepartmental Initiative," May 18, 2017, http://www.city.cleveland.oh.us/5.18.2017HealthyHomes Initiative.

17
Daniel Williams, "Mayor Jackson, Cleveland City Council and Local Organizations Announce Lead Safe Cleveland," January 22, 2019, https://clecityhall.com/2019/01/22/mayor-jackson-cleveland-city-council-and-local-organizations-announce-lead-safe-cleveland.

the City of Cleveland, nongovernmental, and private-sector entities to advocate for funding, public policies, and programs to combat lead contamination. [17] This partnership resulted in a landmark local lead-poisoning prevention law, passed by the Cleveland City Council in July 2019. The law requires owners of rental properties to obtain lead-safe certificates as a precondition to inclusion on the city's rental registry. To support lead mitigation, the coalition created the Lead Safe Home Fund, which had raised just over $10 million by the end of 2019, although the estimated need is closer to $100 million. [18]

▶ SUSTAINABILITY, CLIMATE CHANGE, AND HOUSING

Urban sustainability has grown in prominence in recent decades, with the imminent impacts of global climate change pushing sustainability to the forefront of current local planning efforts. In 2018 *Site Selection* magazine ranked Ohio ninth among all states in sustainability and the Cincinnati metropolitan region first among major US urban areas. [19] Ohio's cities face less immediate threat from climate change as they are not coastal and are not prone to catastrophic weather events. Yet all of them have municipal sustainability offices and climate action plans. These initiatives demonstrate the pervasiveness of sustainability and climate action planning at the municipal level.

Green Cincinnati
The City of Cincinnati established its Office of Environment and Sustainability in 2006 to oversee municipal programs related to sustainability, including the development of the 2018 Green Cincinnati plan. As highlighted on the city's website, the sustainability office works on emissions (e.g., greenhouse gas inventory, air quality), energy (e.g., solar infrastructure, energy aggregation), food (e.g., urban agriculture, waste), the green economy (e.g., brownfields, LEED), mobility (e.g., biking, electric vehicles), and recycling. [20] The office does not provide online advice, resources, or support for sustainable housing rehabilitation such as energy efficiency improvements.

In 2018 Cincinnati developed Green Cincinnati: Building a Sustainable & Equitable City. The plan was built on a prior Green Cincinnati plan, developed in 2008. The new plan frames the past and future as opposing forces: "Cincinnati is a unique city with a rich history of culture and industrialization. This legacy is part of our story and central to our city's character, but the changing economic and environmental realities have prompted our government, businesses, and communities to embrace a more sustainable path."[21]

The Green Cincinnati plan includes eight sections, the first of which focuses on the city's built environment. The plan notes that in 2015 residential buildings produced 7.7 percent of the city's greenhouse gas emissions. [22] Among other goals and recommendations, the city aims to reduce residential energy burden by 10 percent and increase reuse of vacant buildings. Although the plan does not explicitly state a focus on reuse of residential structures, it projects an average size of 2,000 square feet, which suggests housing rather than larger industrial or commercial spaces. Of the three cities' plans, Cincinnati's is the only one to explicitly reference historic preservation, although it does not provide guidance on interagency collaboration or ways to integrate sustainability into preservation decision-making (or vice versa). The most explicit reference to historic preservation is a citation of the National Trust for Historic Preservation's 2016 report *The Greenest Building*, which shows lower greenhouse gas emissions for reused buildings compared to new construction. [23]

Green Cincinnati provides contradictory insight into the costs and benefits of rehabilitating and reusing existing buildings, which include all extant structures in the city. It states that reusing vacant structures is more cost-effective than new construction but also categorizes the feasibility of vacant building reuse as "hard" because "the cost of repairs substantially exceeds the value of the repaired building." The plan sets a goal of bringing ten buildings back into productive use in 2018, reaching a goal of fifty structures per year within five years. [24] It does not state what type of buildings this goal applies to and only implies that the goal applies to privately owned buildings without outlining incentives that would drive this reinvestment.

Sustainable Columbus and the Columbus Climate Adaptation Plan

The City of Columbus established its Sustainable Columbus initiative in 2005 to coordinate environmental initiatives. According the Sustainable Columbus website, there is a strong emphasis on energy efficiency and greening strategies, including green buildings. In terms of residential improvements, Sustainable Columbus provides information on home energy audits, residential energy efficiency, and weatherization. [25]

In 2018 Columbus adopted the Columbus Climate Adaptation Plan. The plan includes eight thematic chapters: extreme heat, air quality and energy, flooding, water quality, water use, ecosystems, emergency preparedness, and vulnerable populations. There is minimal focus on the city's housing stock, aside from cursory mentions of the increase in frequency and intensity of flooding and the impact of extreme heat on vulnerable populations that lack residential cooling systems. Preservation is discussed only in reference to the natural environment, such as preserving wetlands, green spaces, forests, water, and nature preserves. [26]

Sustainable Cleveland and the Cleveland Climate Action Plan

Sustainable Cleveland 2019 was a ten-year initiative launched in 2009 by the Mayor's Office of Sustainability. Through Sustainable Cleveland, the city coordinated activities around a yearly theme (from 2011 to 2019) including energy efficiency, local foods, renewable energy, zero waste, clean water, sustainable transportation, vibrant green space, vital neighborhoods, and engaged people. [27] The Sustainable Cleveland advisory committee included more than ninety members, with no representation from the Cleveland Landmarks Commission, the Cleveland Restoration Society, or any other preservation-focused organization.

The 2018 focus on vital neighborhoods resulted in the Neighborhood Climate Action Toolkit, "an assets-based approach to building thriving and healthy neighborhoods." [28] The Neighborhood Climate Action Toolkit

As of this writing in 2020, coalition members include the City of Cleveland (Mayor's Office, City Council, and Departments of Building & Housing, Community Development, and Public Health), Cuyahoga County Board of Health and Department of Development, Case Western Reserve University, the Cleveland Foundation, Enterprise Community Partners, Environmental Health Watch, Federal Reserve Bank of Cleveland, the Bruening Foundation, the George Gund Foundation, Mt. Sinai Health Care Foundation, Saint Luke's Foundation, Sisters of Charity Foundation of Cleveland, Third Federal Foundation, and the United Way of Greater Cleveland.

18
Rachel Dissell and Brie Zeltner, "Cleveland City Council Passes Historic Lead Poisoning Prevention Law," *Plain Dealer*, July 24, 2019, https://www.cleveland.com/metro/2019/07/cleveland-city-council-passes-historic-lead-poisoning-prevention-law.html.

19
Adam Bruns, "Investors, Tenants Seek More Sustainable Locations," *Site Selection*, July 2018, https://siteselection.com/issues/2018/jul/sustainability-rankings-investors-tenants-seek-more-sustainable-locations.cfm. In 2017 *Site Selection* ranked Cincinnati first and Cleveland fourth. Cleveland was not in the top ten in 2018.

20
City of Cincinnati, "Office of Environment & Sustainability," https://www.cincinnati-oh.gov/oes.

21
City of Cincinnati, Green Cincinnati Plan, May 2018, 9.

22
Green Cincinnati, 32. Other sources of greenhouse gas emissions included commercial uses (33.72 percent), transportation and mobile sources

(31.25 percent), industrial uses (19.71 percent), and solid waste (2.73 percent).

23
Green Cincinnati, 40, 68–69.

24
Green Cincinnati, 66, 68–69.

25
City of Columbus, "Sustainable Columbus," https://www.columbus.gov/sustainable.

26
City of Columbus, Columbus Climate Adaptation Plan, December 2018, https://byrd.osu.edu/columbus.

27
Sustainable Cleveland, "Action Areas," https://www.sustainablecleveland.org/action_areas.

28
Sustainable Cleveland, "Neighborhood Climate Action Toolkit," n.d., https://d3n8a8pro7vhmx.cloudfront.net/sustainablecleveland/pages/149/attachments/original/1462888931/NEIGHBORHOOD_CLIMATE_ACTION_TOOLKIT-FINAL.pdf?1462888931, 1.

29
"Neighborhood Climate Action Toolkit," 2.

30
City of Cleveland, "Office of Sustainability," http://www.city.cleveland.oh.us/CityofCleveland/Home/Government/CityAgencies/OfficeOfSustainability.

31
City of Cleveland, "Cleveland Climate Action Plan: Building Thriving and Resilient Neighborhoods for All, 2018 Update," https://drive.google.com/file/d/1Z3234sMp7S7MjaXvMgcZtcAaYs4x2oHE/view?usp=sharing, 26.

identifies historic buildings and community history as local assets and identifies "passing down cultural traditions" as a potential climate action project. 29 While these are positive connections to historic preservation, the plan does not directly address housing preservation or rehabilitation.

The website of the Mayor's Office of Sustainability provides some suggestions for residents, such as installing low-flow toilets, adding rain barrels or rain gardens, planting trees, air-drying dishes, and replacing old appliances with Energy Star brands. 30 But these tips, while helpful, fail to connect to broader rationales for preserving existing housing. They also do not assist residents, many of whom live below or near the poverty line, with ways to afford these improvements or with ways to meet immediate rehabilitation needs such as weatherization.

In 2018 the City of Cleveland published the Cleveland Climate Action Plan: Building Thriving and Resilient Neighborhoods for All. Of all three cities' climate action plans, Cleveland's most directly addresses the vibrancy of residential neighborhoods. The plan puts forth a threefold goal that the city's housing should be affordable, healthy, and energy efficient. It also emphasizes the city's predominantly African American neighborhoods, where housing improvements are greatly needed. According to the plan, Cleveland's recent economic gains can underpin programs to improve aging housing through energy efficiency improvements such as adding insulation, air sealing, and efficient heating and cooling systems. These basic rehabilitation efforts help support the long-term functionality and preservation of the city's housing. The plan also recognizes the need for a coordinated approach, recommending "layering healthy homes, lead, and weatherization."31

Summarizing Sustainability in Ohio's Three Cs

Overall, Ohio's three major cities all actively engage in sustainability initiatives that increasingly address climate change. Cleveland's climate change action plan directly links sustainability and climate preparedness to housing rehabilitation and lead abatement. Cincinnati's plan encourages historic preservation but falls short in providing concrete implementation strategies. Columbus's plan does not address older housing or historic preservation. In addressing housing through a sustainability lens, the emphasis is on improving energy efficiency and greening strategies. None of the plans argue for or justify housing rehabilitation as an essential, large-scale form of reuse.

While long-term housing preservation is rarely stated as an explicit sustainability goal, the small-scale improvements recommended by these cities, such as improved insulation and energy-efficient appliances, may indirectly lead to that outcome. For example, weatherization can improve energy efficiency and reduce monthly operating costs. This helps residents remain in their homes, increases affordability, and gives residents increased discretionary funds to spend on other maintenance and rehabilitation projects.

The disconnect between sustainability initiatives and historic preservation is starker. This likely reflects persistent silos between the environmental and preservation fields and the view of preservation as a niche activity rather than a core element of sustainability. The lack of preservation's inclusion in collaborative sustainability initiatives and climate action planning reflects this disconnect. Sustainability leaders in each city convened a broad coalition of partners from the public, nongovernmental, and private sectors. No preservation organization from any sector in any city was included. 32

32
Common public sector partners were the sustainability office; public health, planning, and parks departments; utilities commissions; housing authorities; sewer districts; transit authorities; and regional planning agencies. Nongovernmental partners included universities, community-based organizations, and religious entities. Private-sector partners included Procter and Gamble in Cincinnati and ArcelorMittal Steel in Cleveland.

▶ PUTTING IT ALL TOGETHER

Cleveland, Columbus, and Cincinnati all have public and nongovernmental initiatives addressing housing rehabilitation, preservation, lead abatement, and sustainability. Housing rehabilitation efforts are designed to retain and improve older and aging housing. While sustainability and climate action planning are broader in focus, they have the potential to bolster housing rehabilitation goals. Despite apparent synergies, there remain disconnects between historic preservation-driven housing restoration, public and/or nongovernmental residential rehabilitation, lead-safe and lead-abatement programs, and sustainability and climate action planning. *FIG. 2*

Ideally, increased synergies in program operation could advance housing rehabilitation by combining resources including professional expertise and financing. Cleveland's Healthy Homes interdepartmental collaboration regarding lead abatement is a good start. Given that sustainability and climate action planning have risen to prominence at the local level and that housing comprises the vast majority of the urban landscape, it would be extremely beneficial to align rehabilitation programs and lead abatement with the sustainability infrastructure in each city. *FIG. 3* Cleveland's climate action plan makes strides in this direction in calling for a coordinated approach to housing rehabilitation. In Columbus, there was a missed opportunity to connect sustainability to preservation given that the Columbus Landmarks Home Preservation Program has a strong sustainability focus but is completely missing from the city's climate action plan.

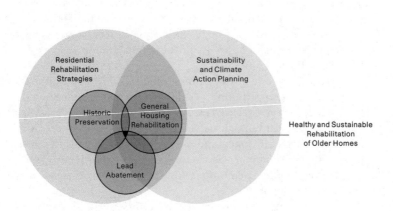

FIG. 2: Disconnects between general housing rehabilitation, historic preservation, lead abatement, and sustainability/climate action planning, with each generally operating within contained boundaries.

33
The New Markets Tax
Credit provides a good
model, targeting census
tracts with poverty
rates exceeding 20
percent and median
family income below 80
percent of area median
family income.

	Cincinnati	Cleveland	Columbus
Current Population (2018)	302,605	383,793	892,533
Population Change (since 1950)	-40%	-58%	137%
Population Change (since 2010)	2%	-3%	13%
Median Household Income	$38,542	$29,008	$51,612
Poverty Rate	27%	35%	20%
% of Housing, Owner-Occupied	38%	41%	45%
Median Value, Owner-Occupied Housing	$129,100	$68,500	$143,000
Median Gross Rent	$709	$700	$928
Vacancy Rate	17%	19%	11%
Median Year Structure Built	1950	1939	1976
% of units built before 1980	86%	90%	56%
% of units built before 1939	41%	54%	12%

FIG. 3: Synergistic approach to housing rehabilitation, with boundaries removed and increased overlap between rehabilitation, preservation, lead abatement, and sustainability.

Even with improved synergy, historic preservationists, including nongovernmental preservation organizations, municipal preservation agencies, and even State Historic Preservation Offices, must actively work to break out of their silos and become part of a broader coalition working to improve the livability and sustainability of urban residential spaces. Preservationists should continue to place people at the center of their work on neighborhood preservation, cultural heritage, and the evolution of older places. To align with health and sustainability goals, preservationists need to develop and prioritize tools that support homes as healthy, sustainable places. In prioritizing people, preservationists should emphasize the value of saving places of daily life, maximizing the use of existing built resources, and adapting older places to modern demands. Much of this is already in the preservation tool kit but can be expanded, developed, and aligned with health and sustainability agendas.

Nongovernmental organizations such as the Cleveland Restoration Society and Columbus Landmarks need to promote the alignment of their existing low-interest loan programs (Heritage Home and the Home Preservation Program, respectively) with residential rehabilitation and sustainability goals. Local preservation regulatory agencies, such as the Cleveland Landmarks Commission, Cincinnati's Historic Conservation Board, and Columbus's Historic Resources Commission, should ensure that their regulatory procedures advance goals of housing retention and rehabilitation, while not impeding (and ideally advancing) health and sustainability.

Agencies and organizations offering tax credits or low-interest rehabilitation loans should consider a bonus credit or rate reduction for incorporating energy retrofits, receiving a lead-safe certificate, and supporting rehabilitation in low-income areas. [33] Ohio's state historic tax credit does not currently apply to owner-occupied housing, but the state could consider expanding the incentive as one way to connect preservation to rehabilitation and sustainability goals. While lead paint is likely present in any home built before 1978, older homes in low-income areas are more likely to suffer from deferred maintenance, elevating concerns about peeling and flaking paint. Because of the deep intertwining of poverty, race, deteriorated housing, and lead contamination, preservation policies should incorporate an equity agenda to target rehabilitation assistance to those most in need.

Within the public sector, historic preservation is primarily a regulatory strategy. Even as the preservation profession has developed popular policy tools such as low-interest loans, tax incentives, and technical assistance, historic preservation is still largely viewed as a niche enterprise that operates on strict regulatory rules.[34] As long as policy makers in housing, public health, and sustainability view preservation in this way, the profession will remain on the fringe of initiatives for which it could be a useful and active partner. The designation and design review of local historic resources should remain an important component of the local preservation function, but it should be just that—one component. To become a more proactive partner in residential rehabilitation, healthy homes, and sustainability initiatives, public-sector preservationists need to find ways to expand their scope. For instance, they could incorporate energy retrofits into the design review process or produce guidelines for retrofitting historic properties. Preservationists working in both the public and nongovernmental sectors could advocate for or launch incentive programs such as low- or zero-interest loans or property tax abatements for targeted rehabilitation and lead abatement in low-income areas. Historic resource surveys, which are direly lacking in all three cities, could help identify areas of residential fabric that retain overall intactness but are in need of rehabilitation. This information, in turn, could help focus sustainability and rehabilitation efforts undertaken by external partners.

There is no simple solution or singular action that preservationists can take to become a full collaborative partner in all locales. There are some actions that would likely help, including more proactive action on the part of preservationists to insert themselves into things like sustainability planning. Preservationists need to put forth compelling arguments about why they should have representation on a lead-abatement task force, a climate action plan, a sustainability advisory group, or the board of a nonprofit housing rehabilitation organization unrelated to preservation. There are a wide range of things that preservationists already do beyond the regulatory function of local commissions that contribute to sustainability and rehabilitation goals. For example, they are highly capable at researching the history of places, connecting history to living communities, understanding the evolution and character of places, adapting buildings and districts, and telling the stories of places, among others. The issue is not that preservationists lack value or have little to contribute; it is that both preservation professionals and preservation policies remain disconnected from broader urban agendas.

If preservationists want a seat at the table, then they must take on the work of demonstrating how the profession, through the knowledge and expertise of its practitioners and the outcomes of its policies, furthers synergistic policy goals such as affordable housing, environmental justice, and sustainability. At present, local preservation regulation is likely more often viewed as an impediment rather than a boost for things like

34
Stephanie Ryberg-Webster, "Urban Preservation: A Community and Economic Development Perspective," in *Making the Past Less Foreign*, ed. Jeremy Wells and Barry Stiefel (New York: Routledge, 2018), 211–228.

affordable housing or sustainability. Preservationists have also not done a sufficient job of promoting how their skills in the areas of research, survey, documentation, adaptive reuse, and building rehabilitation are valuable to sustainability, affordable housing, or environmental justice endeavors. Because of the ingrained perceptions about preservation, waiting for a seat to be offered is not a viable strategy, and the burden falls to preservation professionals to take action and make their case.

There are limitations to simply promoting and demonstrating value. Building relationships across fields and sectors is imperative and requires dedicated time and effort on the part of preservationists, who are likely already functioning with limited support, resources, and capacity. This is likely especially true in the fiscally strained shrinking cities, such as Cleveland, that are prevalent in the Rust Belt and the Midwest. While advocating for additional funding and resources is important, preservationists also have to make difficult choices about how to use or redirect existing resources.

Additional research should continue to explore the synergies between housing rehabilitation strategies and between those efforts and urban sustainability. Future research should also incorporate the many housing programs that are not covered in this essay—code enforcement, point of sale inspections, home energy assistance, and paint programs—to explore a wider range of municipal housing programs across a wider range of cities. Scholars should also analyze and compare other cities, including growing cities and smaller municipalities, to develop a more robust understanding of preservation, housing, and sustainability connections. Additional research should dive into the pervasiveness of and reasons for the disconnect between climate action planning and housing rehabilitation. Do municipal leaders who spearhead sustainability plans intentionally exclude municipal preservation agencies, nongovernmental and private-sector preservation professionals, and others who promote and advocate for historic preservation? Does the disconnect reflect a lack of understanding about preservationists' potential contribution? Are local preservationists ill-informed about the connections between their work and sustainability/climate change efforts? Are local preservationists unaware of other synergistic work happening at the local level?

In many cities, sustainability and, increasingly, climate action planning figure prominently in local planning and policy. Preservation, on the other hand, often remains a niche enterprise. As such, the burden of finding and promoting synergies and increasing collaborations falls primarily on preservationists. Those working to save and rehabilitate older and historic buildings need to build connections outside the preservation silo. They need to make compelling, public arguments about how preservation contributes to housing rehabilitation and sustainability. They need to embrace and demonstrate flexibility and resourcefulness. They should do this to become proactive partners in advancing a more sustainable and healthy future for cities, for neighborhoods, and, most of all, for the people who call them home.

An Interview with Lisa T. Alexander

Addressing Equity in Place

Lisa, as a lawyer and a legal scholar, can you speak to how historic preservation became a dimension of your work and your research?

LISA T. ALEXANDER

My interest in historic preservation emerged from my interest in gentrification, which seems perhaps counterintuitive.

White flight from communities in the urban United States reached an apex in the 1970s, resulting in economic woes and disinvestment in low-income, predominantly minority communities such as Harlem, the Bronx, and other places. The narrative was that these were places of despair and crime, almost lacking in anything of significant value worth retaining. Then, in the late 1990s, we began to see a return to major cities, like New York, Chicago, and San Francisco, of middle- and upper-class whites, people who probably had previously flown to the suburbs. These new residents now wanted to live in cities, and many of them wanted to live in the same neighborhoods that had been characterized in the late 1970s as places of despair, because some of those places now had affordable housing, or rents that younger people, or others coming into the city, could afford.

Those neighborhoods then began to be described as affordable places to live that were also funky, interesting cultural spaces. For example, the Mission District, a low-income Latino community in San Francisco, had an existing culture of mural painting, Mexican food, and other kinds of art. As communities like these began to gentrify, their culture began to be talked about in positive ways. At many moments, this took shape as cultural appropriation, where new people coming in were interested in the funky aspects of the culture in those neighborhoods but were not interested in preserving the individuals who lived in those communities and produced that culture. New buildings were built near the Mexican restaurants or the funky murals without creating opportunities for low-income people who produced that culture to remain in the neighborhood.

Meanwhile, historic preservation law has traditionally been understood as a gentrifying force—you have a building, and you want to preserve its older, historic character, so you get tax credits to do that, and you end up gentrifying communities and displacing, arguably, the original residents who lived there when it was a lower-income neighborhood. So I thought, "How do we use law, if at all, to preserve or demarcate urban cultures without gentrifying those communities and removing that culture?" I was interested in how historic preservation law could be used to preserve the culture produced by low-income people and keep those people in place to benefit from gentrification and revitalization rather than be displaced by it, while also giving proper credit and homage to the culture that those low-income communities produced. That's how I became interested in historic preservation law—and I think this is an unusual angle on historic preservation law, particularly within the legal community.

You use the term "cultural appropriation." Can you explain how the forces of cultural appropriation and cultural displacement function and how they affect low-income BIPOC communities? How can the tools of law be used to work against those effects?

In an article called "Hip-Hop and Housing: Revisiting Culture, Urban Space, Power, and Law" that I wrote for the *Hastings Law Journal* in 2012, I began to discuss this in relation to low-income individuals who lived in communities like the Bronx, which in music industry circles is well understood as the birthplace of hip-hop music in the late 1970s—before hip-hop was even a fully commercialized art form. It was when it was happening in the streets, the playgrounds, the community rooms, and the basements of low-income housing developments in the Bronx, Harlem, Brooklyn, and other parts of New York. I argued in the article that hip-hop was a way for some of the individuals who lived in low-income communities to come together and have fun, enjoy themselves, and socialize in the face of difficulties. But it was also a way of developing a counternarrative about what their neighborhoods were like, and what it was like to be there. Some of the music talked about the crime and the problems that existed in those communities. But a lot of it was also saying, "You say that my community is not a great place to be. But I'm the best rapper, dancer, or breaker in this community, and these communities actually have things in them that are valuable, special, and unique." So that became a counternarrative that people involved in old-school hip-hop started to articulate in the late 1970s.

When those same communities faced gentrification in the late 1990s, the fact that these communities had been the birthplaces of hip-hop suddenly made them cool. The fact that these were funky, low-income communities of color became a reason to live there but, apparently, not a reason to make sure that the people who produced that culture could remain in place. Therefore, the production of that culture began to dwindle.

The contexts that allowed you to produce the art forms of hip-hop—tagging, graffiti art, and breakdancing—in the 1970s began to change because different people lived in the buildings, and zoning and law-enforcement efforts in these communities also began to change. Hanging out in a park late at night, blasting loud music, and rapping over it was not going to be allowed in a community where more moderate-income whites lived and complained about the zoning and the noise—the culture could not happen in the same way. Other aspects of lower-income or working-class communities of color, like bodegas, began to be seen as eyesores. Then, you slowly get more Whole Foods and Starbucks and corporate, commercial stores in your neighborhood. As these legal and demographic changes occur, it becomes more difficult to produce the organic culture that comes from walking on streets together, being in parks together, and hanging out in almost unregulated spaces. The new residents also ask for new things to be in those spaces. They argue, "We don't want that hip-hop park to be a hip-hop park. We want it to be paved over with rubber, and we want new playground spaces, so that our kids can play without worrying about crime, glass, and basketball." The new residents start requiring different things, and that begins to contribute to a cultural displacement of the original residents.

Cultural appropriation creates a situation where people want to use the old history of the culture that was produced in that place as a reason to sell new real estate and encourage new people to move there, without keeping the original residents there and without creating or retaining opportunities for the culture of present residents to be produced. Cultural displacement processes move in new people without providing affordable housing for existing people; call things nuisances when they weren't nuisances before; and enforce loitering and other laws differently than before. Then you have people who want to put up new buildings, and they say, "This new building is right near the Cotton Club in Harlem. It's going to be $8,000 a month to live here, but you'll be in this cool neighborhood that used to be the birthplace of jazz."

In my work, I coined the term "cultural collective efficacy," which borrows from the work of sociologists Robert Sampson and Mario Small and others. They argue that individuals living in poor, low-income, or moderate communities can sometimes find ways to help produce and maintain collective well-being and collective identity, which can help mitigate the negative effects of living in low-income or poor neighborhoods. Sampson talked about this with respect to crime, claiming that communities with strong social networks had higher levels of collective efficacy and could mitigate crime. Others have built upon that to talk about how culture can have that effect on individuals.

For me, cultural collective efficacy is the way in which people in low-income communities build community and positive social capital around culture. In many ways, when their neighborhoods gentrify, if they do have positive identifications with cultural social networks, these networks can make it easier for them to fight gentrification and insist that they actually be beneficiaries of the revitalization happening in their communities. Cultural collective efficacy is a way to fight cultural displacement and cultural appropriation.

This question of empowerment brings up challenges in relation to existing historic preservation policy tools and legislation, which focus more on the physical dimensions of places rather than on their social-spatial dimensions. How can these limitations be confronted through law?

The patriotic, historical underpinnings of historic preservation law are often tied to physical buildings and high art and high architectural styles, to the benefit of elite individuals with large sums of money. But there needs to be a new movement to celebrate, identify, and protect culture that is *not* high culture or high art, or culture that comes from predominantly European sources, or from people with large amounts of money and income. Historic preservation practice should recognize the other forms of root cultural practice that have been produced in communities.

For example, it's well understood by researchers that in part of the area that is now New York City's Central Park, there was a community called Seneca Village, which was an important, vibrant African American community in the nineteenth century. The community had houses and buildings, but they weren't considered high art or representative of the most popular architectural styles. So the village was razed to make Central Park in the 1850s, which was seen as a form of high art. There was little to no effort to see what was there as something of value, or as a community with rich histories and traditions that should be preserved. Eminent domain was used to take over the homes of the individuals who lived in Seneca Village with very little attempt to memorialize that particular community's history. That's just one example of many throughout the United States.

I think historic preservation law has done a poor job of seeing those forms of culture that are produced at the root level, when they are not attached to buildings—root culture that is produced through music, through churches, and through all kinds of other forms of social connection and geography. My interest in historic preservation law is to understand what else needs to be in the historic preservation law tool kit to stop that tendency to ignore the existence of these communities, the culture that was produced in them, and their historical significance.

My *Hastings Law Journal* article on hip-hop and housing discussed a moderate- to low-income affordable housing building in the South Bronx, in which a DJ, known as one of the first DJs of hip-hop, DJ Kool Herc, lived. DJ Kool Herc, whose family was Caribbean, had access to and used record players that were commonly used in Jamaican culture to play disco and other music. He began spinning in the parks and the playgrounds where the neighbors gathered, and hip-hop culture began to be produced in that space.

About twenty-five years later, the affordability and the historic status of the building were threatened; the legal protections that the owner had agreed to that kept the housing affordable for thirty years had expired. The residents were at risk of being kicked out of their apartments because they could not afford the market-rate rents. What they did was to appeal to this culture that had been produced at that site. The building itself wasn't necessarily a high architectural art form that was so beautiful that you would want to preserve it in the traditional historic preservation sense, but they argued that they had produced something of value here: "It's the birthplace of hip-hop. It's well understood as a place of historical significance, and therefore, you shouldn't be able to kick us out."

Notably, that argument had no legal significance in terms of property law. If your housing is affordable, but you're a renter, not an owner, and the protections that allow your rent to be affordable no longer exist in the contracts that govern the property in which you live, then the landlord is not obligated to keep you there. The fact that it was a place where culture was produced is traditionally not understood as sufficient to protect you and keep you in place, so their argument had no clear legal hook in terms of giving them rights to remain. But what I found fascinating about this case study, and why I wrote about it, was the political and social effort of the residents to say, "We actually produced something of significant value to New York, to national and global culture here, so you shouldn't be able to displace us." They got pretty far with that argument. Local city officials worked to find a way that the building could be preserved, and the residents were able to get some subsidies to try to remain in the building as renters and pay affordable rents. The building was also designated as a historic place, and there is a marker there.

I think this case expands how we traditionally understand historic preservation law by asserting that people should have rights to remain and not be culturally displaced, even if they're not owners or not getting the traditional tax abatement to beautify the physical aspects of their homes. There was culture produced here, and that should lead to efforts to mitigate cultural displacement.

Another good example is the Tenth Street Historic District case. Tenth Street was an example of a historic freedom colony in South Dallas, Texas, where low-income African Americans had moved after emancipation. For many years, it was a vibrant African American community. Then, with white flight and the social upheaval of the 1960s, it began to be a much more low-income minority neighborhood. But there's significant history there, and because its rich history was somewhat recognized and documented by the local people, the Tenth Street district became a historic district.

But the city then decided that even though this was a historic district, there were so many low-income, dilapidated, code-violating properties that it tried to condemn and demolish many homes there. The lawyers who brought this case against the city's efforts found that among all the historic districts within the city of Dallas, the city had never tried to get rid of homes in predominantly white historic districts, but here was this effort to get rid of code-violating properties in predominantly minority, low-income, African American districts. The lawyers argued that the city's actions were a violation of the Fair Housing Act, because it was disparate treatment—low-income African American historic districts were being treated differently based upon race, while white historic districts were treated better and were not facing that same impact of cultural and physical displacement.

This is an example of using a different form of law to say, "We have a right to remain in this community even though our homes aren't that elaborate or expensive. Rather than shutting down our properties and displacing us, you should put money into helping us stay in our homes, and revitalize them, and get tax credits for them, because we are in a historic district. You shouldn't treat historic districts differently based upon race." That was an interesting example of expanding the legal tool kit to include things like the Fair Housing Act, along with more traditional historic preservation tools, to make sure that we're preserving important communities and their histories and utilizing the same resources to preserve them that we would use in high-end white communities with historic districts.

And I actually do think that these efforts to expand the legal tool kit need to happen on a case-by-case basis at the local level, which can then be broadened as national best practices. The local level is important because solutions need to be tailored to the place that you're in and the dynamics there. There are ways now, especially with technology and social media, of finding different examples around the country at local levels, enabling us to compare and identify those best-practice examples that could be scaled up and replicated nationally. So I think that bottom-up—from the local, to the regional, to the state, to the national—is a better way to go about these issues, rather than a top-down creation of national policy that has to happen the same way all the time.

In what ways can preservationists change work on the ground in order to support shifts in law and policy toward greater equity?

The historic preservation tool kit needs to be expanded significantly in terms of how we figure out what counts as culture, how we document it, how we figure out its relationship to geographic space, and how we think about the laws that can be used to keep some of the original producers of culture, or their descendants, in place so that they can benefit from that culture, rather than be displaced by it.

My colleague Andrea Roberts has written well, and extensively, about Texas freedom colonies, where freed African Americans created communities and lives after emancipation. There are sometimes very few buildings remaining in those communities that you can use as a basis for preservation. Sometimes what we have are just oral histories of who lived there and what happened there that you can preserve. So you need new tools to find that history, since you're not going to be able to find a physical building that you can rehabilitate and put a plaque on to say, "This happened here." You need to interview people and find other techniques to understand that history and the significance of the place. And perhaps you need to use legal tools like a historic district, combined with affordable housing protections, so that we can both know that this existed and keep in place some of the people whose ancestors were in these communities.

Technology has given us some important tools, but I don't think those tools displace the critical work of interviewing. In my "Hip-Hop and Housing" article, that was a lot of what I had to do. I had some books that had been written about DJ Kool Herc in this period of time, and those were instrumental. But I also went and found some of these older hip-hop artists in New York and interviewed them about their relationship to space, their relationship to Herc, their relationship to the building or the old-school hip-hop movement, where this occurred, and why it was significant. That kind of oral interview and history needs to be a broader part of the tool kit.

I also think preservationists need to be aware of the temporal aspects of law and gentrification. If you're waiting for a community to be fully gentrified—when it's obvious that there are lots of higher-income, predominantly white people living in a neighborhood that was once African American or Latino—it's going to be hard to do this kind of preservation work. People will have been displaced by then, and that displacement will not be easy to measure. It won't be easy to find out where they went or ended up. There will be very few physical markers of what historically occurred there and what the community was like. By the time you get to that stage of gentrification, real estate processes and other forces will have erased a lot of those physical spaces.

When I was a lawyer working with community groups in Chicago doing community development, there were often legal tools that we could use to give communities more control over the land and space in their communities—community land trusts, for example. Often the communities would say, "That legal tool works differently from regular, traditional ownership. We don't want anything weird and crazy. We don't know what that is. We're not worried about gentrification, because we're a low-income community. We'd rather have industry come to us and provide us with jobs, food, and opportunities. We don't want anything that would look like unconventional ownership to dissuade businesses from locating here or to push businesses out."

Then, what I would say was, "I understand, and that's completely your choice. You need to know the advantages and the disadvantages of these legal tools. But if you want control over this land and how it develops, you're going to need to get that legal control now, when it's low-income, when no one wants to be here, and when people think there's nothing here of value. Because if you wait for industry to come in and people to find value, it will be much more difficult to get control and guide how this place develops." Even if you feel you're not in a desirable, high-income community, if you see that the downtown is revitalizing two miles away from you and you want to do something about that, you need to do something now. You need to preserve the history now. Because once the community has changed, and there are higher-end people and different real estate interests involved, you will not be able to have as much control over how it develops.

From a preservationist's perspective, this means going into low-income communities that exist now. You need to talk to people while it's a poor community. Because when it is not, going back and finding that oral history is going to be difficult. The narrow definition of what historic preservation practice and law has consistently seen as things of value worth protecting—high art and culture and architectural styles produced by individuals in high-income communities—is not going to enable us to identify and document the communities that have root culture being produced. Once it's gentrified, it's going to be hard to fully capture what occurred there. That's why I would say it's important for preservationists to document early and to see value in places that traditional public discourse might say are not places of high value.

This importance is heightened by the constant flows of new people to cities. It's also affected by climate change and other processes where physical space can be totally changed in a moment. For example, in New Orleans before Hurricane Katrina, there was a culturally rich community in the Tremé neighborhood and some of the public housing neighborhoods that were later revitalized. They had music, zydeco, and the art and culture of various Zulu tribes during Mardi Gras celebrations within New Orleans. We knew something about that—people had captured that in the wake of Katrina, and then there were TV shows about it.

After that hurricane and disaster, many communities were reconstituted in ways that the city thought were good for the city, putting land to the "highest and best use," without revitalizing areas that were made unusable by the hurricane. But there was a whole history in that place. When the neighborhood was revitalized, that history was not fully recognized, captured, or documented in place and preserved. Often, in the wake of a hurricane, people will say, "This was a low-income community, and we don't want to keep it a low-income community. We want to revitalize it in positive ways." But then, half the people who lived there when it was a low-income community are displaced, without a right or the means to return. The culture they produced is not preserved, if preservationists hadn't been documenting it.

There's a temporal element here that is intertwined with law, but it exists independently of how preservation decides whether there's something of value, whether we should interview communities to hear more about and document that value. We should do that work before the community is completely changed. That's one of the biggest things that I think preservationists need to think about. Preservation of root culture needs to happen when a community is low-income, before the space has been legally reconstituted for revitalization—before eminent domain has been used, before tax credits have been allocated to developers to revitalize it, before the public housing units that might exist in an urban community have been fully revitalized.

> *You're making a clear and rational recommendation that as preservationists, we need to be focusing on the most vulnerable communities. That is particularly germane in the context of climate change and communities at risk. How do you see these interconnected environmental, economic, and social dimensions of preservation playing out in the next generation of policy?*

There has been a focus within property law scholarship and practice that land and properties should be put to their highest and best use. "Highest and best use" has often been defined in primarily economic terms. The argument is that "whatever interventions can improve the exchange and sales price of the land or the property taxes that can be derived from the land should be the top priority, since that will put the land to the highest and best use—meaning that people will pay the most for it."

For example, in a disaster-relief situation, local officials will look at where the most property taxes are coming from, where the sales taxes are highest, and where they think improvements can be put on that land to bring it to the highest and best use. All of that is influencing decision-making and priorities in terms of revitalization after a disaster has struck, and often, the focus is not going to be on vulnerable, low-income communities.

But what is also true—and in some ways, the current moment of the coronavirus has really amplified this—is that our fates are intimately connected. In a disaster, if there are vulnerable individuals who aren't getting the services and help they need to remain in place, that can eventually affect moderate- and high-income individuals. In some ways, our fates are more connected than we'd think. I do think finding ways to support vulnerable communities before the actual crisis of an environmental disaster hits needs to be an important focus. If our priority is only on where money flows, or what we think is going to be the highest and best use, then what we're doing is focusing on short-term monetary, financial issues at the expense of longer-term issues.

These communities being vulnerable, overlooked by the field of preservation, and subject to environmental catastrophe means that the problem will be moved somewhere else and dealt with in a more expensive way at another time. There's value in understanding vulnerable communities, fortifying them, and keeping residents, who lived in these communities during periods of disinvestment and strife, in place, in ways that will actually benefit those people and communities in the long run. In displacing the low-income or vulnerable populations, cities and villages will still have to figure out where this population goes and how it fares. Failure to deal with those social costs and distributional questions in the present only defers the problems and arguably makes them more expensive and worse in the future. That's a reason to document these vulnerable communities before they're in a state of crisis, whether the crisis is created by environmental degradation or economic dislocation from rapid gentrification.

In all this, people who focus on legal analysis and scholarship, practicing preservationists, and those thinking about historic preservation law from an academic perspective need to collaborate more frequently to resolve these problems. That synergy is going to be important going forward.

Barriers to Equitable Redevelopment: Insights from Detroit Neighborhoods

Randall Mason

Addressing Equity in Place

Disaster sometimes knocks down institutions and structures and suspends private life, leaving a broader view of what lies beyond. The task before us is to recognize the possibilities visible through that gateway and endeavor to bring them into the realm of the everyday.
—Rebecca Solnit, A Paradise Built in Hell

1
Mike Sheridan, "How Detroit Battled Its Way Out of Bankruptcy," *UrbanLand*, May 7, 2018, https://urbanland.uli.org/capital-markets/detroit-battled-way-bankruptcy.

2
Thomas Sugrue, *The Origins of the Urban Crisis: Race and Inequality in Postwar Detroit* (Princeton, NJ: Princeton University Press, 2014), xvi.

3
Rebecca Solnit's *A Paradise Built in Hell* (Viking, 2009) offers hope along these lines.

4
For instance, Detroit Future City; the Heidelberg Project; and the city's efforts on Neighborhood Plans and the Strategic Neighborhood Fund, the Fitzgerald Revitalization Project, and efforts to promote tactical preservation.

► PROSPECTS FOR PRESERVING
NEIGHBORHOODS OF DETROIT

The City of Detroit's bankruptcy in 2013 could reasonably be interpreted as the death knell of any progress toward sustainability and equity in that city. The massive failure of both market and governance was the culmination of decades of macroeconomic shifts, systemic racism, broken politics, predatory lending, and failures of urban policy at all levels. The bankruptcy erased $7 billion in debt, drastically reduced public services, and marked something of a before-and-after, capping the decades during which huge swaths of the city were abandoned, demolished, or otherwise left behind. 1 The city's population in 2013 stood at less than 40 percent of its 1950 peak, while the "total value of property in the city," as Thomas Sugrue has noted, "fell by 77 percent (in constant dollars) in the half century beginning in the 1960s."2 Detroit became a poster child for ruination and abandonment.

The bankruptcy was disastrous by any measure, yet its ruinous aftermath perversely revealed some opportunities for preservation and redevelopment. Multiple regeneration strategies have been attempted and are still underway (along with an anything-is-welcome development climate that has transformed downtown Detroit into a "glowing success"). Detroit beyond downtown is a testing ground for sustainable and equitable redevelopment. In such a harsh environment, anything that grows qualifies as a success. Addressing the needs of a limited number of Detroit neighborhoods, inching these parts of the city along paths of regeneration, is vastly inadequate to the depth of the crisis. But making incremental change, while forces for structural change gather force, at least builds the agency of community leaders and their nonprofit and city partners. Is it too much to hope that profound progress can eventually be an outcome of such profound loss, and can appear first in modest, innovative redevelopment projects—in small changes in the direction of change? 3

In terms of historic preservation, the destructive afterlife of Detroit's run as a leading industrial metropolis left seemingly little to preserve. FIGS. 1, 2 The landscape of twentieth-century Detroit—its proud achievements (massive growth, great architectural works, a 139-square-mile mosaic of communities) and its shameful failures (redlining, urban renewal, rebellions)—was erased, literally, economically, and metaphorically. Still, a number of thoughtful preservation-led strategies have been held up as beacons of hope for rebuilding neighborhoods and cultivating community agency. 4

The city's de facto strategy of retreat from some neighborhoods and selective strengthening of others is itself a radical preservation policy. When is a neighborhood too deteriorated to warrant talk of preservation?

FIG. 1: *While the Russell Woods neighborhood, a local historic district, remains quite intact, Nardin Park (to the bottom) has lost many buildings to abandonment and foreclosure. The Dexter Avenue commercial corridor (running top to bottom) was once an active west side thoroughfare; many lots and buildings stand empty, some since the 1967 rebellion. Photograph from Google Earth.*

FIG. 2: *East Warren Avenue, running from left to right, is the original commercial core and main street of the Morningside and East English Village neighborhoods, on Detroit's east side. Many of the commercial buildings on Warren are vacant; high levels of foreclosure and vacancy also mark the surrounding blocks of single-family homes. Photograph from Google Earth.*

Studies in neighborhoods like Russell Woods, Nardin Park, and East Warren/Cadieux face such realities. In the absence of viable markets, can an ethic of conservation, backed by policy and investment aligned with valuing what people and buildings still exist, be a way forward? Many of the projects and places Detroit holds out as signs of hope center in some way on the idea that preservation is not an end but a process, one that can be steered toward better outcomes. The act of building on existing cultures, no matter how tattered, is a foundation for hopeful acts of sustainable and equitable development—a declaration that erasure was not complete, and that Detroit lives another day to fight for its future.

Against the backdrop of Detroit's story, this essay explores some of the barriers to realizing "equitable redevelopment" as a strategy for substantially and historically disadvantaged neighborhoods. Straddling incremental and systemic change, it builds on recognized equitable development principles designed to counter gentrification and move redevelopment processes "toward equity." Equitable redevelopment attempts to temper neighborhood change by taking culture seriously (by incorporating preservation practices and policies).

This essay aims to make connections between experiences working on the ground with the City of Detroit and its partners (through a three-year project of research and neighborhood preservation studios at PennDesign) and this volume's aim to reconceptualize and generate new language for preservation policy. [5] These studios focused on applying "tactical preservation" strategies—partial, provisional means of adapting and activating neighborhood fabric to advance equitable redevelopment outcomes—in several neighborhoods in both Detroit and Philadelphia. One lesson we learned was that preservation planning is an unrealized strength in amplifying and anchoring redevelopment, design, and the policies guiding them in local culture.

After introducing equitable redevelopment concepts, this essay briefly raises some ideas for thinking systemically about neighborhood change and historic preservation's potential roles in those processes—a necessary precursor to advocating for systemic change—before outlining three barriers encountered in trying to implement equitable redevelopment in these contexts: *capital* (providing more access to it), *trust* (building it through heritage work), and *ownership* (imagining broader ways of defining and sharing it, as a matter of culture, not just commodities).

As I write (in early June 2020), widespread protests continue to resonate across the country, bringing ugly realities of historically disadvantaged neighborhoods and citizens—as shameful an American built heritage as the Jim Crow-era statues being toppled at the moment—into the bright light of politics and policy reform. And, yes, historic preservation is implicated. Preservation policies have long reinforced notions of white supremacy, and attempts to critically reform of the field have, as yet, accomplished little.

The force of this moment, in our professional realm, means that any effort that does not lead to *systemic* change is likely to be discredited by progressives, neighborhood-based leaders and stakeholders, leaders of the Black Lives Matter movement and associated organizations, and by public opinion. Rightly so. This is an opportunity for deep, lasting, profound change against structural racism and white supremacy. Preservation has earned a reputation of dealing only in surface appearances. But if integrated with other development, housing, and planning policies, preservation can push past incremental, superficial changes toward more profound results. Preservation professionals and organizations can be forceful agents for change if they wish.

5
This partnership between PennDesign and the City of Detroit received support from the John S. and James L. Knight Foundation.

6
PolicyLink, www.policylink.org; Alexander von Hoffman, *The Ingredients of Equitable Development Planning: A Cross-Case Analysis of Equitable Development Planning and CDFIs* (Joint Center for Housing Studies of Harvard University, 2019), www.jchs.harvard.edu/sites/default/files/Harvard_JCHS_Ingredients_Equitable_Development_Planning.pdf.

7
Angela Glover
Blackwell, "Promoting
Equitable Development,"
Indiana Law Review 34
(2001).

8
For example,
PolicyLink, "Creating
Change through Arts,
Culture, and Equitable
Development: A Policy
and Practice Primer,"
2017, https://www.
policylink.org/
resources-tools/
arts-culture-equitable-
development; CUNY
Institute for State and
Local Governance,
"Equitable Development
Guidelines." March
2018, https://islg.
cuny.edu/sites/
our-work/equitable-
development; Sasha
Forbes, "Principles for
Parks and Equitable
Development," Natural
Resources Defense
Council, https://www.
nrdc.org/experts/
sasha-forbes-aicp/
principles-parks-and-
equitable-development.

9
Environmental
Protection Agency,
"Creating Equitable,
Healthy, and Sustainable
Communities: Strategies
for Advancing Smart
Growth, Environmental
Justice, and Equitable
Development," 2013,
www.epa.gov/
smartgrowth/creating-
equitable-healthy-
and-sustainable-
communities. Marisa
Zapata and Lisa Bates
have analyzed the
pursuit of equity and
equitable planning
through federal
sustainable community
grantmaking, reflecting
on the long-standing
discourses of equity
within the planning field.
Marisa A. Zapata and
Lisa K. Bates, "Equity
Planning or Equitable
Opportunities? The
Construction of Equity
in the HUD Sustainable
Communities Regional
Planning Grants,"
Journal of Planning
Education and Research
37, no. 4 (2016): 411–424.

▶ EQUITABLE (RE)DEVELOPMENT

Equitable development has gained prominence as a strategy for addressing long legacies of discrimination that have devalued historically disadvantaged neighborhoods and in turn made them valuable to predatory investors. More specifically, equitable redevelopment is a means of countering or defusing gentrification. In its various guises, equitable development strategies and principles are designed for strengthening community (the existing community, that is) and achieving improvement without displacement.

While the concept of equitable development is well established, the literature is surprisingly sparse.6 The phrase and the concept were originated by Angela Glover Blackwell and were promoted as a "toolbox" by PolicyLink, the organization she founded and led for many years.7 It proposes an alternative to gentrification outcomes typical of laissez-faire development, particularly the capture of economic value by "outside" investors. It marks two important shifts: first, the community is empowered, taking greater agency over consequential decisions and a measure of actual power in shaping outcomes, and second, ownership of assets and benefits from rising property values (private goods) and community conditions (public goods) are retained by the community early in the process.

This is accomplished, the model assumes, by securing the power of local institutions and residents, by integrating actions across sectors (housing, parks, arts and culture, education, etc.), by timing (securing ownership interests before improvements drive up values), and by rewriting policy and reworking governance. The outcomes achieved, ideally, center on equity in both of its senses: fairness and the value of something owned. Equitable development is a Goldilocks solution, a "just right" combination of incremental change and systemic change, shifting and reforming existing means of directing urban policies as well as the interventions of architects, planners, preservationists, artists, and others through community partnerships (not just engagement) as forms of local, collective ownership. To use a different metaphor, this is a kind of "hacking": using existing real-estate and planning policies ("code"), reprogramming and adapting them to change the rules of the game, and inviting new local players to make new moves. Equitable development has been internalized and adapted (with less radical ideas often winnowed out) by those interested in real estate, parks, and community development, among other areas of intervention.8 The version promoted by the Environmental Protection Agency's Office of Sustainable Communities is thoroughly integrated with sustainability and public health.9

"Ethical redevelopment," a reformulation from the University of Chicago's Place Lab partnership, takes the model a step further by centering projects on the cultural values, histories, and processes of the community. Place Lab foregrounds arts and culture as central participants in equitable development, while reinforcing the agency of communities to decide and "own" strategies for themselves. Reporting on and synthesizing the work of Theaster Gates and colleagues in Chicago as well as the work of other cities implementing this approach, Place Lab's 2017 progress report outlines nine strategies for an approach to redevelopment deeply engaged with locality, culture, creative practice, and the specificities of place. It is not a normative model but instead derives a philosophy from work already undertaken, offering the principles as a sort of open-source code to be used by others elsewhere. 10

Perhaps the leading example of implementing equitable development is the 11th Street Bridge Park project, in Washington, DC. The project's strategy is purposeful, and equity is central to all aspects of the massive project. The project's "lessons learned" (so far, as the planners are in a long implementation process) highlight deep and meaningful engagement well before planning begins: building the engagement and organizational structures early; shifting control of the process and the properties affected to local communities; and assertively using data and metrics to evaluate outcomes along the way. 11

Building on this evolution of ideas and projects, the notion of "equitable redevelopment" offered here positions historic preservation planning, practices, and policies as core cultural elements used to reduce barriers to equitable development at the neighborhood scale. "Preservation planning" refers to projects or policies specifically integrating cultural distinctiveness and/or conservation of the built fabric; it could refer to specific project types (such as adaptive reuse) or different processes for carrying out non-"preservation" functions (for instance, producing affordable housing by investing in rehabilitation of existing properties instead of new construction). The idea of inflecting all aspects of a community's decision-making by explorations of its own culture and heritage is a central idea of Place Lab's ethical redevelopment and is meant to work on two fronts: First, by integrating an existing community's cultural values and processes with the usual factors of planning (economy, mobility, housing, ecology, and others), preservation planning can protect local histories and assets and practices, strengthen community identity, and be used to address the significant cultural barriers faced by redevelopment efforts. Second, this centering of community values and decisions on existing cultural narratives and assets (physical and psychic representations of the community) goes hand in hand with adaptation- or rehabilitation-based redevelopment strategies. There are many versions of this idea established in preservation for individual sites and buildings, but few in whole neighborhoods—the exceptions are notable, including the National Trust's Main Street approach and the work of the Reinvestment Fund (a community development financial institution based in Philadelphia). 12

▶ NEIGHBORHOODS AS SYSTEMS: CIVIC INFRASTRUCTURE

The current moment of widespread protest (as of June 2020) reinforces that the only profound change is systemic change. In committing to systemic change, it is incumbent on us to open up questions about how the systems work and why. Urban systems are enormously complex; the narrow question considered here is how neighborhoods work to meet social needs and maintain quality environments. What follows takes a planning perspective (as opposed to a sociological, anthropological, or

10
Place Lab, "9 Principles for Ethical Redevelopment," 2016, https://issuu.com/ artsandpubliclife/docs/ ethred_9pbooklet_ single.

11
Oscar Perry Abello, "Why History Matters in Equitable Development Planning," Next City, March 7, 2019; 11th Street Bridge Park's Equitable Development Plan, 2018, bbardc. org/wp-content/ uploads/2018/10/ Equitable-Development-Plan_09.04.18.pdf.

12
Lisa T. Alexander describes intersections of cultural processes and legal practices in "Hip-Hop and Housing: Revisiting Culture, Urban Space, Power, and Law," 63 Hastings L. J. 803 (2012); Mark Stern argues "why culture matters" to social well-being at the neighborhood scale in "Historic Preservation and the New Geography of Exclusion," Preservation and Social Inclusion, ed. Erica Avrami (New York: Columbia Books on Architecture and the City, 2020).

13
On the basis of extensive literature reviews and case studies, we generated the "civic infrastructure" conceptual model of the systems underpinning redevelopment. Elizabeth Greenspan and Randall Mason, *Civic Infrastructure: A Model for Civic Asset Reinvestment*, vol. 1 (PennPraxis, 2017), and *Civic Infrastructure: Sustaining and Sharing the Value of Parks, Libraries, and Other Civic Assets*, vol. 2 (PennPraxis, 2018), www.design.upenn.edu/pennpraxis/work/civic-infrastructure-research-and-summit.

architectural perspective) on how neighborhoods work that connects the physical environments, the processes reshaping them, and the societal processes and institutions organized to shape individual decisions that accumulate to produce the conditions of the place. The goal of greater sustainability and equity, no matter how it is specified, means rewiring how neighborhood change works and how power and resources are distributed. This is accomplished partly through public policy, to be sure, but also by reworking the other means of governance.

The systems of a neighborhood, described by a resident, would include spaces and processes of making/keeping a home, moving around, making a living (economy), gathering daily needs (shopping), getting educated (schools, libraries), playing (sports and games), engaging in informal social life (sidewalks), and governing (city hall). Culture, too, is part of neighborhood systems: it is manifest in the park and the statue in the square, in arts programming based in the park and the library, in the character of buildings and spaces, and in other parts of the landscape shaped by human use or design. The cultural landscape is, in other words, the whole "place."

From the planning and preservation perspective, how to manage change is the central question for understanding the system. "Civic infrastructure" is the working model of change explored in my previous research centered on public spaces and assets and how they get redeveloped. The "Civic Infrastructure" research project examined how cities make decisions about designing and maintaining public assets like parks, libraries, and rec centers. 13 This notion of infrastructure encompasses the hard assets and soft processes by which citizens, communities, governments, other institutions, policy and development processes, cultures, and creativity form an "ecology" of relationships to make, use, manage, interpret, and maintain their public assets. We found through our research and case studies that governance is the lifeblood of "ecology." Governance is defined broadly and includes public policies alongside institutions in the public, private, and NGO sectors; it relates to the work of many different professionals, advocates, and fields at the interface of people and environment. It involves leadership, partnership, trust, negotiation, and conflict. When it is working well, it keeps the civic infrastructure alive, flexible, adaptive; it connects the different scales of neighborhood, district, city, and region. It operates and connects several distinct scales of process and place: the site, the system, and the citywide policy.

Regarding the prospects for equitable redevelopment, the most notable and vexing aspect of governance in American cities is its fragmentation. The "ecology" is highly disturbed in most places. This stems not just from the American political system of federalism, weakly linking national, state, and local scales of governance. More pernicious, in relation to neighborhood change, is fragmentation across sectors and governmental functions. The space of the neighborhood is governed by a collection of poorly integrated departments and jurisdictions, a loosely predictable collection of NGOs and community groups. Because of this, practical, spatially coherent coordination or leveraging between steps and achievement of complex, long-term outcomes like sustainability or equity are made extraordinarily difficult.

127

FIG. 3: *Overhead view of a typical North Philadelphia row house block.*
Photograph by Bradley Maule.

The fragmentation of governance is easily highlighted with an empirical example exploring how a single, coherent neighborhood space is actually governed. Consider the photograph in figure 3. *FIG. 3* How many departments, owners, groups, regulations, and relationships do you encounter if you simply walk from a house at the top of the photo, across the street, to a house at the bottom of the photo? When you get to ten, you can stop counting (housing, planning, zoning, preservation, transportation, street tree, parking, police, block association, city council, and so on).

In terms of governance, neighborhoods are a landscape of invisible bureaucracies, policies, expertise, and power—all siloed in terms of bureaucratic structure, discourses, communities of practice, and legal standing. The resulting misalignment between different functions and processes makes it nearly impossible to co-manage neighborhood space holistically (whether the street, play space, open space, commercial space, and so on). Plus, there inevitably is competition between the distinct interests making up this fragmented field of governance: parking versus parks; safety of traffic versus safety of pedestrians; property owner interests versus renter interests; historic preservation versus real estate development; and more. Historic preservation policy is but one voice in this cacophony, usually making things worse and failing to challenge the status quo of fragmentation. (Exceptions to this aspect of preservation policy include heritage areas, greenline parks, and some cultural districts, designed as "partnerships" to counter fragmentation.) All in all, the governance system imposes fundamental barriers to neighborhood change, compounded in neighborhoods of profound disadvantage.

Our civic infrastructure model suggests that integration across the scales of site, system, and policy should be a focal point for managing change. Preservation policy and practice tend to remain very focused on the site scale, however. This presents major challenges to making policy relevant to sustainability and equity, as these issues require systemic-scale interventions. Preservation policy, simply put, needs to get broader,

14
Erica Avrami,
"Preservation's
Reckoning," in
*Preservation and Social
Inclusion*, 10.

15
As Martin Luther King Jr.
and others have argued,
these are all related.
Jeanne Theoharis, *A
More Beautiful and
Terrible History* (Boston:
Beacon Press, 2018),
3–27 and 123–141.

encompassing more aspects of environmental and social process, not just regulating property, supporting organizations and projects representing culture in broader senses than what is reflected in historic buildings, and aligning not only with curatorial outcomes but also with social goals like affordable housing, criminal justice reform, food access, and more. Preservation policy, in other words, needs reimagining as *cultural* policy.

Erica Avrami also addresses such policy bottlenecks vis-à-vis neighborhood change: "While more inclusive storytelling and decision-making are gaining traction and prompting innovation at the project level and among some practitioners, shifts in preservation governance structures and the policy toolbox have been slower to develop, with exploration of inclusive practices happening in more ad hoc ways." She continues, "How government policy will evolve to better ensure just representation and processes may hinge, in part, on the question of government's role in just outcomes."[14] In light of the civic infrastructure model, I would add that innovation and adaption *outside* government will be decisive in solving problems typically associated with government policy. And using the broader concept of governance (encompassing policy but going beyond it) centers on all three sectors and their interrelationships.

▶ THREE BARRIERS

Equitable redevelopment, as introduced above, models more sustainable and equitable change by incorporating cultural factors explicitly into the civic infrastructure of neighborhoods. This model is powerful as an ideal but faces substantial barriers in practice. These barriers are economic, legal, and cultural. Some are obvious, others hidden. The overriding barrier is the national system of lightly regulated, government derisked development (supported by progrowth politics, market-protecting public policies, and systematic racial-class discrimination) that makes gentrification the default redevelopment process for underinvested neighborhoods. Gentrification processes are relentless, driven by our national obsessions and devotions to private property ownership, racial segregation, and the free circulation and accumulation of capital. [15]

Making equitable redevelopment the rule rather than the exception—truly sustainable and equitable—would mean significant systemic change. On the ground, change can tilt toward equitable and sustainable outcomes if these specific barriers are addressed: *capital* access (perhaps most obvious); *trust* (apparent in distrust of outsiders, newcomers, experts, and government); and *ownership* (the biases and exclusivity of conventional private ownership, diminished prospects of public ownership and decent maintenance thereof, plus a typically narrow conception of ownership relating only to property). These three factors have come up again and again in work I've undertaken with students and professional colleagues in neighborhoods across several US cities with long legacies of disadvantage, disinvestment, and discrimination and thus most urgently in need of equitable redevelopment (namely, African American or otherwise racially diverse neighborhoods in Philadelphia, Detroit, and some other US cities).

129

Based on dozens of conversations with professionals, public officials, community leaders, and citizens, in the projects described above and others, these particular factors stand out as barriers to achieving equitable redevelopment outcomes. These barriers are more cultural than technical in nature; they do not derive from building codes, zoning provisions, or building performance but rather are accumulations of many decisions and preferences, aggregated socially and over time, which take on the "natural," invisible qualities of "just the way things happen" or "the way we do business." These barriers are systemic and are woven into the structures that guide power and decisions—and thus guide understanding of what is possible.

Each of these three factors points to distinct institutions, policies, and cultural tropes as points of intervention. Reducing any one of the barriers would ease the way for equitable redevelopment; understanding the connections between them is also important. (One could think of each constituting a loop in a complex systems diagram.) Each barrier also points to opportunities for changed policies that would enable equitable redevelopment and encourage further adaptation and "hacking" of preservation practices and policies.

Capital

Financial capital is required to acquire, maintain, and profit from property ownership. It is the lifeblood of neighborhood change and the neoliberal real-estate development process that equitable redevelopment seeks to rewire. Gaining access to capital and to equity in property *before* property values rise in a neighborhood is a linchpin of equitable (re)development.

Access to capital for housing and business development is an enormous barrier to equitable redevelopment. Structures imposed by the country's dominant culture are inscribed in public policy and political economy, most shockingly in the housing market. Policies built on the culture of white supremacy have long prevented capital access by Black people in particular. [16] There is ample housing policy literature on the hundreds of community development finance institutions, city government programs, federal housing policies (and a few development policies, such as opportunity zones), and foundations and their program-related investments, not to mention corporations and speculators, all of whom are involved in circulating capital through neighborhoods, for better and for ill.

While the *variety* of sources of capital has increased in recent years, the overall *amount* of capital hasn't seemed to increase, nor has the amount of capital controlled by communities themselves (which are defined, in one respect, by being capital poor), and the "quality" of the capital (how many strings are attached, what competition is involved) available to disadvantaged neighborhoods continues to deteriorate. [17] The expertise, technical knowledge, and time needed to participate in the many existing programs are a significant part of the barriers to capital access. From a business or property owner's perspective, there are (in any given place) so many sources of subsidies, tax benefits, zoning bonuses, etc., each with particular application and bureaucratic requirements, that it is very

16
Richard Rothstein, *The Color of Law: A Forgotten History of How Our Government Segregated America* (New York: Liveright, 2018); Keeanga-Yamahtta Taylor, *Race for Profit: How Banks and the Real Estate Industry Undermined Black Homeownership* (Chapel Hill: University of North Carolina Press, 2019).

17
Brett Theodos, Eric Hangen, Carl Hedman, and Brady Meixell, "Measuring Community Needs, Capital Flows, and Capital Gaps, Urban Institute," November 2018, www.urban.org/sites/default/files/publication/99313/measuring_community_needs_capital_flows_and_capital_gaps.pdf; Emily Dowdall, the Reinvestment Fund, personal communication, June 22, 2020.

18
Russell Hardin, *Trust*
(Cambridge: Polity
Press, 2006); Robert
Putnam, *Bowling Alone*
(New York: Simon
& Schuster, 2000);
Trust, Russell Sage
Foundation, www.
russellsage.org/
research/trust; Lee
Rainie, Scott Keeter, and
Andrew Perrin, *Trust
and Distrust in America*,
Pew Research Center,
www.people-press.
org/2019/07/22/
trust-and-distrust-in-
america.

19
Mindy Thompson
Fullilove, *Urban
Alchemy: Restoring Joy
in America's Sorted-Out
Cities* (New York: New
Village Press, 2013).

20
Diana Walters, Daniel
Laven, and Peter
Davis, eds., *Heritage
and Peacebuilding*
(Woodbridge, UK:
Boydell Press, 2017);
International Coalition
of Sites of Conscience,
https://www.
sitesofconscience.
org; Randall Mason,
"Valuing Traumatic
Heritage Places as
Archives and Agents,"
in *Values in Heritage
Management: Emerging
Approaches and
Research Directions*,
ed. Erica Avrami, Susan
Macdonald, Randall
Mason, and David
Myers (Los Angeles: J.
Paul Getty Trust / Getty
Conservation Institute,
2019).

difficult to gain access as a practical matter. We have heard this again and again in Detroit, Philadelphia, and other cities; recent experiences with the COVID-19 PPP stimulus loans demonstrate the extent of this problem, which is structured by our culture of fragmented governance.

Trust

Lack of trust—or an abundance of distrust—is a second barrier. Distrust runs in many directions, along every social cleavage in the United States (class, race, sector, locality, etc.), and by many accounts has been getting worse for some time. [18] As a social phenomenon, trust isn't a simple thing. More trust isn't always better. As political scientist Russell Hardin has argued, *trustworthiness* is really what we're after. Because trust is inherently transactional (not just about what one person, actor, or organization possesses but how it relates to others and how it affects decisions directly via perceptions of risk), it is an important lubricant to governance—an ingredient of "soft" civic infrastructure. There are no laws, policy requirements, formal measures, or institutions charged with producing trust; it is diffused throughout culture in myriad ways.

Enough trust needs to be built in order for the geographically nested governance/civic infrastructure systems to work. Without trust, fragmentation spreads. Trust can be built, or distrust repaired, by positioning heritage and its preservation as a trust-building process—a practice that builds on uses of heritage in peace-building processes in postconflict arenas. The postconflict uses of heritage since the mid-1990s in Rwanda and in the Balkans are cases in point. Building peace and trust mirrors psychologist Mindy Fullilove's prescription for "urban alchemy" to advance holistic, therapeutic restoration of long-damaged neighborhoods. [19]

Trust builds over time and has a historical dimension. Detroit city government is distrusted by some citizens because of a long legacy of discontent, maltreatment, discrimination, and failed service delivery—up to, including, and since the historic bankruptcy in 2013. But other cities suffer from their own versions of the loss-of-trust narrative. Indeed, distrust has arguably become part of the cultural heritage in Detroit neighborhoods. Over a half century, they have become distant from centers of power, disconnected from market and state circuits of capital and power and access, damaged physically (needing both public and private investment), and too often abandoned by the municipal government. This situation, developed over generations, highlights Hardin's insight that trust is a double-edged sword: neighborhoods have little reason to trust and don't want to risk it, yet some measures of "outside" assistance/ inputs are needed and are trusted warily. Municipal governments, for their part, have a poor record (though some good intentions), and they need to trust the local circuits of power, authority, and assets in order to have their investments succeed in the longer term.

Can social trust be rebuilt? This is a bottomless question, but in the realm of preservation, there have been a number of efforts to build trust through engaging heritage. Facing up to historical problems that have become more or less invisible can provide a social platform (and even physical spaces) for peace-building, postconflict reconciliation, and transitional justice.[20] Even if heritage discourse and historic preservation practices/policies can't "solve" the absence of trust, they can at least make it visible and confront the prevailing power structures. This brings to mind James Baldwin's pithy advice about the writer's role in reflecting on morality: "Not everything that is faced can be changed, but nothing can be changed until it is faced."[21]

Ownership

Ownership should mean more than legal possession or control of private property. It should also encompass culture and identity, associations we can "possess" in a different sense, both individually and socially. Adopting more generous, or multiple, definitions of ownership could help foreground the cultural means of advancing neighborhood sustainability and equity.

The legal/property conception of ownership is the default and the clearest index of power and wealth in our society. Private property ownership plays an outsize role in all aspects of American society and inscribes inequity into neighborhoods and every other landscape. Ownership of culture or cultural identity is a common and very democratic way of thinking, though not easily translatable to policy—and therefore it is deprioritized. But acknowledging cultural ownership claims should directly support engagement, collaboration, and more equitable sharing of power beyond property rights.[22] How to bring these two conceptions of ownership onto a more equal basis?

Conflict between these two conceptions of ownership was embedded in American society from the arrival of Europeans, who turned land into property, redefining "ownership" as a legal concept. The transformation of land from a shared cultural space to a commodity traded in markets was catastrophic. It destroyed a pillar of Indigenous societies. White supremacy guaranteed, through slavery, land grabs, and myriad other legal moves, that property ownership prevailed over other cultures and lives.[23]

Property ownership dominates preservation policy, and this aspect of policy has become a desultory practice, narrowed to parsing how little can be regulated, how minimal incentives can be to still reshape decisions, how policy decisions can bracket as much of the messiness of culture as possible (lest it end up a casualty in resurgent culture wars). Preservation policy is so thoroughly structured around private property ownership, its regulation by the state, and the politics thereof that we've lost sight of the cultural possibilities of historic preservation. The original reasons for creating preservation policy asserted that culture, memory, and history—as represented in certain geographies and histories, buildings and land—are matters of public good. Public good should not just be residual to private goods owned as property. It should be created, and supported by policy, as a societal asset. Instead, preservation policy remains largely consumed with regulation of private property. (Exceptions to preservation policies' narrow focus on property regulation prove the rule—national parks, for instance, where the government fully exercises its agency to conserve, to interpret for the long-term public good, and to carve out a genuine cultural public good at least partially insulated from exigencies of the market.)

21
"As Much Truth as One Can Bear," New York Times Book Review, January 14, 1962, 38.

22
The federal Traditional Cultural Property policy takes this approach, identifying places with clear associations unaligned with property ownership. National Park Service, www.nps.gov/history/tribes/documents/tcp.pdf.

23
William Cronon, Changes in the Land (New York: Hill & Wang, 1983); Vann R. Newkirk II, "The Great Land Robbery," Atlantic, September 2019, https://www.theatlantic.com/magazine/archive/2019/09/this-land-was-our-land/594742.

24
Caroline Cheong,
"Connecting Historic
Preservation and
Affordable Housing," in
*Preservation and Social
Inclusion*, ed. Avrami
(New York: Columbia
Books on Architecture
and the City, 2020).

25
Solnit, *Paradise Built in
Hell*, 313.

26
PennDesign Historic
Preservation Studio
reports, 2018 and 2019,
www.design.upenn.
edu/historic-
preservation/work.

When it comes to neighborhoods, standard preservation practices and policies work best on properties and objects—the landmark building, the remnant district, the designed landscape. But neighborhoods are systems that require a different approach. How do we use systemic models of neighborhood change to drive policy reform or "hacking" to result in more sustainable or equitable policies/outcomes? Without some sense of how the systems do or don't work, we are unlikely to "see," let alone overcome, these barriers.

Equitable redevelopment strategies aspire to change the structures of ownership, how power is distributed and conceptualized in neighborhoods. Perhaps the core principle of equitable development is that assets and benefit flows have to be owned by the community itself, in terms of political economy and also legally and culturally. Practically, this requires more profound power sharing and shifting than standard types of collaboration and typically one-way "engagement strategies." It should also stimulate new thinking about the kinds of civic infrastructure that can be (re)built to abet these shifts. For instances, land trusts, B Corporations, and other forms of shared equity arrangements—which deal with cultural as well as property ownership—should thrive and spread. [24]

▶ REUSING PRESERVATION POLICY TO
RESHAPE NEIGHBORHOOD CHANGE

Detroit neighborhoods, east side and west side, symbolize the runaway success of the automobile-fueled industrial economy. Today, after decades of abandonment, demolition, and deterioration, many exist only in tatters. Wide commercial avenues and seemingly endless residential blocks of single-family homes lend the neighborhoods grand scale; but so many buildings are empty or half-missing, their lives disappeared or displaced. These neighborhoods, depending on your outlook, are either symbols of failure or signs of hope. Reasons to retreat, or opportunities for equitable redevelopment.

Rebecca Solnit's *A Paradise Built in Hell* voices a paradoxical optimism about disasters and how they bring out the best in communities. [25] In that spirit, I'm optimistic that preservation policies and practices can tilt these neighborhoods toward hope if we weave them into an integrated strategy of equitable redevelopment. In several neighborhoods, such redevelopment is well underway, and there is much to be learned from those experiments. [26] But the transformation of a building or a lot is not enough to sustain truly equitable redevelopment. It will take rebuilding of the civic infrastructure and a serious appraisal of how governance works, and it will take capital, trust, and renewed senses of ownership. There are plenty of ideas out there for addressing fragmentation and lack of trust—the UN's Sustainable Development Goals, UNESCO's Recommendation on the Historic Urban Landscape, cultural landscape frameworks, various notions of resilience and reconciliation—but we need to acknowledge and face these wicked problems first.

What will doing this work look like? Though preservation is at heart a cultural practice, preservation policy in the United States seems very far from the expressive, polemical, creative possibilities of preservation. In public policies, preservation is tamed by obsessive regulation of property (and a few incentives), and we should be trying to set it loose. Based on trust-building, preservation policies can valorize more forms of cultural expression and heritage (art, food, sports, music, etc.), invest in the most highly used, shared spaces (commercial districts, parks, "the street"), and genuinely share power with community-based cultural "owners." It will be hard to overcome any of the barriers outlined here, let alone all of them. Plus, American cities and neighborhoods are hamstrung by the abiding absence of any national cultural policies or institutions (an absence that has exacerbated, I think, our fractured and fractious culture). 27

27
The United States lacks real national cultural policy, let alone a "culture ministry." I believe the absence of national cultural-policy discourse may have something to do with the recurrent culture wars, divisiveness, and lack of common ground that characterizes American society.

Historic preservation policies could—if hacked, reimagined, and adopted broadly—advance the cultural relevance of many kinds of noncultural, nonpreservation organizations. Foundations, community organizations, schools and universities, and other kinds of nonprofit organizations adopt policies to guide their work; despite what prevailing public policies may call for, these other institutional policies can influence outcomes (especially at the neighborhood scale) substantially. Why couldn't the policies of all these types of organizations commit to preservation *as a way of pursuing* their core missions? Preservation, because it centers on culture, can be a welcome, alloying agent to redevelopment processes. Cultural value and cultural process are mostly invisible in redevelopment processes, but foregrounding the ability of preservation planning to encompass the environmental, design, economic, social, *and* cultural aspects of the neighborhood redevelopment process brings advantages. Taking cues from Place Lab and other efforts at creative placemaking and arts-and-culture development, historic preservation policy can be tasked with being a means to advancing sustainable and equitable outcomes (not just an end in itself).

Lessons from American Vernacular Houses:
People, Planet, Prosperity, Peace, and Partnerships

Claudia Guerra

Addressing Equity in Place

My grandfather built this house for himself and his bride, my grandmother, in the 1890s. The county records say it was built in 1900, but my family remembers it being built before then. They would have built it with help from my grandmother's family, the Michons. They were French and were a family of builders. They built many things here in San Antonio and in Kerrville, where they moved in the late 1800s. The bathroom was added on later. I don't know when. They only had an outhouse at first. They lived in the two-room house for a few years after my mother was born, until they built a bigger house, a three-room house [chuckles], on the other side of the property. They had relatives living in other houses around them.

—Descendant of Alejandro Perez and owner of the Perez House 1

1
Oral history collection is a component of the City of San Antonio's approach to historic preservation research. Oral histories conducted for property-specific research are used to inform the decision-making process and are filed with records on that property and may be obtained by request. Larger collections for major projects and initiatives may be found on the Office of Historic Preservation's YouTube channel. Collecting oral histories from shotgun house owners, as well as from the people who live in shotgun-type houses, gives us the opportunity to learn more about the meaning of these structures. In speaking to the owner of the Perez House, we learned about her family's deep historical connection to San Antonio as well as her financial struggle with building maintenance and her commitment to affordable rent, while also learning deep San Antonio history. This story was collected over several conversations beginning in April 2020.

The Perez House stands on a picturesque lane near downtown San Antonio. Given its location in one of the busiest sections of the city, it's surprisingly quiet. Only the sounds of birds chirping and the yapping of a Chihuahua, which seems very angry that a car is traveling down this very narrow lane, can be heard. Situated in the city's historic core, known as the original thirty-six square miles of the city, the modest home is a three-room shotgun-type house owned by the same family for more than 120 years. It has been continually occupied throughout that time. Next door is another shotgun-type house. In fact, the two-block-long street where the Perez House stands is dotted with several examples of Texas vernacular housing from the turn of the early twentieth century. Shotgun houses, two-room cottages, and three-room bungalows cluster along the lane, which itself reveals Texas vernacular development and cultural patterns. People sit on their porches and watch the occasional car passing by. The street is composed of narrow parcels containing dense

FIG. 1: *The Perez House has belonged to the same family for more than one hundred years. The home was built in San Antonio in the nineteenth century by Alejo de la Encarnacíon Perez, who survived the Battle of the Alamo when he was an infant. The current owner, a descendant of Perez, leases the home at below-market rates to ensure housing remains affordable in an area that is vulnerable to gentrification.*

2
Mitja Bervar and Andrej
Bertoncelj, "The Five
Pillars of Sustainability:
Economic, Social,
Environmental,
Cultural, and Security
Aspects," Management
International
Conference, Pula,
Croatia, 2016.

collections of American vernacular construction—box frame construction with board and batten siding, horizontal lap siding, gravel and dirt driveways, dense tree canopy, and picturesque gardens with front yard ornaments, all of which creates a sense of place reminiscent of small Texas towns, though squarely situated in a highly urbanized section of the nation's seventh-largest city. FIG. 1

These architectural types and neighborhood patterns have long been representative of labor-class housing but have only recently achieved recognition as a form worthy of preservation. Many still see these houses as "shanties" or "shacks" that should be demolished and replaced with newer, larger structures. Though their groupings and locations rate high on density and walkability scales, and also offer a tight-knit social fabric, the neighborhoods they are located in have become vulnerable to demolition for redevelopment. Even so, a few savvy investors have begun purchasing these small homes, renovating them, and either renting them or flipping them for high prices. Both scenarios can mean the displacement of low-income tenants or homeowners as much as the revitalization and continuity of this housing type and the neighborhoods where they stand.

Shotgun houses, in particular, are a rapidly disappearing cultural resource across the nation. San Antonio, Texas, is no different from other cities in this regard. A visible reminder of San Antonio's cultural heritage, the Perez House and other shotgun houses like it are nineteenth-century examples of the wisdom of traditional building knowledge—knowledge that should be understood as a key contributor to a sustainable future. Shotgun houses illustrate the interwoven elements of sustainability: economy, society, culture, and environment. The city's Office of Historic Preservation (OHP) has undertaken a project to inventory and document the remaining shotgun houses in the city in an effort to not only preserve them but also promote them as affordable and sustainable housing, as well as a means to preserve people and planet while ensuring peace and prosperity.

▶ SUSTAINABILITY

The most common definition of sustainability is the use of existing resources in ways that won't compromise the resources needed by generations to come. Mitja Bervar and Andrej Bertoncelj, among others, expand the traditional measures of environmental health to include:

> economy (material well-being through sustainable growth), equity (social well-being through social cohesion), ecology (environmental well-being through natural harmonization), culture (cultural well-being through intercultural dialogue) and security (peace and sustainable stability). 2

The San Antonio OHP's Shotgun House Initiative is rooted in the idea that culture and social well-being are vital parts of sustainability. Collaboration with the city's Office of Sustainability, which is responsible for San Antonio's "Climate Action Plan," ensured the inclusion of cultural heritage as an integral element in the plan's adaptation response to a changing world.3 The OHP's vision of sustainability is an interconnected commitment to the continuity of living heritage that builds on local traditional knowledge and social fabric to perpetuate environmental, cultural, and economic well-being.

The OHP's Living Heritage Initiative works within the framework of the United Nations 2030 Agenda as well as the New Urban Agenda adopted in 2016 at Habitat III, the United Nations Conference on Housing and Sustainable Development.4 The OHP's living heritage work began in 2014 as part of a move toward a more equitable preservation framework, with the goal of creating an inclusive system that recognizes cultural properties as well as local intangible heritage. In 2017 the OHP hosted the first Living Heritage Symposium, where Ege Yildirim, the ICOMOS Focal Point at the time, introduced the 2030 Agenda. The previous year, the OHP presented at Habitat III in Quito, where the New Urban Agenda was presented. We invited presenters and participants from that event to the Living Heritage Symposium as well; the resulting action plan adopted at the 2017 symposium included an endorsement of both initiatives and a commitment to integrate them into the OHP's Living Heritage work. At the core of the 2030 Agenda are seventeen sustainable development goals (SDGs), a set of action items intended to reduce poverty, improve living conditions, provide access to education, enhance health and well-being, and increase equity, all while addressing climate change and ensuring a healthy planet. The SDGs are intertwined, rather than stand-alone, and are categorized in five overarching themes known as the 5 Ps—people, planet, prosperity, peace, and partnerships.

Notably missing from the seventeen SDGs is a goal specific to culture. However, UNESCO's "Culture for the 2030 Agenda" clarifies that culture is an innate element of the human condition. The document underscores how culture is a major driver of sustainable development. Together with the Paris Agreement of the UN's Framework Convention on Climate Change, the 2030 Agenda provides the world with an action plan toward creating a sustainable and resilient global community. The year 2020 introduced a decade of implementation of the seventeen goals and their 169 accompanying targets created to measure achievement of those goals.

Like the 2030 Agenda, the New Urban Agenda's intent is to create resilient, equitable, and prosperous communities. As implied by its name, the New Urban Agenda is focused on urban environments, and it proposes that cities have the ability to provide science-driven solutions for improved quality of life—including reduction of poverty, inclusivity, well-being, health, and planetary protection—by focusing on the financing, governance, planning, and development of municipalities. The New Urban Agenda "acknowledges that culture and cultural diversity" are vital to "sustainable development… and recognizes that culture should be taken into account… in address[ing] the adverse impact of climate change." The agenda is committed to "leaving no one behind" and to socioeconomic and cultural diversity among its 175 principles focused on improving living conditions in the world's cities.5

The 2030 Agenda, the New Urban Agenda, and various thoughts on sustainability guide the San Antonio OHP's shotgun house study.

3
City of San Antonio, *SA Climate Ready: A Pathway for Climate Action and Adaptation* (San Antonio: City of San Antonio, 2019).

4
United Nations General Assembly, *Transforming Our World: The 2030 Agenda for Sustainable Development*, 2015, https://sdgs.un.org/2030agenda and https://sdgs.un.org/goals; the United Nations Conference on Housing and Sustainable Urban Development, *The New Urban Agenda*, 2016, https://unhabitat.org/about-us/new-urban-agenda.

5
UN Conference on Housing and Sustainable Urban Development, *New Urban Agenda*.

Intent on retaining historic, affordable housing in working-class neighborhoods, the Shotgun House Initiative works toward achieving the 5 Ps.
Planned goals include creating a noncontiguous cultural heritage district,
developing recommendations for affordable housing, developing potential
treatment recommendations based on culture and traditional building
methods should the structures be designated landmarks someday, and
training contractors in traditional building methods.[6] With these potential
outcomes, the shotgun house study will contribute to interwoven goals that
guarantee housing, create economic prospects, develop a historic building
trades workforce, and increase educational outcomes for the understanding
of diverse cultural backgrounds while promoting planetary protection.

Cultural Heritage
Districts in San Antonio
are separate from
Historic Districts
and do not come with
regulatory frameworks.
Cultural Heritage
Districts are primarily
honorific but are used
to build awareness and
promote the culture
of the district. OHP
staff review proposed
demolitions in Cultural
Heritage Districts,
notifying neighborhood
associations and grass-
roots preservationists
of proposed changes
while encouraging
discussions between
developers and the
community to achieve
compatible outcomes.

► PEOPLE AND PLANET

The SDGs for people and planet aim to provide people with resources
so that they may live in dignity and equity in healthy environments that
manage and sustain natural resources. Understanding culturally significant structures and their connection to the environment is an important
first step in achieving those aims, and the San Antonio OHP's Shotgun
House Initiative is a part of that broader goal. Through interviews with
property owners (including many who have generational ownership of
their property), archival research, and analysis of building materials and
methods, the initiative is gaining an understanding of the significance of
the homes and the people who own them and live in them.

> *My grandfather and grandmother fell in love when they lived next door to
> each other on Pecos Street. They both came from early settler families, and
> the families were well known in San Antonio. My great-grandfather, my
> grandfather's daddy, was Alejo de la Encarnación Perez. He was known
> as the baby who survived the battle of the Alamo in 1836. Baby Alejo was
> eleven months old when he and his mother, Juana Navarro Alsbury, shel-
> tered at the Alamo during the battle with her brother-in-law, James Bowie.*

Alejo and Juana survived the battle; Bowie did not. Alejo would go
on to serve in the Confederate army, afterward becoming a city policeman
and marshal. City directories confirm that the Michon and Perez families
lived next to each other in the late nineteenth century in the 600 block of
South Pecos Street. Sanborn maps show that several blocks of South Pecos
Street consisted of shotgun housing, except for the Michons' home, a two-
story dwelling. Alejo would survive the devastating flood of 1913 before
his death in 1918. His descendants would survive later historic floods.

An estimated three hundred historic shotgun-type houses still
stand in San Antonio. Though not all shotgun houses have the same
momentous association with San Antonio's past as the Perez House, they
are associated with significant periods in San Antonio's history, most
notably during periods of population growth that are further discussed
in the next section. While it is possible that shotgun houses in San Antonio
were influenced by shotgun-type housing in New Orleans and other
areas of the southern United States, no direct linkage has been found.

However, we do know that San Antonio residents had traveled back and forth to Louisiana since early colonial days, when both the French and the Spanish vied to establish outposts in the region. And we know that similarities in economies, culture, climate, and resources could have influenced shared building technologies. Whether they were influenced by homes in Louisiana or not, the houses were lived in by both tenants and property owners and were built as an economically affordable form of housing. FIG. 2

7
Michelangelo Sabatino and Bruce C. Webb, "Introduction: Vernaculars in the Age of Digital Reproduction," *Journal of Architectural Education* 63, no. 2 (2009): 4–5.

8
Sabatino and Webb, "Introduction."

Michelangelo Sabatino and Bruce C. Webb have argued that the needs that created historic vernacular buildings are the same as those that drive today's sustainability movement: climate, site, materials, and economy. Past societies needed to "wisely" use limited local resources. "Ordinary builders of the past," they explain, "understood passive and active cooling and heating techniques as embodied phenomena rather than technology."[7] The shotgun house, like other American vernacular houses built before 1920 in San Antonio's historic core and its three historic districts, offers traditional building wisdom that can help sustain both people and planet because of its small footprint, conservative use of locally sourced materials, economic accessibility, and contributions to the social fabric. "When we speak of contemporary architecture that is sustainable," Sabatino and Webb continue, "we rarely speak of the cultural or even anthropological dimension that was key to the vernacular tradition that generated 'green' buildings *ante litteram*."[8]

Like all parts of the planet, San Antonio is vulnerable to environmental change. As this essay was being written in late summer 2020, San Antonio experienced one of its hottest periods on record, with temperatures

FIG. 2: *A late 1880s shotgun cottage at 1105 Guadalupe Avenue on the city's historic Westside. The home is a designated landmark largely due to the ongoing efforts of these organizations to preserve the city's working-class community. The Esperanza Peace & Justice Center recently purchased the home and has agreed to participate in the city's study to develop best practices for the maintenance and financial needs of low-income property owners of vernacular housing. Courtesy of the San Antonio Office of Historic Preservation.*

It should be noted that there is no intent to romanticize these houses. Many, both jacales and other American vernacular homes in San Antonio, did not have access to running water or other necessary amenities. The point, rather, is to understand the housing type as offering solutions that are conducive to climate, economy, and culture.

reaching 104°F. We are told it will only get hotter. Hot, dusty, yet prone to flooding, San Antonio has historically experienced extreme weather events from droughts to floods. In 1913, 1921, and 1940, historic floods wiped out entire neighborhoods, most of them in historically Latino communities west of the San Antonio River, nestled between numerous creeks that flow through the community. Substandard infrastructure and a lack of adequate housing made these Latino neighborhoods vulnerable to flooding. A Spanish-language account of the 1940 flood states that while Anglo-American residents lost pianos, carpets, and furniture, Mexican American families lost mothers, fathers, and children. Many of the houses were jacales, a form of wattle-and-daub construction. Though derogatorily referred to in tourist postcards as "Mexican Mansions," the jacal, with its small footprint and economic accessibility, offered many of the early lessons of sustainability that the later shotgun-type house would introduce and to which Sabatino and Webb refer. Both the jacal and shotgun-type houses used easily accessible materials, the small square footage provided an economy of materials needed, and the construction method made them types that property owners could build themselves, often in a short time.[9]

Shotgun houses are both financially efficient and appropriate for San Antonio's hot, humid climate. Vernacular architecture by its very nature implies that people build it based on their needs, with resources at hand, and influenced by culture and location. The shotgun house, with its narrow, hall-less form, allows for cross ventilation and airflow conducive to comfort in San Antonio's warm environment. This form, therefore, responds to the climate, the culture, and the economy of San Antonio's working classes.

▶ PEACE AND PROSPERITY

The SDGs for prosperity and peace aim to provide prosperous lives in societies that are just and inclusive. Toward that end, the San Antonio Shotgun House Initiative aims to develop a trained workforce skilled in historic building trades to increase the economic prospects of local contractors and skilled workers. A current dearth of skilled workers means that historic properties go unmaintained and allows a handful of contractors to inflate the price of renovation work. A trained workforce will increase the number of skilled workers who can share in the prosperity while allowing for more affordable maintenance of these small homes—a practice that will in turn help keep property owners and tenants from being displaced.

Have you seen the enormous building going up two houses down from the house my grandfather built? It's one reason why our property taxes are going up. I can't afford to rent the house at a low cost anymore. We've always rented to low-income families. In the 1970s we rented to refugees from Laos. It was too hot for them in San Antonio so they moved to Kansas, but we still stay in touch. For the last ten years or so, we've rented to a single mother and her daughter. Her daughter now goes to San Antonio College. Keeping their rent low helps them pay for college. I want to, need to, renovate the house for them. I want to keep it as affordable housing, but the improvements will cause my property taxes to rise, and I don't know if I can afford that because the rent doesn't cover the property taxes.

10
Herbert Gottfried
and Jan Jennings,
*American Vernacular:
Buildings and Interiors,
1870–1960* (New York:
W. W. Norton, 2009).

In San Antonio, shotgun housing began as an affordable housing design sometime in the nineteenth century and became prolific at the turn of the twentieth, as civil war in Mexico and famine and political turmoil in other countries such as Italy and Prussia brought many newcomers to San Antonio. By the early 1900s, San Antonio began issuing building permits as the city expanded rapidly, and affordable residential housing was in high demand to meet this influx. Newspaper listings of building permits issued for "Box Houses" where shotgun houses were built indicate both a building boom and the name given to these building types at the time. The type was especially affordable. Construction methods—mainly box and strip, also called board and batten—offered no insulation but were basic and ensured that homes could be built quickly and inexpensively. Kitchens in the rear meant heat would dissipate to the outside rather than the interior, while front porches provided shading. The small footprint also made it an easy form to build on the small, narrow lots developers were platting at the turn of the century. Moreover, the form allowed cultural norms of extended families living close together to build in general proximity to each other. Clusters of homes on single parcels in Spanish-speaking communities were called *vecinidades*.

The development of the city's built environment propelled real estate expansion and provided jobs to many people escaping poverty, war, and famine in different parts of the world. Carpenters, stonemasons, quarrymen, and ironworkers are listed in city directories as occupants of vernacular housing, in addition to rail workers, blacksmiths, and other skilled laborers. Herbert Gottfried and Jan Jennings discuss how vernacular homes can be defined by the geography and ethnic communities they are situated in, as "historically, people with a common culture tend to reinforce and disseminate that culture through the things they build; and *building materials and techniques*, in the sense that both may be unique to an area or a time period." Gottfried and Jennings view vernacular architecture through the continuity of aesthetic systems, which they refer to as "cultural impulses." Vernacular architecture, they claim, is largely in the hands of the builder and influenced by the "availability of local materials" instead of simply trends. [10]

The entire 600 block of South Pecos where the Michon and Perez families lived, as well as several blocks above and below, was razed sometime after 1952, due to urban renewal policies and construction of the highway that now divides downtown from San Antonio's Westside. Urban renewal projects of the 1930s, 1950s, and 1970s transformed the city's built environment and included the demolition of hundreds of shotgun houses and jacales. The urban renewal programs of the 1930s in particular removed many of the jacales along with groupings of small wood frame houses clustered together and dubbed the pejorative *corrales*. These small homes, which also included adobe structures, represented housing typical of the nineteenth century. They were located along waterways near the city center but lacked access to basic sanitation and necessities like indoor plumbing

11
Jim Coleman and Henry
Fletcher, "The Value
of the Vernacular," in
*Habitat: Vernacular
Architecture for a
Changing Planet*, ed.
Sandra Piesik (New
York: Abrams, 2019),
46–52.

and electricity. After the city was ravaged by cholera, yellow fever, and tuberculosis epidemics, these homes and the neighborhoods they were located in were seen as unsanitary and targeted for demolition. The city's first public housing was completed here, in 1941, after Eleanor Roosevelt toured the area in 1936 and advocated for public housing funding in 1939 under the newly created US Housing Authority. Today, community elders recall how the new public housing dispersed families that once lived close to each other. While all agree that better living conditions were needed, not all agree that the demolition of these important cultural residential types was the appropriate answer. Many feel that the demolitions were spurred by land grabs and greedy development. *FIG. 3*

"For these buildings to survive," claim Jim Coleman and Henry Fletcher about vernacular housing types, "they need the skills that went into making them to remain living traditions."[11] Preserving these houses will provide affordable housing, training for a workforce, equity, and an adaptive approach to climate change. Training a new generation of craftspeople skilled in traditional building trades will preserve historic buildings of all calibers, but more importantly, it will create a workforce and microbusinesses. In turn, this will potentially develop appreciation for historic building elements—for instance, creating value for wood windows built locally one hundred years ago, rather than vinyl windows imported and transported thousands of miles using gallons of fuel. This approach can develop cultural values while sustaining economic and environmental needs. Developing prosperity and preventing displacement can provide security and promote peace.

FIG. 3: *A row of shotgun houses stood on the south side of Rawlins Alley in 1968. The alley connected North Salado and North Medina Streets on the city's Westside. The homes were demolished shortly after the photo was taken under urban renewal practices that decimated affordable housing and displaced community members in residential neighborhoods near San Antonio's downtown. Courtesy of the UTSA Institute of Texan Cultures.*

12
Thwink.org. Thwink is
a small research group
dedicated to solving
social problems such as
sustainability through
systemic change.

The United Nations 2030 Agenda is based on the premise that sustainability can be successful only when all sustainable development goals are intertwined and achieved. As one nonpartisan research group has argued, "it is crucial to harmonize three core elements: economic growth, social inclusion and environmental protection. These elements are interconnected and all are crucial for the well-being of individuals and societies."12

What lessons can we learn from this American vernacular? How can the housing type address issues of affordability? Of climate change? Of sustainability and equity? While the San Antonio shotgun house study is not complete, we are working with the premise that preserving economical housing built using local materials and with local values can offer affordable housing, cultural sustainability, and the conservation of existing embodied energy.

The shotgun housing type embodies the ideas of intangible heritage and cultural significance; it also represents the affordable housing of the early twentieth century, offering potential for today's ongoing need for affordable housing. While unsustainable designs (large square footages, imported materials, materials manufactured inefficiently) "devour" resources, shotgun dwellings provide sustainability through their small footprint and basic construction methods—not least because they were built at a time when old-growth wood materials were available and used in these buildings. However, there are some considerations that also must be taken into account with this building type that extend beyond the structure itself:

1   Fractionalized ownership: Many of these homes are shared by families, which can cause title issues; many lack formal titles or deeds. Families sometimes can't prove ownership, creating housing instability.

2   Property descriptions: Land ownership is often not formally captured in county records, making it difficult for property owners to receive equity financing.

3   Disinvestment: Most, if not all, of the shotgun houses in the San Antonio study exist in communities that were redlined beginning in the 1930s. Decades of disinvestment in the community and the lack of financing capabilities have resulted in the erosion of many homes into severe disrepair, making it a potentially expensive enterprise for working-class families to fully rehabilitate a property. Policies such as redlining have created inequities in today's built environment, but emerging preservation work can effect positive change and build resiliency in communities dealing with architectural and spatial exclusion.

4   COVID-19 has disrupted the OHP's ability to engage with property owners as we had hoped. Typically, we would hold in-person meetings with property owners. We can and do hold digital and telephonic broadcast meetings, but many of the property owners are not likely to be digitally engaged as these homes exist in areas with less connectivity to the internet.

13
PlaceEconomics,
Opportunity at Risk (San
Antonio, TX: City of San
Antonio, 2019).

▶ THE FINAL P: PARTNERSHIPS

In order for the OHP's shotgun house study to achieve the vision of promoting people, planet, prosperity, and peace through the work of historic preservation, the final P of Agenda 2030's SDGs, "partnerships," must be incorporated. Achieving sustainability requires strong cooperation among partners sharing a collective vision that prioritizes people and planet. Some of the partnerships and ideas being explored as a next step in the shotgun house study include the development of public/private/ academic partnerships to assist homeowners and small developers and to create a trained workforce.

As the writing of this essay was concluding, the City of San Antonio was entering into a partnership to develop policy to rehabilitate not only shotgun housing but also other American vernacular housing. Spearheaded by Councilwoman Shirley Gonzalez, an elected official whose district contains an abundance of shotgun houses, the collective partnership brings together the University of Texas at San Antonio; Neighborhood Housing Services of San Antonio, a nonprofit housing development organization; MicroSA, a microbusiness nonprofit specializing in skilled workforce training; and three city departments. Our goal is to rehabilitate three shotgun-type houses in a pilot study to determine rehabilitation costs, financing structures that include the creation of grants and low-cost loans, a method for assistance in title clearance and deed acquisition, and workforce trainings all framed within best practices under the Secretary of the Interior's Standards for the Treatment of Historic Properties as well as sustainable and green building practices. The hope is that the study will create a system that can be replicated not only throughout San Antonio but also across the nation.

As with many cities nationwide, pressure to develop in San Antonio has increased. The most valued areas for redevelopment are part of the historic core of San Antonio. Close to downtown and in areas where property values are low or devalued, some of these properties are ripe for redevelopment. At the same time, there is a need for affordable housing. A study commissioned by the Office of Historic Preservation and prepared by the real estate and economic development firm PlaceEconomics, "Opportunity at Risk," shows the extent to which San Antonio's historic housing, built before 1960, is at risk of demolition while largely housing long-term residents, primarily Latino, 33 percent of whom are at or below 60 percent of the city's median income. [13] The COVID-19 pandemic has highlighted and exacerbated inequities in these communities, including housing instability. As cities such as San Antonio work to allocate resources to stabilize and improve housing availability and affordability, shotgun-type houses offer historic lessons for modern approaches to sustainable living.

More than Repairing Cracks in the Facade: Building Systemic Change in Times of Crisis

Jennifer Minner

Reimagining Preservation's Purview

During the pandemic of 2020, an eerie period of silence descended upon many cities. Playful and shrill birdsongs punctuated silences in the absence of car traffic.1 And yet how could one enjoy the birdsongs and fresh air when so many vulnerable, underserved communities and people, especially Black, Indigenous, and people of color (BIPOC), were afflicted and struggling with COVID-19?2 Many took to the streets despite risks to their own health, responding to George Floyd's last words, "I can't breathe," and motivated to respond to the depth of racial injustices, historic and contemporary. These uprisings were signs of a growing consensus that transformation could not be assured without collective action. The air had been poisoned; people's lives were threatened by cascading social justice, public health, economic, and environmental crises.

I write about preservation and policy at a time when there are multiple intricate fractures on the facade of American life that run deep and appear to be growing. The United States is reeling from a global pandemic, a climate emergency, racial injustices, and the social and economic fallout from them all. In a recent scan of various expressions of concern, sadness, and anger on social media, I paused on a post: "May the buildings we burn light the way."3 At this time, I feel challenged to explain my view that preservation should have a prominent place in public policy. What relevance does care for the material world have when we are struggling with a public health crisis? Why should we spend a moment considering preservation policies when so many are unemployed and unsheltered? What relevance do those of us who are (or have been) purveyors of historic plaques and "certificates of appropriateness" have when we realize the depth of racial inequities built into the communities where we live? What is the significance of preservation when there are so many other pressing environmental concerns? How should the many actors and educators who operate within preservation or in relation to it organize to address pressing needs?

Within domestic interiors, as the pandemic grinds on, we become aware of the places where paint is peeling, where mold grows, where air does not circulate. Interior deterioration is sure to intensify where there is a lack of resources as well as willful neglect on the part of property owners unmoved by tenant needs. Many people now face evictions; even substandard places of shelter may be out of their grasp. Many main streets and commercial corridors appear gap-toothed with boarded-up windows, Band-Aids covering the pandemic's mortal threat to independent businesses' existence. Black-owned businesses in America have been particularly hard hit by the pandemic.4 This adds further injury to already hurting BIPOC communities, where people live with the consequences of historic policies of segregation and redlining, where African Americans were denied loans for homes and businesses and, worse, were subject to violence and destruction when Black neighborhoods were deemed too successful by white society.5 Communities of color and low-income neighborhoods were also targeted for urban renewal, resulting in displacement. Later, after racist housing policies were outlawed and urban renewal had failed, African Americans became targets of predatory lending by the private sector.6 These racist policies, enacted by the public and the

1
Jennifer Ackerman, "What Birds Do for Us and What We Can Do for Them," New York Times, May 29, 2020, https://www.nytimes.com/2020/05/29/opinion/sunday/coronavirus-lockdowns-birds-nature.html.

2
See Sandra Garcia, "Where Did BIPOC Come From?," New York Times, June 17, 2020, https://www.nytimes.com/article/what-is-bipoc.html.

3
Dylan Stevenson, "May the buildings we burn light the way," Twitter, May 31, 2020, 11:05 a.m., https://twitter.com/abrakadylan/status/1267109859016749058.

4
Associated Press, "Black Businesses Hit Hard by COVID-19 Fight to Stay Afloat," New York Times, June 1, 2020, https://www.nytimes.com/aponline/2020/06/01/business/bc-virus-outbreak-black-businesses.html.

5
Richard Rothstein, The Color of Law: A Forgotten History of How Our Government Segregated America (New York: Liveright, 2017).

6
Keeanga-Yamahtta Taylor, Race for Profit: How Banks and the Real Estate Industry Undermined Black Homeownership. Justice, Power, and Politics (Chapel Hill, NC: University of North Carolina Press, 2019).

7
In *How to Be an Antiracist* (New York: One World, 2019), Ibram X. Kendi uses the term "racist policies" in place of "systemic racism" or "institutional racism," so that the term can be more widely understood.

private sectors for decades, resulted in enormous racial disparities in the amount of wealth that could be accumulated and passed on to heirs. 7

This systemic racism has carved indelible spatial and material patterns into the landscapes and buildings that comprise US communities. Those patterns affect the contours and topologies of daily lives. Historical patterns of access to or denial of land and capital shaped whole neighborhoods, cities, and generational fortunes. Patterns of production and consumption are etched into the glass and concrete, the bricks and mortar, the stones and tiles, the vinyl, aluminum, and asbestos shingles of the buildings we live in. Tradespeople and laborers built these places and continue to maintain them. These materials represent a vast system of commodities, of products and services. Our built environment represents the essential foundation for human life and livelihoods. When we pay attention to the flows of materials and methods of caring for the built environment, we can become aware of their relevance to equity and sustainability, to recovery and resilience, and to the potential for collective power.

I write this essay in 2020 for readers in the near future. I ask the many actors who comprise preservation as it exists today about areas of progress by 2021 and beyond. I define preservation in terms of the institutions that scaffold and give shape to preservation. Preservation is all of the following and more: a system of governmental programs and regulations; a set of private actors that have the potential to invest in and contribute to collective good or harm; a network of assistance and advocacy through the nonprofit sector; and a field of knowledge about the built environment constituted by educators and academic research. In this essay, I ask if the actors within this system, set, network, and field have embraced a wider agenda that includes care for the built environment and action toward equitable local recovery and climate action. Are we contributing to equitable opportunities through support and expansion of skilled green jobs? Are we helping to build a more robust and creative imagination and awareness of the built environment and inspiring action toward addressing crises of public health, housing, economy, and climate change?

The following are policy considerations and proposals that could contribute to important transformations both within preservation and within a larger network of actors. I propose and discuss a series of questions or "problem sets" for the preservationists of the future to consider, looking back. These arrays of evaluation, written to policy makers, professionals, and the public, are organized into the following domains of action: green and equitable recovery for climate action; rebuilding alliances and equity preservation; conservation, circular cities, and the paradox of thrift; public imagination, visibility, and remembrance; and the transformation or maintenance of the status quo. My hope is that this essay will soon become antiquated as policy makers, professionals, scholars, and students are able to provide robust answers to these queries. May the crises of today become a period of distant memories of the obstacles eventually overcome—a time that future generations pause to learn from.

FIGS. 1, 2: *Climate strike in Denver, Colorado, October 2019.*
Photographs by the author.

FIG. 3: *Sunrise on the Green New Deal mural in Ithaca, New York,*
August 2019. Photograph by Erik Amos.

8
Rep. Alexandria
Ocasio-Cortez (D-NY-
14), "Recognizing the
Duty of the Federal
Government to Create a
Green New Deal," Pub.
L. No. H.Res.109 (2019),
https://www.congress.
gov/bill/116th-con-
gress/house-resolu-
tion/109/text.

9
See, for example, City
of New York, "Action
on Global Warming:
NYC's Green New Deal,"
website of the City of
New York, April 22, 2019,
https://www1.nyc.gov/
office-of-the-mayor/
news/209-19/action-
global-warming-nyc-
s-green-new-deal; and
Eric Garcetti, "Mayor
Garcetti Launches
L.A.'s Green New Deal,"
website of Mayor Eric
Garcetti, City of Los
Angeles, April 29,
2019, https://www.
lamayor.org/mayor-
garcetti-launches-
la%E2%80%99s-green-
new-deal.

10
City of Ithaca, "Green
New Deal," City of
Ithaca, New York (blog),
n.d., https://www.
cityofithaca.org/642/
Green-New-Deal.
The Town of Ithaca, a
separate unit of local
government from the
City of Ithaca, has also
adopted a Green New
Deal resolution and
targets.

11
In Ithaca, preservation
advocates have been
directly involved in
the creation of equity
indicators for Ithaca's
Green New Deal as
well as building energy
retrofits research
and policy, the creation
of green jobs, and
developing deconstruc-
tion policies.

12
Carl Elefante, "The
Greenest Building Is...
One That Is Already
Built," Forum Journal 27,
no. 1 (Fall 2012): 62–72;
Erica Avrami, "Making
Historic Preservation
Sustainable," Journal of
the American Planning
Association 82, no. 2
(April 2, 2016): 104–112,
https://doi.org/10.10
80/01944363.2015.11
26196.

- *Are local, state, and national policies related to the built environment addressing the climate crisis while serving frontline and vulnerable communities and leading us to an equitable recovery from COVID-19?*
- *How is preservation contributing visibly and substantively to those efforts?*

The 2019 federal Green New Deal House bill proposed a vision for unifying climate action with social justice, striving to unite environmental goals with action to rectify oppressive conditions. Appearing many months prior to the pandemic, this resolution sought "to achieve net-zero greenhouse gas emissions through a fair and just transition for all communities and workers" while providing "millions of high paid jobs," and "to promote justice and equity by stopping current, preventing future, and repairing historic oppression of indigenous communities, communities of color, migrant communities, deindustrialized communities, depopulated rural communities, the poor, low-income workers, women, the elderly, the unhoused, people with disabilities, and youth (referred to in this resolution as 'frontline and vulnerable communities')." [8]

Also in 2019, just a few blocks away from the National Trust for Historic Preservation's Past Forward conference, Indigenous and youth of color activists organized a climate strike and invited Greta Thunberg to speak. *FIGS. 1, 2* The youth climate strikes and the youth-led Sunrise Movement have galvanized support for Green New Deal policies and for addressing climate injustices. Support for the Green New Deal has also materialized in the form of public artwork *FIG. 3* and in local government public hearings.

Cities both large and small, from New York to Los Angeles, have adopted local Green New Deal resolutions. [9] These resolutions are a first step in developing policies and programs to unite sustainability, equity, and stewardship of and investment in the built environment. Relatively Lilliputian in size, the City of Ithaca, New York, adopted a local Green New Deal resolution to address racial equity while transitioning to being a carbon neutral city by the year 2030. [10] However, in many communities, preservation's role in Green New Deal-related policies and programs has received little to no attention and support from preservation advocates, landmarks commissions, or policy makers. How many preservation advocacy groups or landmarks commissions can say that they have made clear the intersections between preservation, climate action, and the redress of historic inequities in their work plans, review processes, or city ordinances? [11] There is also a dire need for the institutions that feed local government efforts and innovation, such as State Historic Preservation Offices, the National Trust for Historic Preservation, and the National Main Street Center, to organize around these connections.

For some time now, preservation advocates have made the case that preservation is inherently sustainable, whereas others have called for making preservation more sustainable. [12] Still, little has been written about direct connections between preservation and Green New Deal policies, or about preservation as a force for climate action, environmental justice, or green jobs. There are a few exceptions to that relative silence.

The preservation journal *Future Anterior* sought submissions for a special issue on "Energy Crises & Climate Exigencies from Preservation's Perspective."[13] Preservation and land use law professor Sara Bronin has critiqued preservationists' avoidance of the debates around the federal Green New Deal, admonishing the preservation community for being too concerned with aesthetics to rise adequately to the challenge of the climate emergency.[14] There is much more that preservation can do to respond to the magnitude of the crises and the scale of the opportunities for supporting green jobs and just transitions.

In considering the role of preservation in advancing Green New Deal-style policies, it is worth pausing here to reflect on the original New Deal, enacted in response to the Great Depression. The New Deal of the 1930s and 1940s invested public resources in America's infrastructure. That infrastructure included historic sites and parks. Recovery efforts employed architects, craftspeople, laborers, and artists not only to build new but also to reinvest in existing sites. Stephanie Gray describes New Deal efforts as attempting to "restore" the nation as "historic preservation became a materialized method of cultural production and national recovery."[15] The National Historic Landmarks program, originally called the Historic Sites Survey, was established at that time, as was the Historic American Buildings Survey. Relief efforts resulted in an unprecedented level of public works, from the conservation of soil erosion to restoration of "historic shrines."[16] In similar ways today, tangible care of buildings and landscapes could be integral to Green New Deal efforts focused on securing "climate and community resilience" and creating "a sustainable environment."[17] However, the idea of incorporating a "conservation corps" that includes historic sites, existing building stock, or forms of creative placemaking has not been articulated specifically in the federal Green New Deal, and there is little evidence of it at local or state levels.

The emphasis in the federal Green New Deal resolution on addressing frontline and vulnerable communities very consciously responds to the omissions and segregationist legacies of the New Deal. Many New Deal policies, including federal housing policies, required segregation and willfully left out people of color. The plans, programs, and legislation of this time helped to codify de jure segregation, shaping urban and suburban landscapes and individual and collective fortunes in the decades that followed.[18] Reimagining what a "Green New Deal" might mean is also an important opportunity for preservationists to address critiques that their efforts have overwhelmingly focused on white-centered histories and fixated on concepts of historic significance and integrity that do more to exclude than to aid social preservation.[19] This is an important opportunity for preservation actors to work together to change both how preservation operates and for whom. In order to bring about such change, there needs to be transformation in both preservation leadership and in the workforce that supports reinvestment in the building stock, so that BIPOC communities both benefit from and drive those efforts.

Government and nonprofit preservation programs can substantially build sustainable and equitable recovery in multiple ways. First, reinvestment in the National Park System alongside parks, open spaces, and historic sites at every level can afford the opportunity to once again pair

13
Fallon Aidoo and Daniel A. Barber, "CFP: Energy Crises & Climate Exigencies from Preservation's Perspective," *Future Anterior* (2020), https://doi.org/10.17613/1KAF-1B71.

14
Sara Bronin, "Why Preservationists Must Be More Green," *The Hill*, October 2019, https://works.bepress.com/bronin/29.

15
Stephanie Gray, "Restoring America: Historic Preservation and the New Deal" (PhD diss., University of South Carolina, 2019), https://scholar commons.sc.edu/etd/5433, vii.

16
Gregory Cushman, "Environmental Therapy for Soil and Social Erosion: Landscape Architecture and Depression-Era Highway Construction in Texas," in *Environmentalism in Landscape Architecture*, ed. Michel Conan, Dumbarton Oaks Colloquium on the History of Landscape Architecture 22 (Washington, DC: Dumbarton Oaks Research Library & Collection, 2001), 45–70.

17
Ocasio-Cortez, "Recognizing the Duty of the Federal Government to Create a Green New Deal."

18
See Rothstein, *Color of Law*.

19
Stephanie Ryberg-Webster, "Heritage amid an Urban Crisis: Historic Preservation in Cleveland, Ohio's Slavic Village Neighborhood," *Cities* 58 (October 2016): 10–25, https://doi.org/10.1016/j.cities.2016.05.005; Ned Kaufman, *Place, Race, and Story: Essays on the Past and Future of Historic Preservation* (New York: Routledge, 2009).

20
Rothstein, *Color of Law*.

21
For discussion of the role of philanthropy and preservation, see Fallon Samuels Aidoo, "The Community Foundations of Allyship in Preservation: Learning from West Mount Airy, Philadelphia," in *Preservation and Social Inclusion*, ed. Erica Avrami (New York: Columbia Books on Architecture and the City, 2020), 157–171.

22
Meredith Burgmann and Verity Burgmann, *Green Bans, Red Union: The Saving of a City* (Sydney: UNSW Press, 2017); Pat Fiske, *Rocking the Foundations*, documentary (Ronin Films, 1985).

jobs and job training with care of shared public spaces. This work can be more directly tied to climate action by employing people to improve green infrastructure, to adapt historic sites to protect against inundation, to move structures when necessary, and to retrofit buildings to reduce greenhouse gas emissions. Cultural heritage organizations may also have a crucial part to play, as support will be needed for those communities who choose to resettle away from climate hazards. New jobs might take the form of helping communities to record their stories and attachment to places. It could mean documenting and helping to share local knowledge that can support community members' adaptation to a changed environment.

Preservation organizations and local, state, and federal government agencies also hold vital information about local history and property records. These organizations should assume an important role in supporting the case for national efforts to address past harms to Black and Indigenous communities. 20 Such support could include helping to build a case for a system of reparations. All of these actions would mean building antiracist frameworks and forms of allyship. Doing so will require building a more inclusive set of preservation institutions that are more representative of racial, ethnic, economic, and cultural diversity in communities. It will also mean recognizing and supporting the work of BIPOC actors and organizations that already do crucial preservation and community development work.

▶ REBUILDING ALLIANCES AND EQUITY PRESERVATION

- *In what ways has preservation built deeper alliances and expanded tool kits to address social equity?*

In order to accomplish goals related to both climate action and equity, it is necessary for the entire ecosystem of preservation, philanthropic and community-based organizations, government agencies, and educational institutions to build deeper alliances and to expand preservation's range of activities. 21 It will also require broad-based and grassroots organizing. In 2020 the death of labor activist Jack Mundey sparked remembrances of the many successes of green bans in Australia. Green bans were union-organized construction stoppages undertaken in solidarity and cooperation with neighborhood residents who were being threatened with demolition and displacement, as well as with environmentalists, preservationists, and advocates for Aboriginal land rights, among other progressive causes. *FIG. 4* The film *Rocking the Foundations* and the book *Green Bans, Red Union: The Saving of a City* document the history of the New South Wales Builders Labourers' Federation in the 1960s and 1970s in Sydney, and the lasting impacts of green bans on the preservation of parklands, working-class neighborhoods, and historic buildings. 22 This advocacy also led to greater government accountability and compulsory public involvement in planning processes, offering one precedent for how political coalitions and action can transform public policy in the interest of preservation.

According to scholar Linda Shi, coalition building that has

FIG. 4: *Builders Labourers' Federation (BLF) green bans mural, Sydney, Australia. Photograph by Jay Galvin (Creative Commons license – CC BY 2.0).*

23
Linda Shi, "From Progressive Cities to Resilient Cities: Lessons from History for New Debates in Equitable Adaptation to Climate Change," *Urban Affairs Review*, February 28, 2020, 107808741991082, https://doi.org/10.1177/1078087419910827.

24
Jennifer Minner, "A Pattern Assemblage: Art, Craft, and Conservation," *Change Over Time* (accepted manuscript, August 2021); Assembly House 150, "Assembly House 150," http://www.assemblyhouse150.org.

learned from the progressive city movements of the past is needed to address contemporary threats of displacement related to climate change. She stresses the necessity of building bridges between (1) frontline communities in hot property markets, (2) communities in under-invested urban centers, (3) rural white communities, and (4) labor unions. Wealth inequality is deeply enmeshed in the spatial concentration of wealth in global cities, which has contributed to housing unaffordability and displacement in the first group, and economic devastation in the middle two. Climate adaptation will shift the geography of desirable settlement, and the question is whether the first three groups can align in a way that benefits their collective constituencies. [23]

Parts of this vision of deep, "multiscalar" organizing can be witnessed in Buffalo, New York. The nonprofit organization People United for Sustainable Housing Buffalo (PUSH Buffalo) advocates for tenant rights and just energy transition at the city, regional, and state levels. At the same time, PUSH Buffalo has retrofitted low-income homes for energy conservation, purchased residential and commercial properties to maintain perpetual affordability, planted green infrastructure with vegetation grown in community-owned greenhouses, and converted a vacant schoolhouse into senior housing in the Green Development Zone. Meanwhile, the Society for the Advancement of Construction-Related Arts (SACRA) program, which is run by the nonprofit arts center Assembly House 150, trains people who qualify for job retraining to learn carpentry, woodworking, and other construction skills, partnering at times with PUSH Buffalo and other community-based organizations. [24] Yet another nonprofit, Preservation Buffalo Niagara, supported the establishment of the African Heritage Food Co-op and worked with organizations in the Fruit Belt neighborhood to resist demolition and displacement in an area

25
Tina Meyers, "High Road Economic Development: Best Practices," Cornell University, ILR School, February 25, 2015, https://digitalcommons. ilr.cornell.edu/cgi/ viewcontent.cgi?article=1114&context=buffalocommons.

26
National Trust for Historic Preservation, "Atlas of ReUrbanism," National Trust for Historic Preservation / Preservation Leadership Forum, 2020, http://forum.savingplaces.org/act/pgl/ atlas; Jennifer Minner, Zachary Small, Ashley Pryce, Claire Meyer, and Olivia White, eds., *Equity Preservation Workshop Final Report* (Ithaca, NY: Cornell University, 2017).

27
Minner et al., *Equity Preservation Workshop Final Report*.

28
Norman Krumholz and John Forester, *Making Equity Planning Work: Leadership in the Public Sector, Conflicts in Urban and Regional Development* (Philadelphia: Temple University Press, 1990); Marisa A. Zapata and Lisa K. Bates, "Equity Planning Revisited," *Journal of Planning Education and Research* 35, no. 3 (2015): 245–248.

of rapid development. All the while, the nonprofit Partnership for Public Good provides an umbrella for nonprofit efforts in the region, convening a host of labor, environmental, and community development organizations. All of these actors work toward "high road" economic development, defined as efforts that emphasize "high quality jobs, environmental sustainability, and broad access to opportunities for a diversity of businesses and workers."25 With the exception of Preservation Buffalo Niagara, these organizations do not identify as preservation advocates, yet their actions form a vital network that accomplishes community preservation goals, such as reinvestment in existing buildings and ensuring resilience of low-income residents in the face of displacement threats.

These observations about Buffalo stem from my own research partnerships with the National Trust for Historic Preservation, Preservation Buffalo Niagara, the Preservation Rightsizing Network, and Assembly House 150. This work began with a community-engaged course I taught in 2017 in which Cornell University students mapped spatial data, interviewed community leaders, and observed a variety of grassroots and local government policies related to preservation and building reuse in Buffalo.26 In listening to community stories, it became clear that preservation regulations and procedures can contribute to wider community development efforts, but they can also present barriers. In the course, we developed a framework for "equity preservation" to invoke multiple meanings of preservation and community development policies toward social equity, the use of sweat equity, and retaining local community control and ownership of land.27 This framework also directly references the legacy of "equity planning" that called for local governments to focus their policy efforts on those most in need and those who have been historically marginalized in planning processes.28 "Equity preservation" also invokes the idea of community-based sweat equity, which involves partnerships among preservation, community development, and arts organizations; community land trusts; local businesses; and jus-

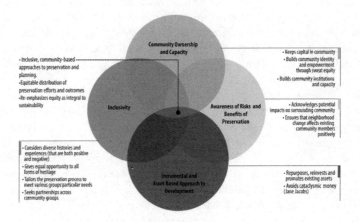

FIG. 5: Framework for equity preservation. From the final report of the 2017 Equity Preservation Workshop course.

157

tice-minded local government agencies. In the wake of the pandemic, which is likely to reinforce prior trends of financialization within American cities, equity preservation should also involve the retention of local ownership and control in the face of mortgage defaults and increasing speculation, in which financial institutions buy up property, taking it out of the hands of local owners. 29 *FIG. 5*

Preservation organizations have forged alliances to support business development and cooperation along main streets, first through the National Trust for Historic Preservation and later through the National Main Street Center. In many local communities, there are efforts that support facade improvement programs, designation of landmarks and historic districts, business improvement districts, and other vehicles for advancing both preservation of building stock and business development. These efforts need to consciously assist, support, and incubate businesses that serve BIPOC communities and that are owned by entrepreneurs of color.

At the National Trust for Historic Preservation, there has been growing recognition of the need to address concerns about cultural displacement in the context of gentrification of Black commercial corridors and neighborhoods. 30 Issues of cultural displacement are difficult to define and assess. According to the National Community Reinvestment Coalition, "cultural displacement" occurs "when the tastes, norms, and desires of newcomers supplant and replace those of the incumbent residents, and can also entail the loss of historically and culturally significant institutions for a community."31 Understanding and responding to displacement as a result of investment takes a sustained commitment to understanding the loss of commercial businesses and institutions. Successfully addressing both recovery and displacement through investment will take concerted efforts at building diversity into preservation leadership and the workforce, and at promoting allyship and antiracist policies in preservation, economic development, business and real estate, and planning, among other allied fields.

Stephanie Ryberg-Webster has written about alliances between preservation and community development organizations that have successfully organized to stop demolitions and preserve ethnic cultural identities in some cases, but she has also demonstrated how preservation policies sometimes impede strong alliances. 32 While there are useful logics to many federal, state, and local government preservation policies, there is a need to revisit the extent to which the specialized procedures and the deployment of concepts such as "historic integrity" are serving wider societal goals of preserving communities. There is also a need to develop new policy innovations that move preservation from primarily a narrow, regulatory system into a more transformative and powerful force that works in concert with other progressive causes. Preservationists need to make a much stronger and more visible case for how their particular skills, related to both in-depth knowledge of material conservation and grassroots organizing to save structures and represent histories, can better serve BIPOC and vulnerable communities, engage in equity preservation, and address the challenges of the future.

29
Saskia Sassen, "Who Owns the City?," in *Shaping Cities in an Urban Age*, ed. Richard Burdett and Philipp Rode (London: Phaidon, 2018), 148–155.

30
Mike Powe, "New Research: Cultural Heritage and the Risk of Displacement in African American Neighborhoods," *National Trust for Historic Preservation / Preservation Leadership Forum* (blog), July 25, 2018, https://forum.saving-places.org/blogs/mike-powe/2018/07/25/cultural-heritage-and-the-risk-of-displacement.

31
Jason Richardson, Bruce Mitchell, and Juan Franco, "Shifting Neighborhoods: Gentrification and Cultural Displacement in American Cities," National Community Reinvestment Coalition, March 19, 2019, https://ncrc.org/gentrification/#_edn1.

32
Stephanie Ryberg-Webster, "Community Development and Historic Preservation: Exploring Intersections in Seattle's Chinatown-International District," *Community Development Journal* 54, no. 2 (April 1, 2019): 290–309, https://doi.org/10.1093/cdj/bsx046; Ryberg-Webster, "Heritage amid an Urban Crisis." See also James Michael Buckley and Donna Graves, "Tangible Benefits from Intangible Resources: Using Social and Cultural History to Plan Neighborhood Futures," *Journal of the American Planning Association* 82, no. 2 (2016): 152–166.

Gillian Foster and Halliki Kreinin, "A Review of Environmental Impact Indicators of Cultural Heritage Buildings: A Circular Economy Perspective," *Environmental Research Letters* 15, no. 4 (April 15, 2020): 043003, https://doi.org/10.1088/1748-9326/ab751e; Luigi Fusco Girard and Francesca Nocca, "Moving Towards the Circular Economy/City Model: Which Tools for Operationalizing This Model?," *Sustainability* 11, no. 22 (November 7, 2019): 6253, https://doi.org/10.3390/su11226253.

34
Tina M. McCarthy and Eleni Evdokia Glekas, "Deconstructing Heritage: Enabling a Dynamic Materials Practice," *Journal of Cultural Heritage Management and Sustainable Development* 10, no. 1 (2019): 16–28, https://doi.org/10.1108/JCHMSD-06-2019-0084; quoted from pp. 23–24.

▶ CONSERVATION, CIRCULAR CITIES, AND THRIFT

- *How has preservation engaged with principles of circular economy and circular city initiatives?*
- *How have preservation practices promoted the ethics of conservation and thrift as useful concepts that can be applied in daily life and patterns of maintaining the built environment?*

Focusing on the social aspects of preservation should not drive preservationists away from developing deeper expertise in material conservation and adaptive reuse or engaging in related scientific research. The virtues of repair and reuse are central to some of the contributions preservation can make to sustainability efforts. While preservation is often focused on regulatory aspects of saving whole buildings in situ, the field can also benefit from scientific partnerships that seek to evaluate the benefits of and develop new methods for increasing building life span and using sustainable and reclaimed materials in retrofitting for energy and materials conservation across the whole of a community's building stock. Both preservation knowledge and wider local and federal Green New Deal efforts can benefit from concerted efforts to develop low-cost, less resource-intensive, and effective means of energy retrofitting across a spectrum of building types.

Concepts of the circular economy and the circular city draw from the idea of urban metabolism, seeking to eliminate waste, including within the built environment, through reuse and repair alongside innovative (and also long-standing and traditional) modes of design and construction. There are various interpretations of circularity, but there are only a few scholars who incorporate cultural heritage as an explicit part of that vision. [33] Although the concepts of circularity and the circular economy are still nascent in the United States, national and local governments in the United Kingdom, the European Union, and China have generated a track record. Preservationists in the United States can learn from those precedents. Nonprofit organizations can advocate for the application of circularity to push government agencies to recognize the value of continued use of existing building stock.

Nonprofit organizations, government agencies, and preservation educators should consider how concepts of circularity can be transformative. For example, lauding the benefits to both job growth and sustainability, McCarthy and Evdokia Glekas point to preservationists' blind spot when it comes to the virtues of deconstruction:

> Building materials exist as a paradox in a heritage discourse that favors whole building preservation. As assemblages they are the foundation of fabric-based authenticity, yet as individual disintegrated components they are not granted heritage status or protection... Deconstruction addresses this inconsistency within preservation practice by offering a treatment that can replace demolition, continuing the ethic of preservation through the process of building removal. Heritage materials are irreplaceable, just as much so as the buildings they were once contained within. Materials reuse represents a point of transformation in the stewardship of the built environment. [34]

FIG. 6: *Demolition of the Chacona Block, Ithaca, New York.*
Photograph by the author.

35
Angela Sandoval, Nicole Tai, Andrew Ellsworth, and Timonie Hood, "Bay Area Deconstruction Workgroup Webinar," May 6, 2020, https://register.gotowebinar.com/recording/4829030187153579782.

36
Thomas William Neumann and Robert M. Sanford, *Practicing Archaeology: An Introduction to Cultural Resources Archaeology*, 2nd ed. (Lanham, MD: AltaMira Press, 2010).

Deconstruction policies, such as the deconstruction ordinance in Portland, Oregon, divert waste from the landfill but also change the economic calculus associated with demolition and disposal versus preservation and adaptive reuse. 35 Some environmental organizations and agencies and preservationists are beginning to collaborate to advocate for building material recovery through deconstruction and reuse. This approach is evidenced by a recent webinar including speakers from the Bay Area Deconstruction Workgroup, a network of advocates extending within and beyond California, and the city of San Antonio, Texas. There are also preservation organizations, such as Historic Ithaca and its Significant Elements architectural salvage store in Ithaca, New York, that already embrace and are sustained by recovery and resale of architectural salvage. However, the ability to salvage and reuse building material in new construction and renovation on a large scale takes public regulatory infrastructure, incentives, and changes in construction and design practices. Most building material associated with demolitions simply ends up in landfills without accounting for embodied carbon. *FIG. 6*

Inspired to action by recent demolitions and by the work of the Bay Area Deconstruction Workgroup, the Just Places Lab at Cornell, which I direct, joined forces with Historic Ithaca, the Susan Christopherson Center for Community Planning, and the Circular Construction Lab at Cornell among others to found the Circularity, Reuse, Zero Waste Development Working Group (CR0WD). CR0WD conducts research and public outreach promoting deconstruction and reuse within New York State communities.

Principles of circularity also relate directly to older ideas about thrift. During the New Deal era, the Keynesian notion of the "paradox of thrift" argued that a drop in individual spending (or saving) had the potential to harm whole communities—an idea with possible ramifications for the role of building materials within the larger question of conserving the environment. 36 The federal New Deal handled this paradox by increasing public spending in ways that were labor-intensive to jump-start

37
Jennifer Minner, "Landscapes of Thrift and Choreographies of Change: Reinvestment and Adaptation along Austin's Commercial Strips" (PhD diss., University of Texas at Austin, 2013). Jennifer S. Minner and Xiao Shi, "Churn and Change along Commercial Strips: Spatial Analysis of Patterns in Remodeling Activity and Landscapes of Local Business," *Urban Studies* 54, no. 16 (December 1, 2017): 3655–3680.

38
Rothstein, *Color of Law*.

39
David Ness, "Growth in Floor Area: The Blind Spot in Cutting Carbon," *Emerald Open Research* 2 (January 24, 2020): 2, https://doi.org/10.35241/emeraldopenres.13420.1; Felix Heisel and Sabine Rau-Oberhuber, "Calculation and Evaluation of Circularity Indicators for the Built Environment Using the Case Studies of UMAR and Madaster," *Journal of Cleaner Production* 243 (January 2020): 118482, https://doi.org/10.1016/j.jclepro.2019.118482.

40
George Lipsitz, "Making Black Lives Matter: Conjuring and Creative Place-Making in an Age of Austerity," *Kalfou* 4, no. 1 (2017): 40–58; Dennis Maher, "Assembled City Fragments," https://www.assembledcity-fragments.com.

the economy—a method with potentially transformative implications for contemporary preservation as well. Positive aspects of thrift can be observed where local entrepreneurs convert the unused bones of former gas stations and other commercial properties to new uses, rescuing toxic sites from states of abandonment. In addition, "landmarks of thrift" appear where legacy family-owned businesses have survived over time—often these properties are time capsules in a larger sea of urban change. 37 In this sense, thrift can produce creative means of conserving material and reducing cost. However, "landscapes of thrift" could also describe the conditions in predominantly Black and Hispanic neighborhoods that were redlined, restricted, and deprived of capital to purchase or improve homes and businesses, while ideas about "safe lending" gave white households in predominantly white neighborhoods access to capital and the ability to accrue much more wealth. This history has had lasting impacts on spatial patterns of racial segregation, greatly impacting the average household wealth of people of color and in turn affecting their access to capital today. 38 Preservation advocates and the public sector should take an active role in helping to redress these negative forms of thrift, while also promoting a vision for the economy that incorporates the active conservation of the built environment.

In addition, principles of conservation and circular economy can be used by preservation advocates and government agencies to question the common assumption that new "green" construction unquestionably serves the interests of sustainability. Adaptive reuse, continued and more efficient use of existing building stock, and the use of recycled building materials through planned deconstruction should become integral to sustainable urban planning and design. 39 Local government agencies and preservation advocacy groups can devise alternative indicators and new methods of accounting for the positive forms of thrift, and they can help cities to revalue forms of conservation, thrift, and circularity that save both embodied carbon and embodied cultures.

▶ PUBLIC IMAGINATION, VISIBILITY, AND REMEMBRANCE

- *How has preservation helped to make care and maintenance of the built environment more creative, more viable, and more visible?*
- *How has preservation allied with the arts to advocate for common goals?*
- *How has preservation aided public deliberation about how we remember the past?*

Preservation ordinances often focus on tangible efforts to maintain a sense of place and the past. However, community preservation can take on many different forms and can be enriched through art and creative practice. Artists such as Rick Lowe, who founded Project Row House in Houston, and Theaster Gates, founder of the Rebuild Foundation in Chicago, use socially engaged art to celebrate Black culture and offer exciting pathways pairing art with community-embedded adaptive reuse. 40 Candy Chang has inspired public engagement in a range of vacant spaces. *FIG. 7* Assembly House 150, founded and led by Dennis

FIG. 7: i wish this was… by Candy Chang and a local community. Photograph by Jason McDermott. Flickr, Attribution-NonCommercial 2.0 Generic (CC BY-NC 2.0).

41
Minner, "Pattern Assemblage."

42
See Cristóbal Martínez, "Cristóbal Martínez," https://cristobalmartinez.net; Cristóbal Martínez, Randy Kemp, and Lisa Tolentino, "Radio Healer," *Extended Abstracts on Human Factors in Computing Systems - CHI EA '10*, 3113 (Atlanta: ACM Press, 2010), https://doi.org/10.1145/1753846.1753928.

43
There are so many more artists and organizations than can be mentioned within the confines of this article. I think also of the installation *Breathing Lights* (2016), which illuminated vacant spaces, and of Emily Barker, whose recent exhibitions call out injustices toward people with disabilities in the built environment. Jonathan Jones, Jay Carrier, and Do Ho Suh also provide vivid means of exploring the intersections of individual memory and collective memories.

44
Nancy Duxbury, W. F. Garrett-Petts, and Alys Longley, eds., *Artistic Approaches to Cultural Mapping: Activating Imaginaries and Means of Knowing*, Routledge Research in Culture, Space and Identity (Abingdon, UK: Routledge, 2018).

45
Jérôme Denis and David Pontille, "The Dance of Maintenance and the Dynamics of Urban Assemblages: The Daily (Re)Assemblage of Paris Subway Signs," in *Repair Work Ethnographies: Revisiting Breakdown, Relocating Materiality*, ed. Ignaz Strebel, Alain Bovet, and Philippe Sormani (Singapore: Springer Singapore, 2019), 161–185, https://doi.org/10.1007/978-981-13-2110-8_6.

46
"Grenfell Tower: What Happened," *BBC News*, October 29, 2019, https://www.bbc.com/news/uk-40301289.

Maher, employs creative practices to strengthen pedagogy in the building trades, making the built environment a beneficiary of new forms of creative reinvestment and care. [41] Cristóbal Martínez and collaborating artists in the Indigenous collectives Radio Healer and Postcommodity offer powerful celebrations of Indigenous knowledge of "hacking" and material reuse and also of creative practices as "sutures" to heal border conditions. [42] These are just a few of the many artists and arts organizations that have ignited the public imagination while demonstrating means of caring for place, material culture, memory, and the built environment. [43] Art, culture mapping, and other creative practices can be an ally of preservation, helping the public to visualize the past, to feel joy and delight, to see things in a new light, and to work toward social justice. [44] Although one might see creative practices as separate from policy, in fact the arts can thrive only with public support, both financial and in terms of flexibility to allow experimentation and public engagement in the public realm. The arts can be essential aids to public memory, to developing visions for the future, and to facilitating greater awareness about conditions in the present.

Many acts of maintenance and repair remain largely invisible to the public. In a study of the workers who maintain wayfinding signs in the Paris subway system, Jérôme Denis and David Pontille expose the skilled work and creativity that goes into largely ignored and overlooked maintenance work. [45] Like childcare and janitorial work, the work of repairing the built environment can remain unseen and undervalued. And yet when that care is missing, societal conditions fall apart. The ways in which buildings are maintained have important social justice implications, as in the tragedy of Grenfell Tower, in London, where the choice of external cladding and use of combustible materials resulted in the deaths of seventy-two people in the social housing complex in a fire in 2017. [46] Those choices privileged the external view of the tower, focusing on "updating" the facade while neglecting to invest in the safety of

47
Matthew Haag,
"Facades on 1,400
Buildings in New
York Are a Threat to
Pedestrians," *New York
Times*, January 30, 2020,
https://www.nytimes.
com/2020/01/30/
nyregion/nyc-scaffold-
ing-building-facades.
html.

48
Jennifer Minner,
"Assembly and
Care of Memory:
Placing Objects and
Hybrid Media to
Revisit International
Expositions," *Curator:
The Museum Journal*
62, no. 2 (April 2019):
151–176, https://doi.
org/10.1111/cura.12291;
Martin Abbott and
Jennifer Minner, "How
Images Construct
Cities: The Art of
Resisting Mega-Event
Amnesia" (unpublished
manuscript, August 8,
2020).

49
Stephen Clowney,
"Landscape
Fairness: Removing
Discrimination from
the Built Environment,"
Utah Law Review 2013,
no. 1 (2013): 1–62.

50
See Andrea Roberts,
"The End of Bootstraps
and Good Masters:
Fostering Social
Inclusion by Creating
Counternarratives,"
in *Preservation and
Social Inclusion*, ed.
Erica Avrami (New York:
Columbia Books on
Architecture and the
City, 2020), 109–121.

51
Roberto Bedoya,
"Spatial Justice:
Rasquachification,
Race, and the City,"
Creative Time Reports,
September 15, 2014,
https://creativetime
reports.org/2014/09/
15/spatial-justice-
rasquachification-
race-and-the-city.

tenants. Issues of neglect are rampant in most communities. In another example, the facades of 1,400 buildings in New York City have been deemed a hazard to pedestrians, victims of neglect by property owners. 47 Meanwhile, many homes, particularly private market rental housing in low-income communities, suffer from problems of indoor air quality.

There are multiple ways of addressing these less visible aspects of preservation and the maintenance of cities, including forms of creative action and artistic practice that reveal the value at stake in the repair of cities as well as the larger systems at work in the built environment. It can mean public remembrance of failures and tragedy, as in public art memorializing those who died at Grenfell Tower. *FIG. 8* It requires public expenditures for the care of public housing and robust building regulations and code enforcement to ensure lives and well-being. It also demands greater inclusion and compensation that recognizes the value of labor in building maintenance and the trades.

Preservation is also a field that is responsible for the care and disposition of monuments. Therefore, it must grapple with mnemonic devices in the public realm, influencing what and how we choose to remember and how we process those memories. 48 Preservation advocacy groups and public agencies must assist in addressing the racial injustices of the past and deliberating about how we deconstruct the monuments of white supremacy and build new monuments and interpretations. The preservation field must work toward inclusivity in public spaces and actively work toward antiracism. 49 By working with cultural organizations and artists, preservation nonprofits and agencies can help to address the excluded and erased histories not readily visible in the built environment. 50 It is also necessary to examine where preservation ordinances and practices may serve to maintain an exclusive "white spatial imaginary" rather than truly representing the diverse communities of the past and the present. 51

FIG. 8: *"Street art in Shoreditch, London September 2017. In memory of victims of the Grenfell Tower fire. Words from a poem by Ben Okri. Artist: Ben Eine." Photograph by Maureen Barlin. Flickr, Attribution-NonCommercial-NoDerivs 2.0 Generic (CC BY-NC-ND 2.0).*

▶ TRANSFORMATION OR MAINTENANCE OF THE STATUS QUO?

- *How has preservation contributed to societal transformations?*
- *How has it contributed to maintenance of the status quo?*

The many actors who comprise preservation today—the nonprofit advocacy groups, the public sector, preservation educators, and the private sector (whether laborers, architects, or investors)—need to be engaged with large-scale transformations. The system of preservation as it is enacted today is too exclusive, too narrowly focused, too white, and too privileged. Preservation has much to build upon, including in-depth knowledge of tangible and intangible heritages, but these should not be used to maintain the status quo. These tools should instead be expanded and applied in the quest for transformative action that effectively responds to the most pressing issues of today. Preservation's ethics of thrift, conservation, and care and its creativity and drive to share buildings and land as cultural resources have profound lessons to offer. These ideas are indicative of great potential to help rebuild equity in local communities and hope in the face of large-scale shocks. The actors involved in the field must seed changes so that preservation can grow beyond the confines of its current regulatory structure. This transformation is necessary so that preservation can actively contribute to the social and economic health of communities, aid in redressing inequities, and contribute to the epic challenges of climate change.

Sara C. Bronin

Reimagining Preservation's Purview

When it comes to the human ability to respond to climate change, laws matter. To slow the global warming that poses an existential crisis for our species, we must be willing to dramatically reshape our laws and legal institutions to encourage or require better behaviors. Within the areas where sweeping reforms are needed, it would be easy to overlook the rather narrow field of historic preservation law.

But recalibrating the way we treat historic places is essential in the climate crisis. In a time of vast uncertainty and rapid change, our historic places have the potential to connect us to our shared history. They often forge our collective identities and serve as backdrops for the moments that endure in our memories. Climate change will inevitably affect these places. We have already seen California landmarks burning, Alaskan cultural sites melting away, midwestern ghost towns exposed, and East Coast artifacts submerged. Others in this volume have considered these sites within their historical and cultural context, as well as the many practical implications of climate change, including the relocation—or the forsaking—of people and structures alike. My fellow scholars have also documented the dramatic impact of human activities—including buildings that overuse energy and are built and demolished wastefully—on our climate.

Keeping their work in mind, I hope to illuminate how our laws play an important role in choosing what is preserved and how. The first legal determination that affects the "what and how" occurs during the designation process. Designation is a formal legal process whereby government authorities apply criteria to determine which resources to list on the jurisdiction's register of historic places. [1] Typically, these criteria include some proof of historic significance, like an important historical event or an association with an important person, and integrity. The National Register of Historic Places, for example, requires significance and "integrity of location, design, setting, materials, workmanship, feeling, and association." [2] Sites that come to lack integrity because of physical degradation can be removed from the federal, state, or local register of historic places on which they are listed. The integrity of a resource—and thus its ability to be listed on a historic register—can therefore be harmed by the effects of climate change. The designation process has been criticized for being too formalistic (in that it focuses on architecture over people), [3] exclusionary of places related to low-income people or underrepresented groups (because those places may have been built with less durable materials), [4] and in need of replacement by a grading system that recognizes that resources may fall along a spectrum. [5] Despite its flaws, the concept of integrity, as well as the designation process as a whole, remains the foundation on which all historic preservation law is built.

Designation is the first legal determination of preservation; this essay centers on the legal determinations that follow, affecting the "what and how" of preservation when someone wants to make a physical change to a site that has already been designated historic. When certain physical changes are proposed, very often a foundational set of standards is applied: the Secretary of the Interior's Standards for the Treatment of Historic Properties ("the Standards"). The Standards are widely accepted as the measure by which such proposed changes should be judged. Indeed,

1
See Sara C. Bronin and Ryan M. Rowberry, *Historic Preservation Law in a Nutshell*, 2nd ed. (St. Paul, MN: West Academic, 2018), chap. 2, which describes the legal process and implications of designation at the federal, state, and local levels.

2
36 C.F.R. § 60.4.

3
See, for example, Vince Michael, "Diversity in Preservation: Rethinking Standards and Practices," *Forum Journal* 28, no. 3 (Spring 2014), which explains that the National Register's integrity criterion prioritizes architecture over culture and creates a binary system without nuance; or Melinda J. Milligan, "Buildings as History: The Place of Collective Memory in the Study of Historic Preservation," *Symbolic Interaction* 30, no. 1 (Winter 2007). "If the resource's features and materials are intact, then the site is worthy of National Register status," Milligan writes, "with physical features ultimately trumping events and people as the deciding factors in making this determination." Milligan, "Buildings as History," 116.

4
See, for example, *Preservation and Social Inclusion*, ed. Erica Avrami (New York: Columbia Books on Architecture and the City, 2020), which describes how the designation process sometimes presents barriers to listing historic resources relevant to underrepresented groups and historic resources that lack physical integrity; Anneka Olson, "Integrity and Incentives: Seeking Equity in Historic Preservation Law," *Access: Interdisciplinary Journal of Student Research and Scholarship* 1, no. 1 (Fall 2017), which explains that the integrity criterion "is also often the automatic disqualifier for vernacular buildings that may have been heavily used and modified," 14; Raymond W. Rast, "A Matter of

Alignment: Methods to Match the Goals of the Preservation Movement," *Forum Journal* 28, no. 3 (Spring 2014), which notes that in an effort to make preservation more diverse, the goals and methods of the preservation movement are misaligned, and "the standard that is most out of alignment is 'integrity'"; Page Putnam-Miller, "Reflections on Federal Policy and Its Impact on Understanding Women's Past at Historic Sites," in *Restoring Women's History through Historic Preservation*, ed. Gail Lee Dubrow and Jennifer B. Goodman (Baltimore, MD: Johns Hopkins University Press, 2003); and Ned Kaufman, "Historic Places and the Diversity Deficit in Heritage Conservation," *CRM: Journal of Heritage Stewardship* 1, no. 2 (Summer 2004), which criticizes the "integrity" requirement for creating a bias against the preservation of working-class and immigrant history, because those historic sites are unlikely to have survived unaltered.

5
See, for example, Patrice Frey, "Why Historic Preservation Needs a New Approach," *Bloomberg CityLab*, February 8, 2019, which argues for a grading system for properties.

6
Federal law generally assigns historic properties to one of five categories: districts, sites, buildings, structures, and objects. The law establishing the National Register for Historic Places, which is the federal inventory of designated historic sites, identifies these five types of historic properties. 54 U.S.C. § 302101. In some situations, the categories matter—for example, only "buildings" can benefit from federal historic tax credits. But the Standards apply to all five types.

7
36 C.F.R. part 68.

8
See text accompanying n. 18 in this essay.

the Standards have been adopted into law by state legislatures, tribal governments, and local historic district commissions all over the country. For that reason, what they say and how they are interpreted have ripple effects on preservation at every level.

In the view of many preservationists, the Standards have capably protected physical fabric within a broad interpretive framework. Unfortunately, the Standards do not adequately address climate-related building adaptations, such as installing energy-efficient windows or solar panels, raising sites, or moving structures. The Standards' omission or lack of specificity about such features has made things difficult for people interpreting them. Too often, interpretations reject such features, and therefore miss opportunities to reduce the environmental impact of the people occupying historic places or of the places themselves. This essay explains the significance of the Standards, analyzes their inadequacy in the climate context, and suggests reforms that recognize the intertwined fate of our tangible heritage and our warming planet.

▶ THE SECRETARY'S STANDARDS

The Secretary of the Interior's Standards for the Treatment of Historic Properties are among the most important foundational rules governing historic preservation practice today. They establish guiding principles for the way people should modify historic properties to meet current needs.[6] The Standards are enshrined in federal regulations promulgated by the National Park Service, a division of the US Department of the Interior.[7] They have impact beyond the federal context, because they have been adopted or adapted by local, state, and tribal governments. In certain jurisdictions and for certain projects, compliance with the Standards is mandatory. This section examines the four treatments covered by the Standards and their broad reach, covering billions of dollars in preservation construction annually.[8]

Four Treatments

The Standards cover four types of treatment of historic properties: restoration, preservation, reconstruction, and rehabilitation.[9] The Standards set forth between six and ten principles for each type of treatment. The principles cover a broad range of construction activities, including repairs, deterioration, additions, archaeological resources, chemical treatments, materials, and finishes, among other things. The Standards generally identify whether such activities "shall" or "shall not" be undertaken. Those who administer the Standards at the federal, state, and local levels often equate these terms as allowing or prohibiting certain activities. According to the federal regulations, identifying the treatment that is appropriate, and thus the activities allowed or prohibited, depends on "the property's significance, existing physical condition, the extent of documentation available, and interpretive goals, when applicable."[10]

The restoration treatment, perhaps the most dogmatic of the four treatments, is usually chosen for interpretive sites, like museums, or highly significant buildings, such as National Historic Landmarks. It "stops the clock" to restore a property to a specific time period. Any materials outside of the chosen time period will be removed, and any deteriorated features will be repaired rather than replaced. For properties receiving the restoration treatment, the Standards mandate that designs for the property that were never built can never be built.

A preservation treatment fits properties where the intent is to retain as much of the historic fabric as possible. The Standards allow for a preserved property to be either used the same way it was used historically or devoted to new uses that maximize the retention of historic fabric. The Standards require maintenance of historic character—including changes that have been recognized during the designation process as having acquired their own significance. In that sense, preservation differs from the restoration treatment, which removes changes to a property that are inconsistent with one particular time period.

The reconstruction treatment is used in limited circumstances, to allow new construction to replicate the appearance of all or part of a historic property that has disappeared. Sufficient documentary or physical evidence about the missing part is required. Reconstructions are therefore not themselves historic, and the Standards say that a reconstruction must reveal that it is new in some way. One example of a reconstruction built in compliance with the Standards is a slave cabin at Mount Vernon, the homestead of President George Washington. The cabin was clearly identified as a reconstruction and provides visitors with a fuller interpretative history of the overall site.

Finally, there is rehabilitation, for which the Standards provide the most flexible guidelines. According to the Standards, rehabilitation is appropriate for projects where fidelity to historic fabric is important but not paramount. The property can have a new use as long as only "minimal change" to historic features occurs. New additions and exterior alterations are allowed, as long as they do not destroy historic materials or disrupt a sense of scale. As is the case with reconstructions, rehabilitations conducted pursuant to the Standards will differentiate new and old materials. At the same time, new work should be "compatible" with the scale, materials, and shape of any remaining historic fabric. New work should be removable without impairing the physical integrity of the historic property. Because of its flexibility in addressing contemporary issues, rehabilitation is the treatment most commonly integrated into historic preservation practice.

Application

By their terms, the Standards apply to projects receiving funding from the National Historic Preservation Fund. [11] However, other programs and projects, both federal and nonfederal, also require the use of the Standards. As a result, the Standards end up governing most preservation construction projects in the United States.

A section of the National Historic Preservation Act, commonly referred to as Section 106, obliges federal agencies whose actions may affect properties on or eligible for the National Register of Historic Places to review their actions in accordance with the Standards. [12] Among the first determinations made is the agency's evaluation as to whether any

9
36 C.F.R. § 68.2 (setting forth the definitions for each of the four treatments). In the Standards, "preservation" is a term of art, not the term for rehabilitations of all buildings, as in common usage.

10
36 C.F.R. § 68.3.

11
36 C.F.R. § 68.1.

12
54 U.S.C. § 306108.

13
36 C.F.R. § 800.5(a)(2)(ii). Adverse effects under Section 106 also include moving property from its historic location, which is something that may be inevitable under climate change. 36 C.F.R. § 800.5(a)(2)(iii).

14
Agencies are required to consult with tribal, state, or local leaders to develop a process that ensures adverse effects will be considered. 54 U.S.C. § 306102(b)(5)(B).

15
54 U.S.C. § 306107. Note, however, that the Ninth Circuit has interpreted that harm-minimization language to simply require the agency to meet a higher standard for planning, not as a mandate for substantive action. *Presidio Historical Association v. Presidio Trust*, 811 F.3d 1154 (9th Cir. 2016).

16
36 C.F.R. § 67.7(a). Note that the Standards for rehabilitation used in the tax credit program are minimally modified from the standards set forth in a separate section of federal regulations that apply specifically to the tax credit. See 36 C.F.R. § 67.7(b).

17
See, for example, *Amoco Production Company v. United States Department of the Interior*, 763 F.Supp. 514 (N.D. Okla. 1990).

18
US Department of the Interior, National Park Service, *Federal Tax Incentives for Rehabilitating Historic*

Buildings: Fiscal Year 2019 (Washington, DC: US Department of the Interior, 2020), 2. Note that the numbers cited do not include the additional money invested in projects approved pursuant to the Standards at the state and local levels, or federal projects developed in accordance with the Standards that did not receive the federal rehabilitation tax credit.

19
Internal Revenue Code § 170.

20
Internal Revenue Code § 170(h)(4)(B)(i)(II).

21
See Reiter v. City of Beloit, 947 P.2d 425 (Kan. 1997).

22
Two scholars conducted a review of jobs posted to Indeed.com that were related to historic preservation in the United States. They found that "three-quarters of all jobs posting during this time were in the area of regulatory compliance," and they assert that "overwhelmingly [local] regulations are based on the Secretary of the Interior's Standards." Jeremy C. Wells and Barry L. Stiefel, "Introduction: Moving Past Conflicts to Foster an Evidence-Based, Human-Centric Built Heritage Conservation Practice," in Human-Centered Built Environment Heritage Preservation: Theory and Evidence-Based Practice, ed. Jeremy C. Wells and Barry L. Stiefel (New York: Routledge, 2019).

23
National Alliance of Preservation Commissions, "Design Guidelines for Preservation Commissions."

effects are adverse. Adverse effects include changes to historic properties that are "not consistent with the Secretary's standards for the treatment of historic properties and applicable guidelines."[13] A finding of an adverse effect triggers a formal review process that involves, among other things, documentation that the agency has considered the effects. [14] The agency need not actually stop or mitigate adverse effects, but if a federal agency imposes adverse effects on a designated National Historic Landmark, the agency must "to the maximum extent possible... minimize harm to the landmark."[15] Lack of compliance with the Standards can thus trigger a finding of adverse effect, and in certain circumstances (like for National Historic Landmarks), lack of compliance can compel additional action.

Federal law also imposes duties on private parties to comply with the Standards. Taxpayers who rehabilitate National Register buildings may apply for a federal rehabilitation tax credit. Before an applicant can receive the tax credit, the Secretary of the Interior must certify that a project meets the Standards. [16] All tax credit applicants must ensure that historic features are retained and preserved. Additions or alterations are acceptable as long as they are compatible with the existing historic fabric. The Secretary's finding that a project does not meet the Standards is usually granted deference by courts. [17] The vast majority of tax credit applicants successfully receive the credit. Between 1976 and 2019, forty-five thousand completed projects leveraged more than $102.64 billion in private investment in rehabilitation, and in 2019 alone, more than one thousand projects valued at $5.77 billion benefited from the tax credit. [18] The Standards have therefore become hugely important in preservation development in all fifty states.

Another federal tax incentive program for preservation provides tax deductions to federal taxpayers for easements they have donated to qualified nonprofit organizations. [19] The Internal Revenue Code requires that these easements prohibit "any change in the exterior of the building which is inconsistent with the historical character of such exterior."[20] Although the Standards are not explicitly referenced in the Internal Revenue Code, in practice nonprofit organizations incorporate the Standards into their agreements with taxpayers seeking the deduction. Thus the Standards are also being interpreted and enforced by private parties on an unknown, ever-growing number of private properties around the country.

In addition, state and tribal governments incorporate the Standards into their decision-making. This incorporation is consistent with the federalist framework of interrelated governmental entities envisioned by the National Historic Preservation Act. I have been unable to find any regulatory review process of any state historic preservation office not conducted in accordance with the Standards. Underscoring this point, the Kansas State Historic Preservation Office was quoted in a case as using the Standards in conducting reviews required by *state law*, explaining that "these standards are used across the nation and provide for consistency in staff reviews."[21]

Finally, local historic regulation, including certificates of appropriateness, are often tied, explicitly or implicitly, to the Standards. [22] The National Alliance of Preservation Commissions has identified commissions from Boise to Roanoke that incorporate the Standards explicitly. [23]

The municipal code of Hartford, Connecticut establishes the Standards for rehabilitation as the key guide to the decision-making of its two historic properties commissions. 24 Boston, another historic city, roughly paraphrases the Standards, then cites National Park Service guidelines that interpret the Standards in a list of publications that "may be considered part of" the local rules. 25 New Orleans, similarly, does not expressly include the Standards in its municipal code but does indicate in supplemental guidance that the historic preservation regulatory process is "guided by principles contained in" the Standards. 26 In Philadelphia at least one lawsuit involving the historic commission has been based on the commission's failure to follow the Standards. 27

There are hundreds of examples of state and local jurisdictions across the country that incorporate the Standards into their decision-making. And, as noted above, projects receiving a federal historic preservation tax credit must also comply with the Standards, amounting to billions of dollars in Standards-compliant real estate development each year. The Standards, and interpretations thereof, are therefore highly significant in historic preservation practice and in real estate development nation-wide.

▶ THE STANDARDS' CLIMATE MISTAKES

With this context, this part of the essay examines how the Secretary of the Interior's Standards for the Treatment of Historic Properties address climate change. As described, the Standards set forth broad principles for the way people should treat historic properties. They have not been amended in any substantive way for decades. 28 Despite changing values over this period, few rank-and-file preservationists or academics have complained about the effectiveness of the Standards. 29

Those who have, have powerfully critiqued the Standards for overemphasizing material fidelity rather than the meaning of the place within its cultural context. 30 That is to say, the Standards prioritize the integrity of the constructed elements of the historic resource, rather than its cultural or intangible elements, and at the expense of a flexible approach to later modifications. This critique originates in the criteria used for the designation of properties in the first place; the designation always includes a criterion of what resources have or do not have integrity. Although the debate about what "integrity" means is beyond the limited scope of this essay, it is important to note that the Standards' inflexibility is influenced by the criteria for listing properties and the fact that those criteria have, similarly, not been changed in decades.

In addition to critiquing the material focus of the Standards, some suggest that they thwart architectural creativity because they make it difficult for new architecture to be both "compatible" and "differentiated." 31 Others criticize the Standards because they make affordable housing projects more difficult. 32 Some believe that the Standards are too vague, which prevents the public from understanding what they intend to accomplish. 33 And then there is the critique that the Standards wrongly forsake sustainable materials in favor of historic ones. 34

All of these views are relevant to the ways the Standards have

24
Hartford, Connecticut, Municipal Code § 28–219(b).

25
For example, the city's standards for Beacon Hill are set forth in City of Boston, "Historic Beacon Hill District Architectural Guidelines."

26
City of New Orleans Historic District Landmarks Commission, "Guidelines Introduction."

27
See *Turchi v. Philadelphia Board of License and Inspection Review*, 20 A.3d 586 (Pa. Commw. Ct. 2011).

28
The precursor to today's Standards was developed initially in 1973 and was expanded to include rehabilitation in 1976. In 1977 the Department of the Interior promulgated regulations for rehabilitation that were used for the tax credit program. In 1992 the department published the Standards with four treatments, as we know them today, and these were formally adopted as federal regulations in 1995. See US Department of the Interior, National Park Service, "A History of the Secretary of the Interior's Standards."

29
Armon White, "Defining Appropriateness" (master's thesis, Columbia University, 2018). White notes that "literature on the Secretary's standards themselves has been largely limited to a simple cataloging of what the standards are," 7.

30
Daniel Bluestone, "Dislodging the Curatorial," in *Bending the Future: Fifty Ideas for the Next Fifty Years of Historic Preservation in the United States*, ed. Max Page and Marla R. Miller (Amherst: University of Massachusetts Press, 2016). This critique originates in the criteria used for designation of the properties in the first place, although the debate about what "integrity" means is

beyond the limited scope of this essay, and some sources are covered in nn. 3–5 in this essay.

31
David Payne, "Charleston Contradictions: A Case Study of Historic Preservation Theories and Policies" (PhD diss., Clemson University, 2013), 245.

32
Elizabeth A. Lyon and David L. S. Brook, "The States: The Backbone of Preservation," in *A Richer Heritage: Historic Preservation in the Twenty-First Century*, ed. Robert E. Stipe (Chapel Hill: University of North Carolina Press, 2003), 109.

33
Gary L. Cole, "Replacing the Secretary's Standards," *Traditional Building Magazine*, July 28, 2015. Cole argues that the Standards should be replaced with a "model historic building code."

34
Jennifer Kuntz, "A Guide to Solar Panel Installation at Grand Central Terminal," *Vermont Journal of Environmental Law* 10, no. 2 (2009): 315.

35
Alanna Casey and Julianne Fontana, "Cracks Preservation Must Fill," Keeping History Above Water, March 15, 2017.

36
See US Department of the Interior, National Park Service, *Preservation Briefs* (Washington, DC: US Department of the Interior, 2011).

37
36 C.F.R. § 68.3(c).

38
36 C.F.R. § 68.3(d)(4).

39
36 C.F.R. § 68.3(a)(2).

thwarted climate goals. A rigid emphasis on specific materials and techniques hinders the creativity we need to make our historic places more resilient and to reduce their impact on a warming planet. It also binds property owners to older materials—particularly old wood and unfired masonry—that are highly susceptible to lichen, fungi, erosion, splash, and smoke damage brought by ever-increasing temperatures, precipitation, and wildfires.[35] The allegation that the Standards thwart affordable housing—an essential societal goal—must be taken as seriously as the allegation that they challenge our ability to address climate change, and perhaps the two problems may be solved together by infusing the Standards with greater clarity and a broader purpose.

The Standards are not the only text we must consider. To supplement the Standards, the National Park Service has issued a series of formal "Guidelines." Over the years, the Guidelines have added detail to the broad Standards. They are sometimes general, updating National Park Service interpretations of all four treatments in the Standards, and are sometimes more specific, focusing on particular concerns or materials. This part of the essay critiques the Standards and their Guidelines, highlighting specific ways in which they undermine the ability of owners of historic places to address the climate crisis.

The Standards

The Standards do not explicitly address climate change or environmental issues. None of the sections describing the four treatments—restoration, preservation, reconstruction, and rehabilitation—refers to sustainability or climate change. No exceptions for environmental measures are made in the preamble to the definitions of the four treatments in federal regulations. What can property owners do, consistent with the Standards, to mitigate the risk, harm, or impact of climate change? In trying to apply the Standards to a few examples, we learn that the answer to this question is "not much."

Take the installation of energy-efficient windows or solar panels as one example. Not all modern energy-efficient windows perform better than historic wood windows in good repair with outside storm windows. In addition, the Department of Energy has found that "the US Department of Energy (DOE) has documented that air loss attributable to windows in most buildings is only about 10% of the total air loss."[36] However, the presence of energy-efficient windows as a replacement for nonfunctional and nonrestorable historic windows can reduce drafts that dramatically affect occupant comfort and can make a difference in electric bills. As noted above, a restoration treatment requires that a property be physically restored to its status at a particular point in time.[37] The reconstruction treatment may occur only in accordance with "the accurate duplication of historic features and elements."[38] Unless the windows or panels were used historically, they are not allowed by the Standards governing restoration and reconstruction. Similarly, for properties subjected to a preservation treatment, the Standards say that "alteration of features, spaces, and spatial relationships that characterize a property will be avoided," and if there is such severe deterioration that repairs are not possible, "new material will match the old in composition, design, color, and texture."[39]

The rehabilitation treatment, which is ostensibly the most flexible of the four, repeats this language but with one change: "the new feature will match the old in design, color, texture and, *where possible*, materials."[40] The Standards do not clarify how modern materials will be considered.

As another example, consider whether the Standards allow raising buildings to withstand floods, which are caused by extreme weather events and sea level rise, both exacerbated by our changing climate. None of the four treatments address raising buildings. Reconstructions require fidelity to historic designs, even if the reconstruction is not itself historic: the Standards ban "designs that were never executed historically."[41] The Standards for restoration and preservation treatments allow only for necessary repairs and some replacement of historic materials—not changes that would raise an entire structure. Rehabilitations allow "exterior alterations" but only if they do "not destroy historic materials, features, and spatial relationships that characterize the property" and if they maintain the "historic materials, features, size, scale, and proportion."[42] Raising a building and still satisfying the Standards for rehabilitation seems virtually impossible, since any increase in height would destroy "spatial relationships," "size," "scale," and "proportion."

Finally, consider how the Standards treat moving structures from their historic location. In many cases, the very location that gives historic structures meaning may be the threat to their continued existence.[43] Moving resources may sometimes be the only way to actually save them. Moving historic homes, bridges, entire Main Streets, and the people who use them may become necessary as sea levels rise or wildfires become more common. Some neighborhoods and archaeological sites are already submerged. None of the four treatments address this issue. Even the Standard describing rehabilitation, intended to be the most flexible treatment, states that "Each property will be recognized as a physical record of its time, *place*, and use."[44] Reconstruction, similarly, requires that the reconstruction be placed "in its historic location."[45] These constraints reinforce the Standards' seemingly total ban on relocation.

While these three examples are certainly not exhaustive, they illustrate the challenges faced by those who wish to change historic properties to address the climate crisis. We turn next to the Guidelines, which on their face aim to clarify certain aspects of the Standards.

The Guidelines

If the Standards have failed to address, or seem to disallow, modifications of historic properties to address climate change, then one might think that the Guidelines fill in the gaps. But the Guidelines make things worse, because their specificity leaves no doubt about what is effectively allowed or disallowed.[46] By their terms, the Guidelines evaluate techniques and materials as either "recommended" or "not recommended." However, it is important to understand that those who administer the Guidelines at the federal, state, and local levels equate a recommended item with approval and a nonrecommended item with disapproval. That said, there have been modest improvements in the area of adaptive treatments related specifically to the flooding of buildings, upon which future reforms can build.

The latest generally applicable Guidelines, issued in 2017, focus

40
36 C.F.R. § 68.3(b)(6).

41
36 C.F.R. § 68.3(d)(6).

42
36 C.F.R. § 68.3(b)(9).

43
See David G. Anderson et al., "Sea-Level Rise and Archaeological Site Destruction: An Example from the Southeastern United States Using DINAA (Digital Index of North American Archaeology)," *PLOS One*, November 29, 2017. This article finds that thirteen thousand historic sites will be lost if sea levels rise by a few feet.

44
36 C.F.R. § 68.3(b)(3); emphasis added.

45
36 C.F.R. § 68.3(d)(2).

46
This is why, below, I use the terms "prohibit" and "forbidden," even if the Guidelines say "not recommended."

47
US Department of the Interior, National Park Service, *The Secretary of the Interior's Standards for the Treatment of Historic Properties with Guidelines for Preserving, Rehabilitating, Restoring, & Reconstructing Historic Buildings* (Washington, DC: US Department of the Interior, 2017). Hereafter, NPS Guidelines.

48
NPS Guidelines, 103, 105.

49
NPS Guidelines, 125. For a restoration, the Guidelines suggest storm windows and insulation but not awnings (202).

50
NPS Guidelines, 153.

51
NPS Guidelines, 153.

52
US Department of the Interior, National Park Service, *The Secretary of the Interior's Standards for Rehabilitation and Illustrated Guidelines on Sustainability for Rehabilitating Historic Buildings* (Washington, DC: US Department of the Interior, 2011). Hereafter, Sustainability Guidelines.

53
US Department of the Interior, National Park Service, *Guidelines on Flood Adaptation for Rehabilitating Historic Buildings* (Washington, DC: US Department of the Interior, 2019). Hereafter, Flood Guidelines.

54
Flood Guidelines, 6.

55
Flood Guidelines, 4.

primarily on buildings even though other types of historic resources are subject to the Standards. The 2017 Guidelines articulate best practices for masonry, wood, metals, roofs, windows, porches, mechanical systems, and interiors, among other things. [47] The Guidelines do not mention climate change once, however, they do in a few places recognize the need to reduce energy usage of buildings being rehabilitated. For example, in the section on windows, the Guidelines state that exterior storm windows and other reversible treatments that promote energy efficiency may be acceptable if the profile of a historic window is not obscured from the street. [48] In the section on mechanical systems, the Guidelines recommend energy efficiency improvements, such as insulating attics and crawl space or adding "appropriate" awnings, to reduce energy usage. [49]

The Guidelines also suggest strategies to ensure that a building is more resilient to natural hazards, although they do not explicitly recognize that such hazards will only become more frequent and intensify with climate change. [50] Resiliency strategies include identifying vulnerabilities and their impacts, ensuring that historic resource maps are up-to-date, and documenting the property and its character-defining features. These strategies generally seem harmless although somewhat ineffective in helping people overseeing construction on a historic site understand what the Standards allow them to do. The Guidelines offer only a vague recommendation to prevent or minimize "the loss, damage, or destruction of the historic property while retaining and preserving significant features and the overall historic character." [51] But no guidance is offered to people needing to address real-time climate threats.

The 2017 Guidelines refer readers interested in sustainability to a previously issued set of guidelines relating to sustainability (the "Sustainability Guidelines"). The Sustainability Guidelines deal with only one of the four treatments, rehabilitation, and like the 2017 general Guidelines, they deal only with buildings. The Sustainability Guidelines offer a highly constrained and conservative series of recommendations related to eight specific material aspects of rehabilitation: windows, weatherization and insulation, HVAC and air circulation, solar technology, wind power, roofs, site features and water efficiency, and daylighting. In each of these areas, charts and photographs explain what types of modifications are "recommended" and "not recommended." Omitted from the Sustainability Guidelines entirely is the suitability of increasingly common mitigation techniques, including preparing and treating wood to protect against fungal growth (caused by increasing precipitation) and making significant topographical and landscaping changes needed to reduce the risk of wildfires. [52]

Likewise, the 2019 Guidelines on Flood Adaptation for Rehabilitating Historic Buildings (the "Flood Guidelines") focus on one treatment (rehabilitation) and one type of historic property (buildings). [53] They are intended to apply only to buildings with a 1 or 2 percent annual chance of flooding, according to flood insurance maps. [54] But they are promising in that they start to address the kinds of adaptations that are necessary now to save buildings from flood risks. These adaptations include filling a basement, changing the site and landscape, moving buildings, abandoning the first story, and elevating buildings. [55] The Flood Guidelines sanction new floodwalls and levees that are scaled to be compatible with the historic character of the property. 56 And they anticipate "unconventional treatments" like floating foundations, hydraulic lifts, and "living with water," which they indicate will need to be evaluated in the future. 57

It is worth evaluating the three example climate strategies just discussed in light of all of these Guidelines. None of the Guidelines make energy-efficient windows viable. They prohibit altering the historic character of windows, changing the appearance of windows in any way, or replacing windows (including the historic glass). Replacement material "that does not match the historic window" is prohibited. 58 Even "new insulated windows" are forbidden if the historic windows can be repaired. 59

Raising buildings is forbidden by the Guidelines, except that if homes are subjected to a preservation or rehabilitation treatment, they may be elevated if elevating homes is part of "local or regional traditions."60 Beyond that limited exception, only repairs or limited replacement in kind are allowed. 61 The Sustainability Guidelines fail to include raising buildings as a recommended treatment, and so, by implication and in practice, they are read to prohibit elevation. The later-issued Flood Guidelines, however, allow raising historic buildings, as long as character-defining features of a historic building are protected. 62 The Flood Guidelines suggest that heights be limited and that any new foundation complement the building's historic character. While this guidance helps, it applies only to the rehabilitation treatment, only to buildings (as opposed to other types of historic properties), and only to those within certain designated floodplains. Extending this guidance to all of the other types of properties—encompassing structures (including bridges and roads), sites (including archaeological sites), and objects—is essential, as many properties will face flooding risks in the years ahead.

The 2017 Guidelines take a hard line against moving or relocating buildings, suggesting in several places that structures be kept in place to retain "the historic relationship" between buildings and landscape features. 63 They prohibit moving buildings onto historic sites. They ban even the relocation of buildings within a site, like an industrial mill complex, and, perhaps worst of all, they prohibit changing the level of a site's grade, which means that topographical changes cannot be made to guard against ground-borne hazards like wildfire and water. 64 The 2019 Flood Guidelines seem to reverse those recommendations, albeit for a fairly limited number of properties. They suggest that moving a building to a new site is possible if there is a documented risk of flooding. It also says that if owners cannot avoid relocating a building to a new site "noticeably different from the original setting," relocating may be acceptable. If a building is moved, the Flood Guidelines suggest moving it in one piece, making minor repairs along the way and protecting fragile features like chimneys and plasterwork. 65 Beyond the scope of this essay are guidelines issued by FEMA and the National Flood Insurance Program, which exempt historic properties from requirements that they be altered to satisfy federal requirements, if doing so would jeopardize their status of being designated historic. 66

The various Guidelines have added specificity to Standards sometimes criticized for their vagueness. Yet they have mostly failed to

56 Flood Guidelines, 18.

57 Flood Guidelines, 53.

58 NPS Guidelines, 48.

59 Sustainability Guidelines, 4.

60 NPS Guidelines, 73, 155.

61 NPS Guidelines, 55–57.

62 Flood Guidelines, 36–42.

63 NPS Guidelines, 66, 138. See also the recommendation of "maintaining the building, its site, and setting in good repair" (153).

64 NPS Guidelines, 138.

65 Flood Guidelines, 49–51.

66 See Sara C. Bronin, "Resilient Heritage: Disaster Policy and Historic Preservation in the United States," in The Cambridge Handbook of Disaster Law, ed. Susan Kuo, John Travis Marshall, and Ryan M. Rowberry (Cambridge: Cambridge University Press, forthcoming 2021).

67
Only a 2012 case
challenging a local law
based on the Standards
came close, but the
property owners even-
tually lost. See Hanna v.
City of Chicago, No. 06
CH 19422 (Cook County,
Ill. Chancery Div. May
2, 2012).

promote reasonably climate-conscious preservation practice. Only the Flood Guidelines start to tackle the serious adaptation strategies we will need to address one consequence of climate change, although the Flood Guidelines' scope is very limited, and they promote interventions, such as raising buildings, that raise equity concerns in terms of impacts on neighboring properties. Overall, the Guidelines—and the Standards they interpret—justify criticisms that they ignore modern problems and are overly focused on the materials they protect rather than the people, neighborhoods, and communities that preservation is meant to serve.

▶ REFORMING THE STANDARDS

How might the Standards and their associated Guidelines be reformed to better harmonize preservation and environmental goals? As noted above, the Standards have in several important respects outlived their value to the field. In focusing on the Standard's deficiencies related to climate change, this essay does not intend to diminish other concerns—and in fact, some of the reforms suggested here could provide other benefits. There are three potential reforms worth considering: eliminating the Standards, revising the Standards, and augmenting existing Guidelines.

Eliminating the Standards

Given their rigidity on the one hand, and their vagueness on the other, should the Standards be eliminated entirely? Eliminating the Standards would offer the freedom and flexibility currently missing from preservation practice today. It would immediately loosen the firm grip of aesthetics on regulatory decision-making. And it would give free rein to people hoping to make radical physical changes to address climate issues—or to express their creativity in other respects.

All that said, I am not yet ready to argue for the death of the Standards. In their defense, the Standards have unified historic preservationists' approach to a sweeping range of actions, including federal agency under-takings, developers' tax credit projects, and smaller-scale local historic districts around the country. They have enabled the development and redevelopment of visually coherent neighborhoods, with deep benefits to property owners who have come to rely on their predictability. And the Standards have justified current laws governed by the Standards, because although they are vague, they provide property owners with sufficient information to understand what is expected of them. Indeed, judicial challenges of the Standards have never been successful. 67

Eliminating the Standards would probably mean the end of historic preservation regulation as we know it, since it would eliminate the criteria to which approvals and denials are tied. Review processes focusing on the Standards occur not just at the federal level, where the Standards have been adopted and formally interpreted through the Guidelines, but also at the state and local levels. So much of this regulation is tied in with the Standards that eliminating them altogether would lead to regulatory chaos. Without the Standards and a coherent body of law interpreting them, decision makers could be charged with arbitrariness—and challengers could win.

Revising the Standards

68
36 C.F.R. § 68.3.

69
Flood Guidelines, 53.

70
Portland, Oregon,
Deconstruction
Ordinance, City Code,
Chapter 17.106 (2019).

Rather than toss out the Standards entirely, preservationists should consider serious reforms to ensure that they reflect how we live today. I hesitate to use this essay to suggest specific language, because there are many things to consider beyond climate, and wide consultation is needed. I also acknowledge that making changes will not be easy, since changing any federal regulations requires an extensive process, with public review and comment—and since reforms to the Standards themselves may not even be popular among preservationists. But based on my observations above, I will offer a few guiding principles for reform.

First, revisions should be made to the prefatory language in the Standards, which states that they "will be applied taking into consideration the economic and technical feasibility of the project."[68] This provision of the federal regulations should be amended to add "climate threats, environmental conditions, and equity" to the list of considerations weighed when evaluating the applicability of the Standards. So far, this essay has clearly made the case for climate and environment to be added. But equity is a critically important addition, because so many decisions in preservation are made without considering impacts on low-income people and people of color. If, for example, the Standards are modified to sanction the elevation of historic resources at risk of water damage or the fortressing of historic resources at risk of fire damage, decision makers should be required to account for the impact on neighboring property owners in reviewing the particulars of an application.

Second, the Standards should add a fifth treatment to the four already listed: relocation. The Flood Guidelines are the first instance in which the National Park Service considers a relocation treatment, albeit only for specific types of properties (buildings) threatened specifically by flooding. Relocations will be increasingly necessary in the years ahead, for reasons other than flooding. Some of the principles laid out in the Flood Guidelines—including taking care to move and site properties in settings as close to their original setting as possible—are worth adopting for all properties.

Third, a sixth treatment—deconstruction—should be added to the Standards. Again, the Flood Guidelines acknowledge that sometimes sites will need to be demolished to save the livelihoods of the people living on them or to save the neighborhoods in which they are located.[69] If demolition must occur, the most sustainable way to do it is to deconstruct historic places. Following the lead of places like Portland, Oregon, a new deconstruction treatment articulated in the Standards can ensure that valuable materials are salvaged for reuse and that construction debris is eliminated from the waste stream.[70] Of course, the Standards could indicate that the deconstruction treatment is a last resort.

Fourth, existing Standards for the four treatments should be revised to incorporate both climate adaptation (techniques and materials that respond to changes in our climate) and climate mitigation (techniques and materials that prevent the harmful effects of climate change). At a minimum, in accordance with the second suggestion above, all references to preserving historic resources in place, without a relief valve for environmental threats, should be eliminated. Doing so will, in turn, eliminate the contradiction that we see now between the Flood Guidelines, which

71
36 C.F.R. §§ 68.3(a)(7),
(b)(7), and (c)(8).

support relocation, and the rehabilitation treatment in the Standards, which does not. Moreover, provisions about adding solar panels and roof-mounted wind turbines to buildings subject to the restoration and preservation treatment should be added to the Standards. These new provisions could state a preference for installations that are out of public view, but if such placement would render installations ineffective, the provisions could simply require that new equipment be removable without significant damage to historic fabric. Similarly, the Standards should loosen strict requirements that all but ban new energy-saving devices, such as modern or insulated windows or high-performance insulation. Finally, revisions should be made to references to "chemical or physical treatments," which occur in the restoration, preservation, and rehabilitation treatments. [71] These treatments should be allowed if they will protect against smoke and mold risks (among others), even if they cause some minor or cosmetic damage or alteration.

Augmenting the Guidelines

Even if all of these changes are not made to the Standards or are not made right away, the National Park Service should continue to issue Guidelines that address challenges posed by climate change. The Guidelines should be extended to cover historic resources beyond buildings, and they should address physical risks other than flooding, from hurricanes, tropical storms, tornadoes, blizzards, wildfires, earthquakes, extreme heat, and drought—which are all becoming more frequent and more powerful as a result of climate change. In addition, the 2011 Sustainability Guidelines should be updated where they clearly thwart environmental goals.

These ideas must be tempered by the one obvious flaw of the Guidelines: they can be changed, rescinded, or replaced as National Park Service priorities change. While they are a good temporary fix, the more permanent solution is to revise the Standards themselves.

▶ CONCLUSION

The law must adapt as the physical context of historic sites evolves. Climate change has already damaged or destroyed many historic places, eviscerating their ability to communicate their significance and their ability to serve as places of memory and connection. At the same time, historic buildings can themselves contribute to climate change by using too much energy or water. We must be freed of the constraints that would prevent us from retrofitting, moving, or otherwise altering historic sites to address these concerns. Even cornerstones of preservation law, like the Secretary of the Interior's Standards for the Treatment of Historic Properties, must be scrutinized. We must implement permanent changes to the Standards and its official interpretations to address the impact and risks of climate change on historic resources.

But necessary legal reform does not end with the Standards. The designation process may need to be overhauled to ensure that the very criteria that qualify a resource as eligible for listing on registers of historic places do not hinder our ability to make changes that can ensure the resource withstands or adapts to the effects of climate change. Local zoning laws, building codes, and tax incentives must be scaled to promote sustainable building reuse. Housing and environmental policies should promote environmentally just investments in our older places. Property tax abatements and credits can reduce energy consumption and carbon emissions while promoting clean energy use. Financial policies providing access to capital should be opened to ensure equitable redevelopment at the neighborhood scale. As I have written elsewhere, disaster laws must be updated wholesale, to ensure that they—the last line of legal defense on the climate battlefield—help us protect the historic places that embody human culture. [72] And future preservation advocates must be educated and empowered by preservation educators. Packaging our ambitions into tangible legal reforms—including and especially the Standards that govern changes to so many historic properties—is the only way we will ever be able to harmonize historic preservation and climate goals.

[72] See Bronin, "Resilient Heritage."

An interview with Vicki Weiner

Reimagining Preservation's Purview

ERICA AVRAMI
You're the current director of the Master's Program in Historic Preservation at Pratt Institute. The school has a history of community development and activism. Can you explain how historic preservation became a part of Pratt's curriculum and mission?

VICKI WEINER
Pratt Institute was founded in the 1880s by Charles Pratt, who was an industrialist and a progressive. He brought an activist bent to the founding of the school, with a mission to educate and train immigrants in Brooklyn so that they would have a ladder toward wealth, and so that they could become homeowners and citizens in America. His wealth came from the oil industry, but he was committed to improving the lives of workers through access to education and safe housing. Pratt has evolved over the years into a premier art and design school that maintains a tradition of fostering education that improves peoples' lives as artists, as designers, as citizens. That has been a through line since its founding.

The school's history is, of course, very complicated, especially when you get to the mid-twentieth century. Pratt is in Clinton Hill, Brooklyn, a community that, like much of the borough, was subjected to racist housing policies and aggressive urban renewal plans that displaced low-income residents and destroyed historic buildings. The administration of Pratt at that time was not progressive—in fact, in the 1950s the school entered into an urban renewal plan with the city to clear blocks around its academic buildings for student housing and campus development. The campus was enclosed by fencing as part of that plan, with a couple of streets demapped to create a superblock campus that the school could control access to via manned entrance gates. This changed the dynamic and relationship with the surrounding residential community and displaced some residents and businesses. The fencing in of the campus made many folks feel they were no longer welcome. On the other hand, Pratt has always been home to scholars and teaching practitioners who felt that sense of Charles Pratt's community-serving mission, even if the administration wasn't always progressive. The institute's Art and Design Education Program, the School of Architecture, and many other departments evolved into serving as community support systems early on, and Charles Pratt himself founded one of the city's first free libraries. And, by the way, we're very fortunate at this moment in time to have a truly progressive administration at Pratt, with a president and other leaders who've placed community service, engagement, and partnership at the top of the school's list of current priorities.

In the 1960s, when there was so much disinvestment all over Brooklyn, there were faculty and students in the Architecture and Urban Planning Departments who were working with community-based groups to help them keep from being displaced, whether by the lack of services in their communities or the city-sponsored plans that sought to demolish blocks of housing and businesses. This was the situation out of which the Pratt Center for Community Development was born. The center was founded in 1963 by a group of faculty and students including Ron Shiffman, who is now Professor Emeritus of Planning at Pratt and who also founded the Graduate

Center for Planning and the Environment (GCPE) within the School of Architecture, where the Historic Preservation Master's Program sits.

Pratt Center—the first university-based community development center in the country—has always focused on partnering with community-based organizations to work on social justice and equity-oriented issues, primarily around affordable housing and economic development. The founders of Pratt Center had a hand in helping community leaders in Bedford-Stuyvesant establish the Bedford Stuyvesant Restoration Corporation, the nation's first federally funded Community Development Corporation (CDC), which is still going strong.

In the 1970s, as the community development corporation movement grew exponentially all over the city but particularly in Brooklyn, one of Pratt Center's community-building strategies was to invite young organizers and volunteers from CDCs in Black neighborhoods to take part in a fellowship program where they were trained in community organizing, data collection and analysis, and community-based planning. The center would then help them to translate their fellowship coursework into academic credits so they could get a master's degree in city and regional planning from Pratt. This initiative, as with much of Pratt Center's work, connected pedagogy to community development very firmly, and since that time the planning master's degree program has had community development at its core.

The Historic Preservation Program was founded in 2004 as a "sister" to the City and Regional Planning Program within the GCPE. For a long time, there had been one or two historic preservation courses within the planning curriculum, but in the early 2000s, Eric Allison and Ned Kaufman led the development of an independent curriculum for a master's degree in historic preservation. They put together a curriculum committee that I and a few others were asked to serve on. In formulating the program, we thought about the unique nature of Pratt as a school, its founding by a social progressive, and its history of supporting communities through a service learning model. I think that because of the proximity to the planning program and Pratt Center, and because of our particular interests in community-based preservation, it naturally became part of the program's mission to focus on teaching the approaches, tools, and skills that would prepare new preservationists to support community development that reflects neighborhood history. We wanted our students to leave the program with the ability and interest to develop historic preservation strategies that address equity issues and social justice. We were also thinking about what Pratt's competitive advantages might be—having a planning department with a strong community activist bent, as well as being in an art and design school that would allow us to implement a curriculum based in interdisciplinarity.

Once it became part of the curriculum at Pratt, was historic preservation readily recognized by colleagues as an integral tool in community development agendas?

At around the same time the Pratt Historic Preservation Program was being founded, I was transitioning from working at the Municipal Art Society, where I was the Kress Fellow for Historic Preservation, to the

Pratt Center for Community Development, where I was a visiting scholar. I had a grant to conduct research on the Fulton Street Mall in downtown Brooklyn, and the Pratt Center offered to house me while Randy Mason and I, along with Pratt and Penn Historic Preservation students and others, conducted the study.

When I first arrived there, I detected that a number of the urban planning staff members were somewhat suspicious of me. I imagined them saying things like "She's a preservationist? Who let the enemy in?" The staff was (and is) made up of progressive activist planners and policy specialists who focus on applying community-based strategies for equitable development in low-income communities, and in their view, historic preservation tools were neither relevant nor useful. As I had time to talk to them about the Fulton Mall project, I think it became clear that I was looking at the broader culture of Fulton Street and downtown Brooklyn holistically, as a place, and that I myself considered the traditional tools of preservation to be ineffective in preserving what was (and is) so important about Fulton Street Mall. And as this became clear, I think we all realized that we had the same goals but were using different approaches and tools to meet those goals. The goals were around preserving the place that is Fulton Street Mall—its buildings, yes, but also its other identifiable attributes, both tangible and intangible. We all wanted to see this place preserved for the people to whom it is important. Where we differed was in what we would consider sacrosanct versus sacrificial. Do you need the buildings to preserve the place? What I learned is, yes, to a large degree, you do— because investment in new buildings would, in economic terms, mean that they would have to yield or generate considerable revenue to cover the developers' costs. In economic terms, preserving buildings can often be (and in the case of the Fulton Street Mall, was and is) pretty important.

It also happens that it's important in terms of the preservation of the place's aesthetics and the mysterious thing we call "sense of place." But a big question arises: can saving the buildings also save everything else about the place? No, it cannot. What was at stake on Fulton Street wasn't just bricks and mortar—it was also the businesses, the signage (much of it illegal), the way space is used by the public, who that public is, etc. It was important in the project and for my colleagues to understand that the mission of historic preservation could extend beyond the buildings to all of the other social attributes of a place. We preservationists are responsible, if we choose to be, for addressing those attributes and figuring out how to preserve them. On a policy level, this means looking beyond the traditional policy tools of historic preservation—because all the New York City Landmarks Law can do is preserve the buildings. That is not irrelevant by any means, but it is also not enough. Once that ideological bridge was established between myself and my Pratt Center colleagues, I think we all realized that we were working toward the same goals, and that it was beneficial for us to pool our approaches and tools, because they are all potentially useful in preserving a place in this broader sense.

Much of your own work as an educator at Pratt has sought to strengthen that intersection of historic preservation and community development. Do you see opportunities for the academy to better support these dual agendas?

I do, but in our selection of projects and partnerships, we're focused on opportunities that may not necessarily result in landmark designations or listings on the National Register—or, at least, those are not the core outcomes we're shooting for. I'm seeing work by students and faculty on community narratives and previously overlooked historic sites that has a large potential role to play in addressing the challenges that low-income communities face.

Our program includes many courses that work with and for a community-based organization as a client; I think that, in and of itself, moves us toward serving both preservation and community development agendas. For example, our Heritage Documentation studio for first-year students recently teamed up with an advanced planning studio within the GCPE to work in a Brooklyn community with an activist organization as the community "client." Our students conducted considerable deep research and then presented a historical narrative of the neighborhood to these clients, who are leaders in breaking down systems of racism and addressing environmental injustices that the community has suffered for decades. After hearing the students' research, the head of the organization said that she had never considered historic preservation to be useful to her organization, but the presentation exposed for her how our approach and tools are highly relevant and could indeed be useful.

The students conducted fairly traditional historical research but then asked themselves how they might relate what they found to the issues and challenges the client was focused on addressing. They were able to add to the commonly told story of the community by answering a lot of questions: How did the area develop physically, and what were the drivers of that development? Who lived here and worked here? What brought people of different cultures here, and when, and why? How have external economic forces shaped the community? How has racism shaped it? In pulling on all of these threads, students came up with a lot of visual material, like a 1930s-era redlining map, which our client may never have seen before. But when you look at that map and you look at the neighborhood today, you can see the negative impact this historic policy had, and you can see that it's still being felt.

Our client found that this way of seeing how past policies, social movements, and urban development shaped the community they live in today—and being able to connect the dots between community history and their own deep knowledge of the neighborhood's assets and challenges—was very useful. Would they be interested in using the traditional tools of preservation, like designating a local historic district or National Register district? They might—but only if it serves as a means of achieving their environmental and economic justice goals. More useful to their efforts are the kind of narratives that preservationists are able to help articulate—narratives that point to historic decisions which put the community at a disadvantage, while also documenting and raising up positive stories of cultural heritage, organizing, and self-determination that form the backbone of the community. Those are the skills and approaches we hope to bring in our engagement with communities—helping to surface the past and connect it to what matters to current residents in the neighborhood, helping to articulate *why* it matters. Preservation has the potential to be fuel for the fires that community organizations are stoking, as they seek enormous changes in environmental and land use policies in their own neighborhoods and more broadly throughout New York City.

How might such stronger intersections between historic preservation and community development translate from education into preservation policy, shifting it toward questions of equity and justice?

Maybe changing policy means not just trying to fix what many think of as a broken designation system. While I definitely support my colleagues who seek to bring equity and inclusion to the historical record represented by these programs, I think we also need to focus on other ways preservationists can make impacts in communities. When exploring and highlighting the Native American history of a community's physical place, you'll sometimes see a light bulb go off about the systemic oppression that has been experienced on that very same land through the centuries. In teaching students these skills through community-engaged projects, we're all learning from one another—community members and students and faculty. Our students also have their eyes opened about so much that is going on in nonprivileged places, and it pushes them out of the bubble that I find many of our preservation graduate students have been living in. It also happens to open up social justice career pathways for them, and if our students leave Pratt and go work for an environmental justice organization, I consider that to be a win.

So while I'd like to see the National Register be more inclusive—and I support the advocates and scholars who are working hard to make it so—I suppose I'm not that personally invested in trying to change the National Register. That's not the policy I've focused on, because National Register listing is not the primary way that heritage conservation benefits the communities I gravitate toward working in, though sometimes it can be a useful tool for them. The skills and approaches that we as preservationists employ to uncover narratives—whether about individual sites, groupings of sites, or whole communities—can inflect the work communities are doing to change policies that impact and harm them. I see great potential in enriching the stories and narratives of communities doing social justice policy work, which is often focused on issues like racism or economic disparity, with the heritage story—if we call it that—of their communities. That's the policy change that I'm excited about. Preservation could encompass a more diverse set of tools that afford community understanding and self-reflection, and inform a much broader range of community goals.

I also believe that if we're serious about shifting our field and its policies toward equity and justice, it's critical that we diversify our student body and our faculty, so that there isn't a gulf between us and the communities we partner with and serve. That's something many of us who lead academic programs are actively working to do.

How do we expand and better apply the preservation toolbox in ways that look beyond simply preventing a building from being torn down and that focus more on people-place relationships?

To me, "place" is not just a building. Of course, a work of architecture, an edifice, shares the attributes of place, and when communities define their place, they might point to buildings that contribute to its character and importance. But place is more than that—it is much richer and much more complex than just a set of buildings.

Our most immediate tools can be targeted toward saving the buildings that contribute to defining a place, but then there are so many other tools that are not coming from historic preservation policy that are needed to save the rest of what makes that place important, special, unique to those who live there. Many of the community groups we work with are fighting to save the community from gentrification, overdevelopment, and displacement. They want to save the people who are there and the places that matter to those people. So when you define place as encompassing both people and edifices, it opens up a whole other set of issues to address, and the need for other policy tools beyond what historic preservation offers.

But do we need our preservation policy tools to remain strong so we can continue to save buildings? Yes, because communities definitely seek to preserve buildings they deem important for a range of reasons, from tangible to intangible. But if you're going to save the *place*, you're going to have to get out of the comfort zone of traditional historic preservation—its "save the building" mode—and into the space where you understand that you are contributing to a very complex set of strategies for place-saving, some of which you, as a preservationist, may know nothing about.

In that sense, our students are often very nervous that they don't have a base of knowledge about other urbanist disciplines. We encourage them to seek knowledge by taking courses within the GCPE and elsewhere within Pratt Institute, but typically they get thrown into an interdisciplinary project before they've had a chance to do that. In those instances, we tell them, "You don't have to walk in as an expert on these complex issues. In fact, we want you to acknowledge and embrace that you are not an expert. You're bringing research and analytical skills that we're helping you to develop, and joining that to what our colleagues from other disciplines and the local experts know about the issues facing this community. This kind of engagement has to be an exchange—they're going to learn from us what we know as preservationists, and we're going to learn from them as well." In this way, we try to teach our students that preservation is not the whole picture; it's not the one tool that saves the day. It's part of a set of tools and strategies for helping communities solve their most challenging problems.

> How can preservationists seize upon and support this expanded idea of place in the face of climate change and the need to adapt and potentially to relocate? What does place mean when it might no longer be fixed to a particular geography?

I think that community and social cohesion are really the core of preserving communities that may have to relocate, and those comprise their own tapestry and set of disciplines that preservationists aren't at the center of. But we have a role in this, certainly, if, for example, water is going to make their buildings uninhabitable and unusable. We have some choices about the buildings: we could adapt them, we could move them, or we could abandon them. But for a community that suffers the trauma of flooding year after year or every five years, how do they maintain their sense of community cohesion if some of them decide, "I cannot take this anymore. I have to get out of here"? Are they going to be able to stay together as a community and preserve an intangible sense of their place somewhere else? Or are they going to have to give up their place?

I feel like these are questions we have to grapple with, and there are no real answers yet. But if we want to be a part of helping to find some solutions for these communities, we have to recognize that, at the end of the day, place may be first and foremost about the people. We have to face the fact that in many cases, we're going to lose physical places and will have to create new places for people to relocate to. As an educator, I see this as a real call to our students to shape these strategies and take up this critical work—how can we preserve heritage if the physical place is gone? There is a lot of important scholarship and practice focused on this now, and our students need to be engaged with it, because as the younger generation, this is going to fall squarely on their shoulders. However, I think the current generation of architectural conservationists and preservationists may have a very hard time with abandoning a physical place and letting it sink. We may not agree about what the right solution is. But if the resources to move vulnerable buildings are not available or would take away from resources to preserve that community's culture, heritage, and sense of cohesion elsewhere, I would side with giving those resources to the people instead of the buildings.

What is the role of preservationists when resources are focused on people rather than on buildings?

I think it's about preservationists joining community efforts to grapple with all the issues that they're grappling with today. Community-engaged preservation isn't just us finding out what people care about, and then suggesting tools to save it. It's a process of sharing and cross-learning between ourselves and community members who are experts about what they know, feel, and do, who they are, and what their identity is. We supplement their knowledge of their place with archival and other particular skills-based research that we do, as well as strategies like designation, adaptive reuse, interpretation, etc., that can be aids in meeting their goals. But I don't think that engagement means saying, "Here's how you might list that building on the National Register. I hope that helps." This is about community struggle, in communities with histories of struggle: low-income communities of color and Black communities. To be effective in helping them preserve their heritage, we have to join them. We can't keep thinking that we're confined to our own field, dropping in to be a little helpful and then dropping out again. Pratt Center has been working with a number of community organizations for decades. The GCPE's engagements with its community partners are sometimes decades long. These are real partnerships. The faculty and practitioners at Pratt and Pratt Center are not traditional technical assistance experts who swoop in, give their clients some information and some answers, and swoop out again.

I think the future of the pathway of historic preservation that I see myself on as a practitioner and an educator is one that is about finding the partners who are in the struggle, being their allies, and joining them in significant, meaningful ways. It's about bringing resources through our privilege as academicians, as people in a graduate program, and often as white people.

That doesn't lead to easy or quantifiable successes right away, or in some cases, ever. But it does impact the process. It does give communities some tools that they hadn't thought of before. It also gives them a new network of allies who become resources for them as they set out to make change toward justice. And while their struggle is often not specifically about historic buildings per se, preserving architecture could be a way to address some of the issues they face. For us, it's finding those matchups.

What role can preservation education play in prioritizing and empowering communities in their struggles to confront issues of climate and equity?

I think preservation programs and educators can provide ways to extend the resources that communities have. Our partnership brings resources, and our heritage and research approach brings new information that they just didn't have the the time, access, or opportunities to consider. It's empowering for them to have new information about how their place evolved, providing clues about what was there before that may answer questions they didn't know they had.

Sometimes it becomes apparent that conditions of the past were better than conditions now, and communities choose to advocate to return to those conditions. For example, our recent Heritage Documentation studio discovered that a major thoroughfare in the client's neighborhood had been a beautiful boulevard with a green median, until it was demolished as the subway was built, and it's currently a pretty hideous artery that drivers speed through. Whether the client will decide that they want to advocate for the city to restore the green median on this avenue or not, the discovery that this place didn't always look so horrible really struck them. It was not an eyesore, it was an oasis—and restoring aspects of that past could transform and improve the place in important ways.

I think that preservation pedagogy and preservation programs can play a major role in elevating that kind of story, and in being a resource for capturing the stories of people who are in the community today. This has been the Pratt Center model all along. What can we do to further community goals, through our teaching and training of new professionals who share a sense of mission to contribute to community improvement?

Do you see the kind of community-focused approach Pratt embraces becoming more prevalent within preservation education and practice?

I completed my master's in historic preservation in the early 1990s. At that time, as a student, I was already being exposed to a pedagogy that recognized the interdisciplinarity of preservation, that recognized that historic preservation careers have pathways that are somewhat different from one another. But as I recall it, despite having some faculty who were working to break the mold, the focus was still on the physical fabric of places and on historically important and significant architecture, defined by high-style buildings designed and built for the privileged. The field still clung to architecture, design, and physical conservation. Since then, I feel that a lot of us trained in those years have forged a more distinctively interdisciplinary and much broader path, and the pedagogy itself has broadened due to our interests.

I think that there will always be an architectural, curatorial aspect to historic preservation. That's a beautiful thing, and we absolutely need that. But that is not the only purpose of historic preservation. As an educator within this discipline, I can see quite clearly that there is plenty of room for different pathways. The term "historic preservation" has multiple definitions and meanings. It means different things to different people, and I'm totally comfortable with that.

I do feel that we are really evolving as a discipline. Sometimes faculty are leading the change, and we, as heads of programs, are also working to identify new definitions of the term for our field, recognizing that preservation is embracing all of these things and that the pedagogy is now responsible for teaching the full range of possibilities to the next generation of scholars and practitioners.

> *As educators, we may be pushing the field, asking tough questions, and trying to create didactic experiences for the next generation of preservationists, but we also have to be cognizant of the professional world they are entering. How do we prepare students to work within yet at the same time challenge existing governance structures?*

I think the governance structure of preservation is a very fixed thing in students' minds. They come into school with a preconceived notion that these historic policies cannot be changed. They need to learn how the National Register works, how the Secretary of the Interior's Standards work, and how the New York City Landmarks Law works, and certainly we teach them. But based on what I see in thesis and studio projects, students need to be pushed to see policy as something other than a rigid, unchangeable structure, and that reflects the fact that in some ways, we're still teaching it as a rigid structure. If we want to inspire those entering the field of preservation to question government systems and seek to change them, we're going to have to teach our students first that this is possible, and, second, how to approach it. I don't think we're quite doing that now, but we're moving in that direction. Our students can be agents of change, and it's our responsibility to teach them the skills they need to think in innovative ways about policy change so that they see how they can be leaders who make change.

Change may also come as our schools' more recent alumni attain positions of power within government agencies—in other words, when a new generation of preservation leaders takes control. At Pratt, our alumni are united into a really great network, and many of them are achieving positions of influence at city agencies and civic organizations, which is new for us since our program is relatively young. Many of them are active participants in the dialogue around how to regulate cultural landmarks in New York City, and others are engaged in issues around sustainability and preservation. I hope that what they learned at Pratt has set them up to figure out how to broaden the policy tool kit so that we can preserve more of what is valued by people in communities, whether it's architecture or not. I see them taking up that charge and finding themselves in a position to make important changes to the field. That's pretty exciting.

Also, we cannot have a conversation about heritage conservation or preservation right now without acknowledging the harm and suffering caused by the COVID-19 pandemic and by the racial biases in our institutions and ourselves. Understanding the Black Lives Matter movement, antiracism, and police brutality has, and has to have, a huge impact on what we teach. We have to change what we're teaching and how we're teaching it.

Most of the policies we work with have come out of our country's history of systemic oppression and racism. As people who want to seek policy change, we need to acknowledge and start figuring out how to address that, how to repair it. I think we're at an inflection point where we need to be much more aggressive in seeking change from within and beyond the academy, in order to meet this important moment and stop perpetuating the harms that racism has caused. One way we're hoping to address this at Pratt is by diversifying our student body and making it possible for interested members of the communities we work with to come to graduate school. This will require finding or building financial resources that we don't have right now, especially in light of the pandemic, but we're very eager to make it much more feasible for community advocates we work with to join us, and to support them in getting a degree in historic preservation.

► Appendices

At the conclusion of the February 2020 symposium, participants met in small breakout groups and as a collective to consider practical steps toward examining and strengthening the intersection of preservation policy with issues of sustainability and equity. Contributors were asked to propose potential courses of action and to indicate critical institutional actors—governmental agencies, universities, professional associations, not-for-profit organizations, community-based organizations, and more—that could be engaged in this work. The intent was not only to gather creative ideas but also to underscore the need for cooperation and to identify moments of leverage that could help to reform preservation's established policy infrastructure. Neither formal recommendations nor a representative consensus, the following propositions provide an extempore agenda to extend the terrains of both discourse and action.

Confront Institutional Policy Barriers

The policy landscape of historic preservation is built upon and within governance structures fraught with histories of systemic injustice. For preservation agencies and organizations to effectively counter and disrupt these legacies, they must fundamentally acknowledge the ways in which preservation policy is complicit in perpetuating exclusion and inequity. This kind of self-reflection and responsive reform compels new institutional commitments of ongoing accountability to the diversity of publics that preservation is intended to serve.

Anticipate Policy Futures

In addition to reckoning with its past, the preservation enterprise must anticipate its future relative to climate and justice concerns. Existing preservation policies are inadequate for addressing imminent and long-term challenges and ensuring equitable approaches to resilience, adaptation, migration, and mitigation. Pivoting and aligning policies to ensure better coordination of equity, climate, and preservation policies across levels of government could be supported by convenings of local, state, and federal agencies. Likewise, meetings of like-level agencies, such as municipal preservation commissions, would allow cities to share ideas and approaches. To build the collateral of exchange, more case-based research is needed on policy conflicts, such as the inequities of exempting buildings that are listed on the National Register (or eligible for listing) from energy codes or the role of historic districting in climate gentrification. Case studies of successful policy integration—such as effective models for incorporating photovoltaics into historic buildings and districts or programs for the salvage and reuse of building materials—would likewise serve to support explorations of policy reform. Awards for best practices in policy integration, possibly offered by a foundation, could further incentivize government agencies and quasi-governmental institutions to invest in future-oriented policy reform. These agencies should also begin drafting new legislation to anticipate these futures and have responsive policies at the ready as regulatory landscapes shift.

Maximize Intersections with Other Disciplines

Historic preservation has always been a multidisciplinary endeavor, relying upon the arts and humanities, the sciences, and the social sciences. Established as a university-level program of study for more than half a century in the United States, the field has both an opportunity and an obligation to capitalize on this interdisciplinary foundation to confront the policy challenges of sustainability and social justice. Universities stand at the vanguard of climate research and education; they likewise play a critical role in redefining how preservation both informs and is informed by other disciplines and professions. These institutions can and should proffer evidence to undergird policy reform and prepare the next generation of professionals who will address, for example, the heritage dimensions of climate-related relocation, reparations through heritage preservation or reconstruction, and more. Preservation programs thus have an affirmative obligation to engage a broader range of disciplinary fields in research and training to meet the challenges on the horizon, including but not limited to the environmental sciences, social and environmental psychology, public health, and social work. Such interdisciplinary engagement could be further cultivated by representing heritage perspectives in climate- and justice-focused conferences and forums, developing webinars and events targeting nonpreservation constituencies, and instituting fellowships and faculty exchanges.

Develop Adaptive Capacities and Coalitions

Expanding beyond preservation's traditional core to effectively contribute to climate adaptation and equitable resilience involves cultivating alliances with entities whose missions intersect with that of preservation, even if they do not define themselves as preservation focused. These alliances might include organizations invested in community development, coastal adaptation, environmental and social justice, economic revitalization, and more. This effort also includes more intentional cooperation with professional associations whose members will serve as expert collaborators in planning adaptation strategies, as well as with artists who can help ignite public understanding of the complex relationships of climate, justice, heritage, and attachments to place. Not-for-profit and nongovernmental organizations, like the National Trust for Historic Preservation, have a central role to play in developing preservation's capacities and coalition building, as a means of leveraging civic engagement and advocacy toward policy reform.

Disrupt Binaries

Designation, a primary tool of preservation policy, creates binary constraints: a place either is or is not recognized as heritage; it is valorized and protected or not. The challenges of desertification, coastal flooding, extreme weather conditions, and greenhouse gas emissions require dramatic changes to built environments, historic or otherwise. Sociotechnical interventions suited to these challenges, like adaptation, retrofitting, relocation, and deconstruction, complicate these long-standing binaries of saved versus not saved. The onus is on all institutional actors to reform preservation policy and practice to deal more robustly with the spectrum between binaries. This work involves developing equity-oriented approaches to triaging affected properties and publics, as well as becoming more fluent with the language of loss and how to mitigate its consequences.

Challenge Norms

Norms of preservation practice in the United States have been substantially influenced by federal policy and guidance, namely the National Register of Historic Places listing criteria and the Secretary of the Interior's Standards for the Treatment of Historic Properties, both of which privilege original design and fabric, as well as formal and material integrity. The diverse approaches required to address climate and exclusion—in varying contexts and with varying publics—unsettle these normative principles and strategies of intervention. Circular economies, which might involve building deconstruction and material recycling as well as adaptive reuse, further trouble what it means to "preserve." All institutional actors, but especially regulatory government agencies, carry the responsibility of redefining these standards of practice to more liberally acknowledge the nonmaterial dimensions of heritage, to sanction energy retrofits and climate-adaptive interventions, and to incorporate relocation and deconstruction within preservation's remit.

Redefine Preservation Tools

Heritage sites survive in large part due to their capacity to adapt to ever-changing social, economic, and environmental conditions. Preservation policy, in safeguarding places indefinitely, fundamentally reinforces long timelines and planning horizons. Policy should be less about how to maintain the status quo and more about how to adjust and readjust to constant change. The range of preservation actors share the responsibility of reimagining the scope and application of policy tools to understand social-spatial relationships, to emphasize adaptive care of the built environment, to visualize the future with communities, and to co-develop priorities and options.

Center People

This redefinition of preservation's tools is premised on centering people in policy and practice. Planning equitable transitions in the face of climate change hinges on co-creating knowledge with publics about their stories and attachments to place, not simply documenting and preserving buildings. Preservation institutions collectively share the burden of enhancing the field's capacity to work with diverse publics and leveraging policy toward community-engaged processes and equitably distributed benefits.

Preservation's Intersection with Sustainability and Equity: A Literature Review

Shreya Ghoshal
Scott Goodwin
Erica Avrami

Heritage occupies a unique position within the built environment in that most municipalities in the United States and most countries around the world have adopted policies to preserve heritage in situ, protecting selected places from physical loss and the market forces of change. The values and narratives associated with heritage places are understood to serve important community-building functions within society (Rose 1981). Through physical and spatial encounters with the past, community members are thought to share and foster common identities and reflections of self. The perpetuation of these places is believed to support social resilience by reinforcing notions of collective agency and endurance through time (Auclair and Fairclough 2015).

At the same time, contemporary research is bringing to light the role of the built environment and its management in exacerbating climate change as well as compounding inequities within and between communities. As the most "fixed" and socially valued elements of the built environment, heritage places and the critical policy space they occupy are together coming under increased scrutiny, compelled by the climate crisis and growing calls for social justice. From the legacy effects of racially restrictive covenants, redlining, and urban renewal to decisions about coastal property buyouts, renewable energy development, and exclusionary zoning, scholarship is beginning to interrogate the vast extent of preservation policy's implications. The literature is also pointing to new potential for preservation policy to become a vital change agent.

This literature review provides background on the multiple policy questions and arenas that relate to the preservation enterprise, in an effort to shed light on the existing state of knowledge as the field looks toward questions of social-spatial justice, environmental sustainability, and their inextricable links. Although greater interest in equity and sustainability is building on the ground in preservation projects and in the operational activities of organizations across the country, the focus in this review is on the kinds of research and actions that can inform systemic shifts in preservation policy and governance structures.

While the topics herein are diverse and the body of literature more extensive than that cited, the emphasis is on identifying points of intersection with preservation, so as to inform new avenues of inquiry, synergies with allied policy arenas, and potential directions for policy reform. Intended as a starting point, this review is organized in the following sections:

Equity and Exclusion
Contested Monuments and Commemorative Disparities
Spatial Exclusion
Socioeconomic Inequity and Affordability
Property Rights and Human Rights

Environmental Sustainability
Climate Change Mitigation
Climate Change Adaptation and Resilience
Environmental Justice

Through a review of the literature on these subjects, spanning both preservation and associated disciplines, clear tensions, gaps, and opportunities emerge that point to a set of key questions facing the field today: If the decisions about what and how to preserve are privileging certain segments of society and certain publics, how can heritage policy be reformed to promote a more just and sustainable built environment? And, if existing policy serves principally to reinforce the environmental and sociospatial status quo, what kinds of transformative policies can be mobilized to meet this profound moment of change?

▶ EQUITY AND EXCLUSION

Confronting preservation's role in perpetuating racially and economically biased policies requires the field to respond to long-standing criticisms around issues of equity and exclusion. The previous titles in this series, *Preservation and the New Data Landscape* and *Preservation and Social Inclusion*, considered these questions largely through the lenses of data collection, representation, and engagement with diverse publics (Avrami 2019, 2020). But these matters are not simply a question of representation (i.e., whose story gets told in the built environment). As a regulator of social-spatial relationships, the built environment constrains and empowers certain communities and community members—physically, economically, ecologically, socially—through its management. Ongoing debates surrounding contested monuments have inspired further dialogue around socioeconomic injustices in the historic built environment. The literature in this section, partially drawing upon scholarship in adjacent fields, begins to explore larger discussions around dismantling legacies of racism and oppression that may be maintained through preservation policy and action, compelling the field to reckon with who, or what, has been privileged in the public realm.

Contested Monuments and Commemorative Disparities
Memorialization is one avenue of scholarship that addresses the topic of sociospatial exclusion and intersects directly with preservation. Inspired in large part by public dialogue demanding action—for instance, the calls to demolish contested monuments—the number of articles and publications related to controversial commemorations has continued to

grow since 2015, and the conversation has only become more critical in light of public mobilization following the height of Black Lives Matter and other social justice movements in 2020.

Previously, scholars and practitioners were divided between two dispositions: support for the continued preservation of contentious memorials—such as Confederate monuments—versus advocates for their removal. Those who supported their preservation cautioned against the potential danger of forgetting negative histories when contemplating the immediate desire to take all contested monuments down (Forest and Johnson 2018). Their assertion that public administrators hold a duty to explore the range of alternatives beyond the binary of removal versus retention was originally embraced by most preservation groups across the United States (Elias, McCandless, and Chordiya 2019). However, the preservation ethos experienced a marked shift following the racially charged events of 2020. Major preservation advocacy organizations have stated that Confederate monuments should be removed and that their continued existence within the built environment represents a privileging of racially biased values against Black and Indigenous Americans in particular (National Trust for Historic Preservation 2020; Society of Architectural Historians 2020).

Over the past decade, municipalities across the United States have attempted to engage with this debate by creating monument review commissions to evaluate particularly egregious cases (e.g., white male figures, Confederate histories, etc.) (New York City Mayoral Advisory Commission 2018). These cities are pushing the academic debate from theory to practice, attempting to create new policies that promote one solution over others. Building on his research into commemorative landscapes, Stephen Clowney has argued that while legal scholars and policy makers often overlook the built environment's historical use as a tool of race-making, creative policies can redress the exclusionary and prescriptive mechanics of racialized public spaces (Clowney 2013). The author advocates for a new policy approach that engages municipal governments with equity-oriented and participatory review in new public space projects. It should be noted that while the conversation surrounding contested landscapes is just coming to the forefront in the United States, other prominent international examples have been analyzed for the past few decades; most notable are the cases of Holocaust memorials in Europe and postapartheid landscapes in South Africa (Walkowitz and Knauer 2009).

As historian and preservation scholar Dell Upton explains, the conversation around racial equity shouldn't just be about whether to preserve or erase fraught histories in the landscape; it should instead question which histories are afforded space in the public realm (Upton 2017). These statues and memorials were erected—mostly during Reconstruction and the post-Civil War era—to enshrine the values of a white supremacist population who remained unchallenged in their claiming of space. As Upton suggests, confronting and demanding changes in policies involving the reclamation of spaces through commemorations requires an acknowledgment of the power dynamics and decision-making processes involved. It therefore becomes an issue of contextualization, a concept with which preservationists are well equipped to engage.

Spatial Exclusion

The debates surrounding contested monuments and narrative power represent a small—but highly visible—fraction of injustice codified in the built environment. Scholarship on spatial exclusion builds on a body of literature in urbanism and the social sciences that examines the discriminatory processes and inequitable impacts of twentieth-century planning and urban design. The past few decades have seen an increase in such evaluative scholarship on urban renewal, redlining, and racially restrictive covenants that have legacy impacts on the sociospatial fabric of US cities, neighborhoods, and communities. In his foundational text "Planning and Social Control: Exploring the Dark Side," Oren Yiftachel argues that such urban and regional planning efforts can be linked to forms of social control that, when left unchecked, lead to regressive goals of social oppression, economic inefficiencies, patriarchy, or racial marginalization (Yiftachel 1998). Yiftachel calls on the field of urban planning to analyze the negative impacts of policy in order to enable policy makers and practitioners to learn from prior mistakes.

Scholarship has sought to bring these inquiries to bear on contemporary practice toward realizing greater social equity (Flyvbjerg 2002; Fainstein 2005). A reexamination of past approaches to urbanism and public policy continues to inform a growing understanding of exclusionary practices and their effects. Studies on racially restrictive covenants, for example, have investigated how residential planning policies encoded racial segregation into socioeconomic landscapes and exacerbated emerging racial prejudices and stereotypes that associated Black residents with declining property values and urban blight (Gotham 2000).

Similarly, Richard Rothstein has explored the impacts of racially biased government policies, "de facto segregation" practices, and their lasting effects on Black and brown households—effects that persist in cities today (Rothstein 2017). Historical analyses of federally backed urban renewal-era development and highway construction projects broadly recognize the disproportionate impact of such projects on Black, brown, and lower-income residential communities (Karas 2015), and some literature explores how confronting those legacies through policy can serve as a form of restorative justice (Mohl 2012).

However, the preservation field has yet to robustly address how it might create policies that engage both legacy built fabric and histories of sociospatial injustice. An understanding that historic preservation is also implicated in such historical equity matters—and that those matters can inform more equitable contemporary practice and policy—is only just emerging in the literature. Despite a broader scholarly reflection on twentieth-century urban policies and planning strategies, there is limited research that approaches the subject of how discriminatory practices are still manifest or reproduced in the built environment itself. Some scholarship has identified architecture's ability to be instrumentalized toward inequity (e.g., racial exclusion) (Weyeneth 2005). However, the notion that such exclusionary architecture persists into the present and may continue to have impacts on cities, neighborhoods, and communities raises important questions for the preservation field, with policy implications.

Sarah Schindler has illustrated the power of the built environment to constrain the behavior of individuals and communities and enact spatial exclusion, and has argued for new policies that leverage this understanding toward greater social equity (Schindler 2015). Drawing on historical techniques used to enact racial exclusion (e.g., physical barriers, transit, wayfinding), Schindler argues that legal scholars, courts, and policy makers overlook the ways that the built environment functions as a form of extralegal regulation. While law addresses the discriminatory impacts of racially restrictive covenants and zoning ordinances, she finds that existing jurisprudence is insufficient to address the harms of the exclusionary built environment, though federal legislation or municipal environmental review may be mobilized toward ensuring that new construction is included. While policy solutions for legacy issues may be less clear, Schindler's research highlights that municipalities have opportunities to address exclusionary architecture as part of much-needed infrastructure rebuilding and repair projects.

1
See https://www.ada.
gov/ada_title_III.htm.

While there is limited examination of preservation's relationship to exclusionary architecture at the scale of the urban landscape, its engagement with accessibility at the building scale suggests how the field might use its policy tool kit toward meeting sociospatial equity goals. One avenue where preservation has been more responsive in creating more inclusive practices and policies is through accessibility compliance in historic buildings. Title III in the American Disabilities Act of 1990 (ADA) prohibits discrimination on the basis of physical disability in the activities of places of public accommodations; it requires that all public buildings—including landmarked buildings—comply with ADA codes (Bronin and Byrne 2012). [1] Legal scholars have analyzed the competing goals of the ADA and the National Historic Preservation Act (NHPA) in an attempt to examine the compromises that must be made in order to promote accessibility in historic buildings (Parkin 2007).

An examination of early literature on ADA compliance for historic preservation reveals that the field was initially opposed to this significant policy change. Legal scholars and preservation advocates focused largely on impacts to historic buildings as part of ADA compliance, despite the obvious implications of continued exclusion by inaccessibility (Fondo 1994). This discourse highlights the often protectionist stance that preservationists take when responding to potential policy change. But over the past three decades, the field has begun to accept the ADA mandate and adopt case-by-case interventions toward accessibility. Still, scholarship continues to probe the nuanced relationship between preservation and disability, challenging assumptions about access and preservation's role in confronting architectural exclusion (Gissen 2019).

There are also significant connections to be made between preservation and the concept of "disparate impact"—the idea that policies are discriminatory if they have adverse effects on particular groups. Generally applied in legal disputes involving housing and real estate, disparate impact was born out of civil rights implications regarding the Fair Housing Act of 1968 and helps to demonstrate the intertwined relationship of spatial, social, and economic exclusion. As defined by the federal court system, the concept concerns policies and practices that are facially neutral and nondiscriminatory but result in disproportionately negative impacts on certain individuals and groups. The US Supreme Court upheld the legal theory in *Texas Department of Housing and Community Affairs v. The Inclusive Housing Project, Inc.*, stating that a policy's intentions—whether good or bad—do not absolve institutions and businesses from responsibility when outcomes create disproportionately negative effects for protected populations. 2

Recent legal scholarship surrounding disparate impact has identified limitations in the application of the theory as a tool for forcing desegregation in cities, but scholars still see potential in its ability to hold governments and organizations accountable for discrimination in housing policy and future urban revitalization efforts (Callison 2016). While this theoretical framework has not yet been applied to the field of historic preservation, many of the concepts of sociospatial exclusion discussed throughout this literature review merit a reflexive dialogue that identifies the field's complicity in negative racially and economically biased outcomes in the built environment.

Socioeconomic Inequity and Affordability

Social and economic benefits are common rationales for preservation policy, yet research is painting an increasingly complicated portrait of its socioeconomic effects. A literature once focused on preservation's ability to enhance property values and promote economic development is now grappling with the possibility that existing policy is compounding socioeconomic inequities—whether as an agent of gentrification and displacement or as a foil to urban densification and a tactic of sociospatial exclusion. Confronted with such criticisms, preservation advocates have often pursued counterevidence over policy reform. However, an emerging body of literature seeks to harmonize preservation policy with affordability and densification and to mobilize it toward greater socioeconomic equity.

The early literature on preservation economics tends to be in agreement that preservation activities yield positive socioeconomic benefits. As an extensive literature review by Randall Mason demonstrates, studies have often sought to express those benefits, whether manifest in preservation projects or through the impact of policy on property values and urban economies (Mason 2005). Scholarship on property values has found that designating historic landmarks and districts can have positive price effects (Leichenko, Coulson, and Listokin 2001), and impact studies on preservation as a development tool have demonstrated that policy can have positive economic effects at municipal and regional scales (Listokin, Listokin, and Lahr 1998). While not without rebuttal, such studies have come to inform a body of advocacy literature that makes the cases for historic preservation and its policy tool kit on the grounds of good economics (National Trust for Historic Preservation 2002; Rypkema 2005).

More recent scholarship has continued to evaluate preservation's policy impacts on cities and neighborhoods, including its role in urban development and revitalization through job creation, production of housing units, and tourism (Gilderbloom, Hanka, and Ambrosius 2009; Ijla et al. 2011; Ryberg-Webster 2014). Further study of property values is also expanding knowledge of historic designation's price impacts (Noonan and Krupa 2011; Thompson, Rosenbaum, and

Schmitz 2011; Zarhirovic-Herbert and Gibler 2012). While such research nuances understanding of preservation outcomes—often by identifying cases where anticipated benefits are absent—its focus on economic impacts and property values typically reify the advocacy view of preservation's current policy toolbox.

Nevertheless, a growing body of research recognizes that preservation policy can also have inequitable socioeconomic outcomes, which are often tied to issues of affordable housing access and gentrification. Preservation has long been associated with gentrification and the exclusion of lower-income residents, though often seen as an antecedent or symptom of those processes (Fein 1985; Smith 1998; Wagner 1998). But scholarship more recently has charged preservation with catalyzing inequitable change. Edward Glaeser has argued that historic districts are responsible for restricting the housing supply and increasing the cost of living, ultimately leading to socioeconomic exclusion (Glaeser 2010). Glaeser's critique is based on a reading of income disparity across historic district lines, and other research has found similar evidence implicating preservation policy in socioeconomic and racial equity issues. One cross-sectional study of New York City found that historic district residents are higher income, more highly educated, and more likely to be white (Ellen, McCabe, and Stern 2016).

Still, scholarship is only beginning to investigate the relationship between heritage policy and neighborhood change, as well as to develop new data to more effectively analyze the relationship between preservation and socioeconomic exclusion. Indeed, accounts of gentrification by way of preservation are often conflicting or inconclusive (Allison 2005). Some studies assert that there is no causal connection between the two, or that preservation can even stave off gentrification (Chusid 2006). Others find a correlation between urban form in historic districts and income inequality, suggesting a direct link between policy and exclusion (Talen, Menozzi, and Schaefer 2015). Brian McCabe and Ingrid Gould Ellen have found that the relative socioeconomic status of New York City neighborhoods improves following historic designation, but with little significant change in rents or racial turnover (McCabe and Ellen 2016). They conclude that historic districting accelerates some of the processes associated with gentrification and that planning for affordable housing is an important concern for policy reform.

A sizable body of literature recognizes the preservation–affordable housing nexus as a critical point of analysis. The field has long defended itself against criticism that its policies create barriers to affordable housing, whether by raising prices or by inhibiting new development and restricting supply. As a matter of national policy, government bodies in the United States have promoted combining historic rehabilitation tax credits with low-income housing credits to encourage affordable housing development through preservation (Delvac, Escherish, and Hartman 1994). Advocacy literature has also sought to make the case that preservation can serve as a tool for rehabilitating existing affordable housing stock (Listokin and Listokin 2001; Rypkema 2002). But an ongoing housing crisis in US cities has focused the debate on preservation's municipal policy tools (i.e., landmark and historic district designations). In 2016 the White House released a report outlining barriers to affordable housing that called out "arbitrary or antiquated preservation regulations" as a significant obstruction (White House 2016).

Some research points to opportunities for affordable housing advocates to work with preservationists to preserve rent-stabilized housing through municipal policy (Milder 2016). Yet much of the literature on mechanisms for preserving affordable housing exists outside historic preservation, instead residing in the distinct field of housing preservation, and with little intersection (Howell 2018; Howell, Mueller, and Wilson 2019). How historic preservation and housing preservation might find common ground to achieve mutual equity goals remains an open question. However, Lisa T. Alexander has offered another possible inroad in her examination of how place-based lawmaking can more effectively promote equitable development and redevelopment. Through a theory of "cultural collective efficacy," Alexander provides a framework for examining urban micro-dynamics and explores how the prism of culture can inform place-based lawmaking—for example, through "historic districts with affordable housing protections"(Alexander 2012).

Notably, academic research has taken an interest in another broad concern within which the subject of affordable housing is subsumed: that municipal preservation policy can restrict residential development and thereby inhibit urban densification. That criticism, articulated by Glaeser and others, holds that landmarking and districting can decrease overall residential affordability by restricting density, compounding socioeconomic inequities across neighborhoods and cities (Glaeser 2005). At a macro scale, researchers have asserted that restrictions to urban densification—including municipal preservation policies—can even compound socioeconomic inequities across regions, hindering national economic growth (Hsieh and Moretti 2017).

These charges have not gone unaddressed by preservation advocates. A study by the National Trust for Historic Preservation's Preservation Green Lab has promoted findings that older districts in US cities have higher levels of residential density (National Trust for Historic Preservation Green Lab 2014). But scholarship also has sought further evidence on the matter. Vicki Been et al. have found that historic districting in New York City has heterogeneous effects depending on local development potential, leading new construction activity to fall across historic districts after designation, while property values also fall in less dense areas where buildings are below their allowable limits (Been et al. 2016). However, the study is inconclusive as to whether historic districts restrict housing supply beyond their boundaries. McCabe and Ellen have also investigated preservation's potential to constrain urban growth and development through restricted densification, leading the authors to propose a restructuring of New York City's preservation decision-making process to allow greater coordination between preservation and planning authorities, and to encourage *as-of-right* development on vacant and not contributing sites in historic districts (McCabe and Ellen 2017).

Given the array of criticisms levied against preservation on socioeconomic grounds, some scholarship is beginning to view its historic districting policy tool as a form of "exclusionary zoning"—a legal practice of limiting housing supply with land use controls that benefit wealthy

203

communities. John Mangin has argued that historic districts remove entire portions of the built environment from the stock of developable land and drive up costs, placing a disproportionate burden on lower-income residents (Mangin 2014). Despite such claims against normative historic preservation tools like historic districts, Elizabeth M. Tisher has argued that preservation policy can in fact be used to promote inclusion (Tisher 2017). Finding that negative views of historic districts as growth control are based on unfounded assumptions—including that cost of living is the only factor in housing affordability—Tisher asserts that preservation can further affordable housing and inclusivity goals if municipalities loosen zoning restrictions while maintaining historic district regulations.

Only a limited amount of research explores ways to reform policy and instrumentalize new frameworks toward greater socioeconomic equity, affordability, and inclusion, such as Jennifer Minner's work on "equity preservation" (Minner 2016). Beyond the literature that engages potential policy responses to questions of affordable housing, densification, or exclusionary zoning referenced above, some scholarship has taken social equity and inclusion as a departure point for framing policy reform. Erica Avrami, Cherie-Nicole Leo, and Alberto Sanchez Sanchez have made the case that municipal preservation policy can be better aligned with public interests and its own stated rationales toward more inclusive and equitable processes and outcomes (Avrami, Leo, and Sanchez Sanchez 2019). Other scholarship views emerging research and criticism to be endemic of preservation's growing relevance to interdisciplinary planning and urban policy. However, as Stephanie Ryberg-Webster and Kelly L. Kinahan recognize, the lack of existing interdisciplinary research on creative preservation planning and policy strategies poses a challenge for the field (Ryberg-Webster and Kinahan 2014).

Property Rights and Human Rights

A growing international discourse and emerging policy instruments surrounding *intangible* (as opposed to *tangible*) heritage has garnered increased attention to questions of the social-spatial construction of heritage as a concept and challenged the material focus of preservation policy (UNESCO 2003). Early concepts of cultural property were object and real property oriented. That heritage may be place based—without the physical trappings associated with expert architectural values—speaks to a growing understanding of how different worldviews shape our understanding of heritage. In the United States, for example, Native American treaties provided early forays into "use" as a form of property right, challenging ownership and boundary concepts (Wolfley 2018). Heritage as use is also emerging in municipal preservation policy through legacy business programs, such as those implemented in San Francisco and San Antonio. 3

Derek Fincham examines the growing body of heritage law and discusses the often competing frameworks of conventional property rights and emerging heritage practices (Fincham 2011). He claims that existing scholarship often focuses on Indigenous groups and repatriation as the sole avenues of study in this debate, rather than exploring broader relationships. Fincham stands counter to Eric Posner, a legal scholar who argues that cultural property should be treated like any other form of property (Posner 2007).

If the overarching objective of heritage and preservation policy/

3
While legacy business programs are increasingly advocated by preservationists, there is still limited understanding of how best to support such business and what elements of programs are most effective as a form of policy, as discussed in Seattle's Legacy Business Report, https://www.seattle.gov/Documents/Departments/economicDevelopment/22820_Legacy_Report_2017-09-25.pdf.

4
This language is used
by the National Park
Service in the National
Historic Preservation
Act of 1966 and other
enabling acts for the
preservation of national
parks, national forests,
and other landscapes.

legislation (in the United States, but also abroad) is considered to be the "safeguarding of resources for future generations," traditional notions of individual property rights become slightly problematic.[4] The efficacy of policy and so-called "heritage law" has repeatedly been called into question—in regard to Indigenous cultural resources specifically, but also for cultural heritage more broadly speaking. Legal scholars point to the difficulties of delineating enforceable rights and methods of prosecution. As Lyndel V. Prott and Patrick J. O'Keefe argue, *heritage* is one of the most difficult terms confronting legal scholars to date due to the lack of consensus and coherence across legislation as to the extent of its bounds (Prott and O'Keefe 1992). The distinction between ownership over tangible versus intangible heritage, for instance, has proven especially difficult for scholars to reconcile.

This critical shift in the discourse has emerged in a postcolonial era to assert the rights of Indigenous and marginalized publics; it highlights the disparities between the *concept* of heritage rights and actual legal practices. Allen Buchanan argues that the development of Indigenous peoples' rights builds upon insights of postcolonialist rhetoric, and emphasizes the solidarity of Indigenous cultures in order to create international networks of advocates fighting to secure standing in the major fora in which international law is made (Buchanan 1993). In his expansive discussion of the international Indigenous peoples' rights movement, Buchanan calls attention to, in particular, the tensions and distinctions between individual and collective rights. He contends that collective land regulatory rights and collective property rights are the most insistent demands by Indigenous groups around the globe, often challenging more individual-oriented property rights within current legal frameworks, but presenting an opportunity to enrich—rather than undermine—heritage law.

In more recent scholarship surrounding the Indigenous peoples' rights movement, multiple legal scholars have analyzed the impacts of preservation and heritage legislation on treaty rights and tribal sovereignty. Samantha M. Ruscavage-Barz's note from 2007 discusses various legislative and planning processes at the state and national level that ultimately failed to protect Petroglyph National Monument in New Mexico from encroachment by a highway extension (Ruscavage-Barz 2007). Despite a not insubstantial set of regulations in place to protect Indigenous rights and culture, she determines that there is a clear disconnect between the letter and the spirit of the laws enacted to protect and preserve Native American sacred sites.

Jeanette Wolfley comes to a similar conclusion in her article chronicling the Dakota Access Pipeline conflict, which highlighted a much larger, ongoing struggle for Indigenous rights, racial equity, and environmental justice in the United States (Wolfley 2018). She describes how most tribes have immeasurably different perspectives on land rights, feeling a spiritual duty to protect the lands for future generations—a task complicated by typical legal frameworks that do not acknowledge collective land rights. Wolfley asserts that energy development projects especially, such as the Dakota Access Pipeline, raise difficult challenges to treaty rights—namely, traditional tribal practices like hunting, gathering, and fishing—tribal landscapes, and tribal sovereignty. The inextricable link between treaty rights and cultural identity compels more ethical engagement with tribes when crossing tribal lands with energy and other development projects, and suggests important points of consideration for preservation policy reform.

▶ ENVIRONMENTAL SUSTAINABILITY

For decades, preservation has engaged sustainability as a discourse, invoking energy savings and recyclability as rationales for its practices and policies that regulate the historic built environment (Fitch 1966; Advisory Council on Historic Preservation 1979a, 1979b). Only as awareness of the climate crisis has grown has new research compelled the field to reexamine past thinking about its role in climate change and to find intersections between sustainability and its policy tool kit. Indeed, scholarship is only beginning to recognize preservation policy's implication in issues of energy code compliance, renewable energy development, coastal adaptation, and disaster assistance. Meanwhile, connections are being drawn between heritage and resilience. But even as the field seeks to realize the potential of preservation to contribute to sustainability goals, there is a sense that the limited scope of existing policies—if not the rigidity of those policies themselves—poses a significant barrier to climate action (Fatorić and Biesbroek 2020). Below, these developments, tensions, and potential avenues for future research are reviewed through the lenses of climate change mitigation, climate adaptation and resilience, and environmental justice.

Climate Change Mitigation
Contemporary research brings to light the role of the built environment and its management in exacerbating climate change. Buildings and building construction account for 36 percent of global energy consumption and nearly 40 percent of energy-related CO2 emissions (UN Environment and International Energy Agency 2017), while the built environment's total energy usage is projected to double or triple by 2050 based on current trends (Intergovernmental Panel on Climate Change 2015). There is growing recognition across disciplines that buildings need to play their part in energy reductions (Munasinghe 1990; Belussi et al. 2019), and the preservation field, implicated across policy and practice, increasingly confronts its role in climate change mitigation. Discussions have coalesced research, advocacy, and policy literature around three primary concerns: energy consumption of existing buildings, development of renewable energy infrastructures, and the circular economy framework.

Regarding energy efficiency, advocacy literature has focused on the perceived "inherent sustainability" of historic preservation. However, research is complicating this view, just as new questions are raised about how long-standing preservation policies may conflict with progressive municipal energy codes intended to mitigate climate impacts. Heritage professionals often assert that older buildings are intrinsically "green" and advocate for preservation on the grounds of energy savings (Elefante 2007). Such claims draw on the notion that embodied energy, or the total energy required to source materials and construct a building, constitutes a significant energy investment that should not be discounted. Advocacy-oriented analyses of the avoided impacts achieved through building reuse support these claims with data regarding the time needed to realize energy and resource savings in building rehabilitation versus replacement, and argue for the additional benefits of preserving green space and keeping existing buildings out of the waste stream (National Trust for Historic Preservation Green Lab 2011).

Yet two issues confound this view and its implications for policy. First, embodied energy is—in economic terms—a sunk cost that remains external to the market. For that reason, instrumentalizing an avoided impacts approach toward climate change mitigation requires significant shifts in real estate development and construction policies that have yet to be realized (Avrami 2016). Nevertheless, literature on pollution points to a potential precedent for policies that internalize externalities associated with energy costs—namely, "green taxes" that operationalize energy reform (Corbett and Wassenhove 1993; Hubbard 1991). Second, embodied energy constitutes a small proportion of energy consumption over the life cycle of a building, and instead what's been dubbed *operational energy* is far more significant (Agbonkhese et al. 2010). As buildings become more energy efficient or carbon neutral, this proportion will change. But at present, energy savings through operating consumption is a primary focus in reducing the built environment's carbon footprint through policy.

However, the preservation field has largely sought exemptions from energy codes, arguing that compliance could compromise the historic fabric of buildings (Drury and McPherson 2008). Indeed, all fifty states in the United States maintain some sort of exemption for buildings included on or eligible for the National Register of Historic Places. But according to recent scholarship, energy retrofits in historic buildings are becoming an increasingly feasible option (Ascione et al. 2017). While policy exemptions are still viewed as a protective measure against the "threat" of retrofits, literature is beginning to see energy efficiency in historic buildings as the greatest opportunity for a sustainable future (Phoenix 2015). Amanda L. Webb, in her review of existing methods, has outlined guiding principles based on more objective evaluative measures by which retrofits can be implemented without harm to historic structures (Webb 2017).

European scholarship has pushed this research a step further to assert that successfully upgrading historic buildings to the current energy efficiency standards opens up the possibility of ensuring the prolonged preservation of heritage resources (Cabeza, de Gracia, and Pisello 2018; Carbonara 2015). Despite the growing number of studies related to the viability of energy retrofits, there are still several gaps in the literature. Definitive methods of balancing multiple criteria, such as sociocultural values versus environmental strain, do not yet exist. Moreover, many of the relevant studies focus on a European context, meaning that research must diversify in order to enable broad municipal policy reform.

When preservation scholarship does engage specifically with questions of policy and energy consumption, it tends to focus on the limitations of current energy policy structures, arguing that both heritage policy and energy codes have not caught up to research on the potential for more energy-efficient historic buildings. Livio Mazzarella discusses updated directives for energy efficiency in the European Union and the fact that those directives still allow for exemptions under architectural heritage designations (Mazzarella 2015). He identifies the lack of international policy dealing with energy retrofits for historic buildings as a point of failure on the road to climate change mitigation, and calls for lobbying action to steer energy policy in a more effective way toward energy efficiency in all existing buildings.

Andra Blumberga and coauthors come to a similar conclusion in their evaluation of regulatory instruments in Europe, claiming that current mechanisms are insufficient for large-scale energy efficiency improvements (Blumberga et al. 2018). Energy codes in the United States employ similar prescriptions, meaning that existing buildings (especially historic buildings) are not part of the policy framework promoting environmental sustainability. Despite continual updates to building energy codes creating more and more stringent sustainability measures, historic buildings in most US municipalities maintain their categorical exemptions. Keeping in mind the well-founded tensions between historic buildings and energy policy, the literature is calling for alternative compliance paths and updated regulatory measures for energy compliance in historic buildings in which policy compels the implementation of these new retrofit technologies and models (Lidelöw et al. 2019).

While the energy consumed by historic buildings plays a central role in the discourse on preservation and climate change mitigation, heritage and preservation policy are also implicated in the development of renewable energy infrastructures that reduce reliance on fossil fuels and contribute to a more sustainable and lower-carbon energy landscape. The utility-scale wind power and solar energy projects that are increasingly significant to the "green-energy" transition often have large spatial footprints that are points of conflict for competing land use interests, including historic preservation.

Preservation advocates often position renewable energy development as a threat to the integrity of cultural heritage. In 2008 UNESCO identified renewable energy facilities—including thermal, wave, solar, and wind power facilities—as among the fourteen principal threats to World Heritage sites (World Heritage Center 2008a). Other preservation-minded organizations have positioned themselves as a check on unconstrained renewable energy development and have argued that preservationists deserve a seat at the table during the early stages of energy development decision-making (Burg 2014). The US National Park Service has called for heritage stakeholders to consider the Secretary of the Interior's Standards when weighing a shift to renewable energy at or near national landmarks (National Park Service, n.d.).

The question of preservation policy's influence on renewable energy development first emerged prominently in the literature around the proposed offshore wind power project Cape Wind, planned for the Nantucket Sound off the coast of Massachusetts in the early 2000s. A controversial invocation of federal historic preservation law dealt a significant blow to that project by lengthening what became a decade-long permitting battle, leading some to identify the National Historic Preservation Act as the biggest obstacle to future wind-power development (Spinelli

2010), and inspiring critiques of preservation policy as a tool of energy NIMBYism in urgent need of reform (Kimmell and Stalenhoef 2011). After Cape Wind, the literature continues to define tensions between policy and renewable energy through various terrestrial and offshore energy and transmission projects.

David A. Lewis has found that preservation interests and renewable energy developers are commonly at odds because preservation is increasingly deployed to thwart such projects, while developers use tactics to circumvent preservation laws altogether (Lewis 2015). Yet by his account, modest policy and administrative reforms focusing on coordination and planning would be enough to reduce adverse impacts to historic resources while encouraging energy development. Changes of this kind to the state and federal frameworks that govern large-scale solar and wind projects suggest how policy reform writ large might better align the field of preservation with sustainability and climate change mitigation.

However, new research into renewable energy microgrids and distributed generation (as an alternative to the "energy sprawl" of rural and offshore development) also reveals how sustainable energy development may collide with preservation interests in urban contexts, and thus collide with municipal preservation policy (Bronin 2010). Through microgrids—distributed networks of small-scale energy generators like solar collectors, wind power systems, or geothermal wells—questions of alternative energy land use are poised to become neighborhood issues. Research has confronted preservation policy's potential to restrict renewable energy development at the building scale (e.g., rooftop solar panels) (Kuntz 2009), and the subject has even risen to the level of popular debate (Appelbaum 2020). Still, how municipal policy might influence the development of urban microgrids or other renewable energy technologies at the utility scale remains an open question.

Scholarship recognizes a fundamental link between energy development and environmental justice that is also relevant to cultural heritage (Outka 2012). Indeed, this interrelationship is apparent in the early literature on Cape Wind, even from competing perspectives: while some authors argued that delaying development out of concern for Native American heritage advanced environmental justice (Ziza 2008), others posited that legal review was instigated by private interests and constituted both NIMBYism and an environmental injustice. Attempting to promote justice across energy development projects, some authors propose reforms that foreground community participation in heritage matters (Poulis 2013). Nevertheless, the topic of how heritage policy can be instrumentalized to advance environmental justice through renewable energy development is given limited attention in the literature. Elena Bryant, writing on renewable energy transmission projects in Hawai'i, has offered a way forward in this regard, arguing that renewable energy development itself can be a form of restorative justice when coupled with considered policies that ensure the rights of people to their natural and cultural heritage (Bryant 2011).

A circular economy and circular cities discourse exists largely in parallel to other preservation-oriented discussions on climate change mitigation. In a circular city, resource flows are cyclical and localized through closed-loop, integrated systems, resulting in reduced resource consumption, waste, and CO2 production (Murray, Skene, and Haynes 2017; Williams 2019). By gradually decoupling economic activity from the consumption of finite resources, cities can transition to renewable energy sources and eliminate waste from systems (Rizos, Tuokko, and Behrens 2017).

While there is a wealth of scholarship on circular principles in the built environment, historic preservation has yet to engage with the concept in a meaningful way. Jennifer Minner's research into "landscapes of thrift," aimed at understanding the relationship between reinvestment into existing buildings and larger processes of redevelopment and change in neighborhoods undergoing transition, is particularly relevant to the broader preservation discourse on sustainability (Minner 2013). Building material reuse—above and beyond normative adaptive reuse practices—has not yet been embraced on a wide scale by any discipline related to the built environment. However, the circular economy framework, which views the built fabric as adaptable, flexible, and recyclable, can provide a potential path toward achieving climate mitigation through renewed understandings of durability and building conservation.

Climate Change Adaptation and Resilience

Beyond mitigation, the impacts of climate change are increasingly the concern of scholarship, advocacy, and policy-making across disciplines and across the globe. Unsurprisingly, preservation is also turning more of its attention to the relationship between climate impacts and heritage—including how preservation figures into adaptation and resilience. While scholarship finds many ways that the climate crisis warrants attention on issues from material decay to environmental justice, policy thinking has coalesced mostly around the topic of sea level rise and coastal adaptation. Confronted with visions for coastal change ranging from adaptation in place, to managed retreat, to unmanaged loss, preservation has engaged variably with these difficult prospects. Even so, a dominant narrative has emerged in the literature that positions heritage as a victim of climate change. By contrast, limited research explores the role that preservation policy might play in addressing the complexity of these sociospatial challenges.

A 2017 literature review by Sandra Fatorić and Erin Seekamp confirms that most scholarship on heritage and climate change is concerned with characterizing climate-induced impacts to historic places (Fatorić and Seekamp 2017). This literature names sea level rise; flooding; extreme weather events; coastal erosion; changing air and sea temperatures; changing soil and sediment conditions; and changing humidity as threats to the material integrity of heritage (Cassar 2005). Impact studies focusing on specific geographies or heritage typologies advance ways of adapting preservation practice to respond to climate challenges on a case-by-case basis. But even as researchers develop vulnerability-assessment methodologies to support broader adaptation planning (Sesana et al. 2019), scholarship rarely addresses what sustainable adaptation might look like beyond the site scale.

A similar inclination is clear in literature published by international heritage organizations. Influential reports produced by UNESCO tie the prediction of adverse impacts at World Heritage sites to international adaptation strategies and policies (World Heritage Center 2007). At these sites, adaptation consists of site monitoring and preventive or corrective actions, while policies focus on raising risk awareness and building local capacities to mitigate impacts to historic sites (World Heritage Center 2008b). Just as UNESCO literature extrapolates a site-scale and impacts-oriented view of adaptation to the World Heritage system that is its institutional mandate, other international organizations have taken an equivalent approach to cultural heritage generally (ICOMOS Scientific Council 2007).

By contrast, literature on preservation policy produced at the national or local scales more often recognizes climate adaptation as a process extending beyond the boundaries of individual sites. The US National Park Service's recent programmatic focus on sea level rise situates historic preservation within a broader discourse on coastal adaptation and seeks to address how the protection of coastal heritage can dovetail with regional or municipal resiliency planning (Beavers, Babson, and Schupp 2016). Because sea level rise has dominated the national discussion on planning for climate change, the principal adaptation strategies under consideration for coastal communities and environments (i.e., adaptation in place, managed retreat, and unmanaged loss) are also recent subjects of concern within preservation.

As the discussion of the impacts-oriented literature suggests, the field most often engages with adapt-in-place strategies for coastal resilience. This is true not only in academic and advocacy literature but also in professionally focused publications. Ann D. Horowitz, writing for *APT Bulletin*, has surveyed adapt-in-place strategies relevant to municipal- or community-scale planning, describing "hard adaptations" (e.g., seawalls), "soft adaptations" (e.g., beach nourishment and dune building), and "non-structural adaptations" (e.g., building elevation and local zoning) as key components of the preservationist's adaptation toolbox (Horowitz 2016). While case studies have explored so-called hard and soft adaptations (Schupp, Beavers, and Caffrey 2015), policy literature more often focuses on building elevation and adaptive retrofits, often through guidelines and standard setting for historical appropriateness (Mississippi Development Authority n.d.; 1000 Friends of Florida 2008). Land use tools, including zoning and building code requirements, tend to be absent from preservation literature, despite holding an important place in other planning and policy literature on coastal resilience (Grannis 2011).

Some literature has moved beyond adaptation in place to confront the reality that aspects of the historic built environment will inevitably be lost to sea level rise. That recognition is apparent in discussions of "triage" as a way of managing heritage (Berenfeld 2015). It is also evident in US national policy literature, which has suggested a system for prioritizing sites for preservation, while recording and preparing others for loss. (Rockman et al. 2016) However, such policy tends to lack detailed guidance on how prioritization should occur, and scholarship is increasingly seeking to fill that gap (Seekamp, Fatorić, and McCreary 2020). Collectively, these discussions align preservation planning more closely with managed retreat strategies for adaptation and coastal resilience.

International policy literature on managed retreat has called out the preservation of cultural heritage as a critical concern for community relocation planning (UN High Commissioner for Refugees 2014; Ferris 2017). However, the preservation community has been slow to respond to this discourse and further build its adaptation toolbox. The field has engaged with the idea of building relocation, often in terms of feasibility and authenticity (Gregory 2008). But the ways that heritage and preservation interface with the land use tools commonly associated with climate-related relocation or managed retreat—for example, coastal property buyout programs, coastal transferable development rights (TDRs), and conservation easements—remain under-explored in the literature, even as other fields examine their policy specifics and social justice implications. The work of Robin Bronen in examining climate-induced relocations in Alaska (Bronen 2011, 2015) and the work of A. R. Siders in exploring the adaptive capacities of communities (Siders 2013, 2019) highlight how questions of human rights, equity, and culture are critical to adaptation, thereby suggesting potential avenues for intersections with historic preservation.

Implicit to the strategy of managed retreat is the notion that a degree of loss can be a means to achieving resilience. While academic scholarship has raised the possibility that the loss of material heritage can support community resilience and inspire creative engagement with the past (DeSilvey 2017; Rico 2016; Holtorf 2018), the nature of the relationship between preservation policy and unmanaged loss as a distinct adaptation strategy is a subject requiring further exploration. Erin Seekamp and Eugene Jo have offered one way forward, arguing that heritage policies accommodating loss and encouraging "transformative continuity" can realize resilience while expanding the preservationists' limited conceptualization of adaptation, often seen only as something done reactively and persistently (Seekamp and Jo 2020).

Indeed, much of the literature on preservation and adaptation views cultural heritage as a passive victim of climate change. However, W. Neil Adger and others have argued that climate impacts and adaptation are in fact mediated by both culture and place—meaning that heritage should instead be understood as an active participant (Adger et al. 2013; Adger 2016). Building on this understanding, some case studies and a growing body of academic scholarship point to how heritage and preservation policy have agency in adaptation.

One line of research recognizes cultural heritage as a source of (or as a resource tied to) historical, traditional, community-based, or local knowledge that may be integral to equitable and sustainable adaptation strategies and resilience (Brabec and Chilton 2015). However, much of the research relating to how multiple knowledge systems might be incorporated into planning and policy exists outside the concern of preservation (Maldonado 2014; Nakashima et al. 2012). Other literature points to the instrumental role that heritage and preservation can play in community resilience more generally. Case studies of communities undergoing climate change adaptation or disaster recovery indicate that preservation activities can support social cohesion (Beel et al. 2017; Wagner, Frish, and Fields 2008). Other scholarship has posited that heritage-oriented development can support resilience by promoting collective stewardship (Laven 2015).

These discussions exist within a broader discourse on community-based adaptation that has more readily addressed questions of policy than the literature on preservation has (McNamara and Buggy 2017). However, international advocacy literature is starting to recognize that preservation has the potential to contribute to adaptation through both knowledge and social cohesion, calling for communities to be placed at the heart of decision-making processes (ICOMOS Climate Change and Heritage Working Group 2019). That same literature also draws attention to the potential for policy and practice to contribute to sustainability goals and to mobilize climate action. New research explores how diverse cultural heritage can be a vector for climate action, and points to its potential to bring dimensions of social and climate justice into transformative change through policy (Fatorić and Egberts 2020). Still, the question of how policy can be instrumentalized at the municipal scale toward sustainable and equitable adaptation as a mode of climate action remains to be fully addressed.

Environmental Justice

The environmental justice movement serves as a relevant example of policy reform from which preservation might learn. Born from the growing recognition that lower-income and Black and brown communities bear greater health and environmental risks, the movement has made important policy inroads at the intersection of equity and sustainability. A 1983 report titled *Siting of Hazardous Waste Landfills and Their Correlation with Racial and Economic Status of Surrounding Communities* and subsequent public demonstrations sparked the movement against environmental racism and led to decades of further studies and critical work on the correlation between impoverished communities and environmental injustices (Scholsburg 2007).

Due to efforts by grassroots activists from the early 1980s through today, the environmental justice movement has measurably improved the ways in which health and environmental policies are administered in the United States and how federal legislation protects Black and brown communities and other marginalized communities. In an article evaluating the movement's impact on public policy, Robert D. Bullard and Glenn S. Johnson offer a historical analysis of the environmental justice movement and its trajectory from grassroots activism to justice by way of national policy (Bullard and Johnson 2000).

In the past decade, literature within the environmental justice movement has shifted from a discussion of research and empirical studies toward an evaluation of proposed policies and the federal response to policy action. In an extensive literature review, Paul Mohai, David Pellow, and J. Timmons Roberts cover nearly two decades of research and contentious literature on environmental racism in order to evaluate emerging policies focused specifically on addressing established environmental injustices (Mohai, Pellow, and Roberts 2009). They conclude with a call to action, asserting that although extensive research has established the disproportionate impacts of climate change on Black and brown communities, not enough analysis of policy options and their compatability with social and environmental justice goals exists. Similarly, multiple authors evaluate the government's response to the climate crisis and discuss the role of corrective justice and courts in the long battle toward equity in the sustainability movement (Konisky 2015). Additional scholarship highlights the paucity of these types of evaluations, suggesting that revisions to existing sustainability plans and creation of new plans need to better reflect the breadth of environmental justice concerns, using racial and gender equity as drivers for policy change (Pearsall and Pierce 2010).

While preservation is recognizing its role in contributing to the climate crisis and compounding social inequities, scholarship that elucidates how this recognition can translate into policy action is limited. Throughout this literature review, there are multiple examples of parallel policy realms from which preservation could potentially learn. The environmental justice movement's specific approach to policy reform provides a case study for how climate action and social justice can work in tandem to achieve measurable change and more equitable outcomes.

▶ POLICY REFORM TOWARD EQUITY AND SUSTAINABILITY

This literature review makes clear that while equity and sustainability are growing concerns within preservation, many important connections to multiple policy arenas have yet to be made. Furthermore, the field has not substantially engaged *municipal* preservation policy—a critical space for the built environment's regulation and management—as part of reconciling tensions between theory and practice or confronting emerging challenges posed by environmental and sociospatial change.

The literature also exposes a number of underdeveloped areas of research as well as potential avenues for policy reform. The discourses around equity and sustainability reveal that the field has often been hesitant to develop or revise policies to confront those issues out of concern for normative ideals of material integrity and authenticity. Even as criticisms are levied, and even as notions of justice and adaptation are more readily taken up, preservation remains inclined toward protectionist approaches. Moreover, while scholarship across disciplines highlights how questions of human rights, equity, and culture intersect with the struggle for self-determination and resilience, there has been limited research on how existing tools can evolve to address those concerns.

Scholarship on sociospatial equity actively pursues more equitable representation in the built environment, but there is a dearth of research on the question of how to contend with the legacy impacts of exclusionary architecture, or how this reflexive approach can lead to actionable shifts in policy. Similarly, literature lacks robust discussion of potential interdisciplinary approaches to harmonize preservation goals with affordability, densification, racial justice, and broader social equity frameworks—for example, the opportunity to bridge gaps between affordable housing and preservation policy, or to find intersections between heritage policy and collective land rights.

Regarding climate change, although preservation increasingly aligns itself with environmental sustainability and climate action, the literature reveals that interest among researchers and policy makers has less often translated into robust policy thinking on the most critical issues facing communities and their built environments. Municipal energy codes, renewable energy development, and circular cities frameworks all point to the important work still needed to scale up preservation thinking and better mobilize policy toward climate change mitigation. Similarly, while preservationists contend with site-specific adaptation and avoiding potential loss, more work is required to understand how existing policies might inform how climate adaptation will occur for communities, cities, and regions, and what new policies might ensure that adaptation is sustainable and equitable. There are existing models for achieving policy reform, like the environmental justice movement, which have potential to inform that work.

Confronted with racial and economic injustice and the climate crisis, preservation faces a reckoning. As the field confronts the reality that its policies may operate counter to contemporary research on sociospatial and environmental challenges, the need for policy reform only becomes more glaring. Existing lines of research as well as gaps identified through this literature review point to only some of the potential paths leading to much needed change. A review of each topic within equity and sustainability discourses suggests that those paths are inevitably intertwined, and creating a more sustainable built environment ultimately means creating a more just built environment.

Bibliography

Adger, W. Neil. 2016. "Place, Well-Being, and Fairness Shape Priorities for Adaptation to Climate Change." *Global Environmental Change* 38:A1–A3.

Adger, W. Neil, Jon Barnett, Katrina Brown, Nadine Marshall, and Karen O'Brien. 2013. "Cultural Dimensions of Climate Change Impacts and Adaptation." *Nature Climate Change* 3 (2): 112–117.

Advisory Council on Historic Preservation. 1979a. *Assessing the Energy Conservation Benefits of Historic Preservation: Methods and Examples*. Washington, DC: Advisory Council on Historic Preservation.

Advisory Council on Historic Preservation. 1979b. *Preservation and Energy Conservation*. Washington, DC: Advisory Council on Historic Preservation.

Agbonkhese, S., R. Hughes, M. Tucker, and A. H. Yu. 2010. *Green-deavor Carbon Calculator*. Newport, RI: 1772 Foundation.

Alexander, Lisa T. 2012. "Hip-Hop and Housing: Revisiting Culture, Urban Space, Power, and Law." *Hastings Law Journal* 63 (3): 803–866.

Allison, Eric W. 2005. *Gentrification and Historic Districts: Public Policy Considerations in the Designation of Historic Districts in New York City*. PhD diss., Columbia University.

Appelbaum, Binyamin. 2020. "When Historic Preservation Hurts Cities." *New York Times*, January 25, 2020. https://www. nytimes.com/2020/01/26/opinion/historic-preservation-solar-panels.html.

Ascione, Fabrizio, Francesca Ceroni, Rosa Francesca De Masi, Filippo de' Rossi, and Maria Rosaria Pecce. 2017. "Historical Buildings: Multidisciplinary Approach to Structural/Energy Diagnosis and Performance Assessment." *Applied Energy* 185:1517–1528.

Auclair, Elizabeth, and Graham Fairclough, eds. 2015. *Theory and Practice in Heritage and Sustainability*. New York: Routledge.

Avrami, Erica. 2016. "Making Historic Preservation Sustainable." *Journal of the American Planning Association* 82 (2): 104–112.

Avrami, Erica, ed. 2019. *Preservation and the New Data Landscape*. New York: Columbia Books on Architecture and the City.

Avrami, Erica, ed. 2020. *Preservation and Social Inclusion*. New York: Columbia Books on Architecture and the City.

Avrami, Erica, Cherie-Nicole Leo, and Alberto Sanchez Sanchez. 2019. "Confronting Exclusion: Redefining the Intended Outcomes of Historic Preservation." *Change Over Time* 8 (1): 102–120.

Beavers, R. L., A. L. Babson, and C. A. Schupp, eds. 2016. *Coastal Adaptation Strategies Handbook*. NPS 999/134090. Washington, DC: National Park Service.

Beel, David, Claire Wallace, Gemma Webster, Hai Nguyen, Elizabeth Tait, Marsaili Macleod, and Chris Mellish. 2017. "Cultural Resilience: The Production of Rural Community Heritage, Digital Archives and the Role of Volunteers." *Journal of Rural Studies* 54:459–468.

Been, Vicki, Ingrid Gould Ellen, Michael Gedal, Edward Glaeser, and Brian J. McCabe. 2016. "Preserving History or Restricting Development? The Heterogeneous Effects of Historic Districts on Local Housing Markets in New York City." *Journal of Urban Economics* 92:16–30.

Belussi, Lorenzo, Benedetta Barozzi, Alice Bellazzi, Ludovico Danza, Anna Devitofrancesco, Carlo Fanciulli, Matteo Ghellere, et al. 2019. "A Review of Performance of Zero Energy Buildings and Energy Efficiency Solutions." *Journal of Building Engineering* 25. https://doi.org/10.1016/j.jobe.2019.100772.

Berenfeld, Michelle. 2015. "Planning for Permanent Emergency: 'Triage' as a Strategy for Managing Cultural Resources Threatened by Climate Change." *George Wright Forum* 32 (1): 5–12.

Blumberga, Andra, Einars Cilinskis, Armands Gravelsins, Amalija Svarckopfa, and Dagnija Blumberga. 2018. "Analysis of Regulatory Instruments Promoting Building Energy Efficiency." *Energy Procedia* 147:258–267.

Brabec, Elizabeth, and Elizabeth Chilton. 2015. "Toward an Ecology of Cultural Heritage." *Change Over Time* 5 (20): 266–307.

Bronen, Robin. 2011. "Climate-Induced Community Relocations: Creating an Adaptive Governance Framework Based in Human

Rights Doctrine." *New York University Review of Law & Social Change* 35 (2): 357–407.

Bronen, Robin. 2015. "Climate-Induced Community Relocations: Using Integrated Social-Ecological Assessments to Foster Adaptation and Resilience." *Ecology and Society* 20 (3): http://dx.doi.org/10.5751/ES-07801-200336.

Bronin, Sara C. 2010. "Curbing Energy Sprawl with Microgrids." *Connecticut Law Review* 43 (2): 547–584.

Bronin, Sara C., and J. Peter Byrne. 2012. Historic Preservation Law. *Historic Preservation Law*, New York: Foundation Press Thomson/West.

Bryant, Elena. 2011. "Innovation or Degradation?: An Analysis of Hawai'i's Cultural Impact Assessment Process as a Vehicle of Environmental Justice for Kanaka Maoli." *Asian-Pacific Law & Policy Journal* 13 (1): 230–299.

Buchanan, Allen. 1993. "The Role of Collective Rights in the Theory of Indigenous Peoples." *Transnational Law Contemporary Problems* 3 (1): 89–108.

Bullard, Robert D., and Glenn S. Johnson. 2000. "Environmental Justice: Grassroots Activism and Its Impact on Public Policy Decision Making." *Journal of Social Issues* 56 (3): 555–578.

Burg, Steve. 2014. "Get Your Wind Farm off My Historic Site: When Visions of Sustainability Collide (Part 2)." National Council on Public History. https://ncph.org/history-at-work/wind-farm-historic-site-part-2/.

Cabeza, Luisa F., Alvaro de Gracia, and Anna Laura Pisello. 2018. "Integration of Renewable Technologies in Historical and Heritage Buildings: A Review." *Energy and Buildings* 177:96–111.

Callison, J. William. 2016. "Inclusive Communities: Geographic Desegregation, Urban Revitalization, and Disparate Impact under the Fair Housing Act." *University of Memphis Law Review* 46 (4): 1039–1055.

Carbonara, Giovanni. 2015. "Energy Efficiency as a Protection Tool." *Energy and Buildings* 95:9–12.

Cassar, May. 2005. *Climate Change and the Historic Environment: Research Report.* Centre for Sustainable Heritage. London: University College of London.

Chusid, Jeffery. 2006. "Preservation in the Progressive City: Debating History and Gentrification in Austin. *Next American City* 12:23–27.

Clowney, Stephen. 2013. "Landscape Fairness: Removing Discrimination from the Built Environment," *Utah Law Review* 1:1–62.

Corbett, Charles J., and Luk N. Van Wassenhove. 1993. "The Green Fee: Internalizing and Operationalizing Environmental Issues." *California Management Review* (fall): 116–135.

Delvac, William F., Susan Escherish, and Bridget Hartman. 1994. *Affordable Housing through Historic Preservation: A Case Study Guide to Combining the Tax Credits.* National Park Service. Washington, DC: Government Printing Office.

DeSilvey, Caitlin. 2017. *Curated Decay: Heritage beyond Saving.* Minneapolis: University of Minnesota Press.

Drury, Paul, and Anna McPherson. 2008. "Conservation Principles: Policies and Guidance for the Sustainable Management of the Historic Environment." English Heritage. https://historicengland.org.uk/images-books/publications/conservation-principles-sustainable-management-historic-environment/conservationprinciplespolicies andguidanceapril08web.

Elefante, Carl. 2007. "The Greenest Building Is... One That Is Already Built." *Forum Journal: The Journal of the National Trust for Historic Preservation* 21 (4): 27–38.

Elias, Nicole S., Sean McCandless, and Rashmi Chordiya. 2019. "Administrative Decision-Making amid Competing Public Sector Values: Confederate Statue Removal in Baltimore, Maryland." *Journal of Public Affairs Education* 25(3): 412–422. DOI: 10.1080/15236803.2019.1601328.

Ellen, Ingrid Gould, Brian McCabe, and Eric Stern. 2016. "Fifty Years of Historic Preservation in New York City." White paper. New York: New York University, Furman Center.

Fainstein, Susan S. 2005. "Planning Theory and the City." *Journal of Planning Education and Research* 25:121–130.

Fatorić, Sandra, and Robbert Biesbroek. 2020. "Adapting Cultural Heritage to Climate Change Impacts in the Netherlands: Barriers, Interdependencies, and

Strategies for Overcoming Them." *Climatic Change* 162 (2): 301–320.

Fatorić, Sandra, and Linde Egberts. 2020. "Realising the Potential of Cultural Heritage to Achieve Climate Change Actions in the Netherlands." *Journal of Environmental Management* 274:1–9.

Fatorić, Sandra, and Erin Seekamp. 2017. "Are Cultural Heritage and Resources Threatened by Climate Change? A Systematic Literature Review." *Climate Change* 142 (1–2): 227–254.

Fein, David B. 1985. "Historic Districts: Preserving City Neighborhoods for the Privileged." *New York University Law Review* 1 (60): 64–103.

Ferris, Elizabeth. 2017. *A Toolbox: Planning Relocations to Protect People from Disasters and Environmental Change.* Georgetown University, United Nations High Commissioner for Refugees (UNHCR), International Organization for Migration (IOM).

Fincham, Derek. 2011. "The Distinctiveness of Property and Heritage." *Penn State Law Review* 115 (3): 641–684.

Fitch, James Marston. 1966. *American Building.* Vol. 2, The Environmental Forces That Shaped It. Boston: Houghton Mifflin.

Flyvbjerg, Bent. 2002. "Bringing Power to Planning Research: One Researcher's Praxis Story." *Journal of Planning Education and Research* 21:353–366.

Fondo, Grant P. 1994. "Access Reigns Supreme: Title III of the Americans with Disabilities Act and Historic Preservation." *Brigham Young University Journal of Public Law* 9 (1): 99–134.

Forest, Benjamin, and Juliet Johnson. 2018. "Confederate Monuments and the Problem of Forgetting." *Cultural Geographies* 26 (1): 127–131.

Gilderbloom, John I., Matthew J. Hanka, and Joshua D. Ambrosius. 2009. "Historic Preservation's Impact on Job Creation, Property Values, and Environmental Sustainability." *Journal of Urbanism* 2 (2): 83–101.

Gissen, David. 2019. "Introduction: Disability and Preservation." *Future Anterior* 16 (1): iii–xiii.

Glaeser, Edward L. 2005. *Triumph of the City: How Our Greatest Invention Makes Us Richer, Smarter, Greener, Healthier, and Happier.* New York: Penguin Press.

Glaeser, Edward L. 2010. "Preservation Follies: Excessive Landmarking Threatens to Make Manhattan a Refuge for the Rich." *City Journal* 20 (2). https://www.city-journal.org/html/preservation-follies-13279.html.

Gotham, Kevin Fox. 2000. "Urban Space, Restrictive Covenants and the Origins of Racial Residential Segregation in a US City, 1900–50." *International Journal of Urban and Regional Research* 24 (3): 616–633.

Grannis, Jessica. 2011. *Adaptation Tool Kit: Sea-Level Rise and Coastal Land Use.* Washington, DC: Georgetown Climate Center.

Gregory, Jenny. 2008. "Reconsidering Relocated Buildings: ICOMOS, Authenticity, and Mass Relocation." *International Journal of Heritage Studies* 14 (2): 112–130.

Holtorf, Cornelius. 2018. "Embracing Change: How Cultural Resilience Is Increased through Cultural Heritage." *World Archaeology* 50 (4): 639–650.

Horowitz, Ann D. 2016. "Planning Before Disaster Strikes: An Introduction to Adaptation Strategies." *APT Bulletin: The Journal of Preservation Technology* 47 (1): 40–48.

Howell, Kathryn L. 2018. "Housing and the Grassroots: Using Local and Expert Knowledge to Preserve Affordable Housing." *Journal of Planning Education and Research* 38 (4): 437–448.

Howell, Kathryn L., Elizabeth J. Mueller, and Barbara Brown Wilson. 2019. "One Size Fits None: Local Context and Planning for the Preservation of Affordable Housing." *Housing Policy Debate* 29 (1): 148–165.

Hsieh, Chang-Tai, and Enrico Moretti. 2017. "Housing Constraints and Spatial Misallocation." *American Economic Journal: Macroeconomics* 11 (2): 1–39.

Hubbard, Harold M. 1991. "The Real Cost of Energy." *Scientific American* 264 (4): 36–43.

ICOMOS Climate Change and Cultural Heritage Working Group. 2019. *The Future of Our Pasts: Engaging Cultural Heritage in Climate Action.* Paris: ICOMOS. https://indd.adobe.com/view/a9a551e3-3b23-4127-99fd-a7a80d91a29e.

ICOMOS Scientific Council. 2007. *Recommendations from the Scientific Council Symposium: Cultural Heritage and Global Climate Change (GCC).* Pretoria, South Africa: ICOMOS.

Ijla, Akram, Stephanie Ryberg, Mark S. Rosentraub, and William Bowen. 2011. "Historic Designation and the Rebuilding of Neighborhoods: New Evidence of the Value of an Old Policy Tool." *Journal of Urbanism* 4 (3): 263–284.

Intergovernmental Panel on Climate Change. 2015. "Buildings." In *Climate Change 2014: Mitigation of Climate Change: Working Group III Contribution to the IPCC Fifth Assessment Report,* 671–738. Cambridge: Cambridge University Press.

Karas, David. 2015. "Highway to Inequity: The Disparate Impact of the Interstate Highway System on Poor and Minority Communities in American Cities." *New Visions for Public Affairs* 7:9–21.

Kimmell, Kenneth, and Dawn Stolfi Stalenhoef. 2011. "The Cape Wind Offshore Wind Energy Project: A Case Study of the Difficult Transition to Renewable Energy." *Golden Gate University Environmental Law Journal* 5 (8): 197–225.

Konisky, David M., ed. 2015. *Failed Promises: Evaluating the Federal Government's Response to Environmental Justice.* Cambridge, MA: MIT Press.

Kuntz, Jennifer. 2009. "A Guide to Solar Panel Installation at Grand Central Terminal: Creating a Policy of Sustainable Rehabilitation in Local and National Historic Preservation Law." *Vermont Journal of Environmental Law* 10:315–336.

Laven, Daniel N. 2015. "Heritage Development and Community Resilience: Insights for the Era of Climate Change." In *The Future of Heritage as Climates Change: Loss, Adaptation and Creativity,* edited by David Harvey and Jim Perry, 248–268. London: Taylor and Francis.

Leichenko, Robin M., Edward Coulson, and David Listokin. 2001. "Historic Preservation and Residential Property Values: An Analysis of Texas Cities." *Urban Studies* 38 (11): 1973–1987.

Lewis, David A. 2015. "Identifying and Avoiding Conflicts between Historic Preservation and the Development of Renewable Energy." *New York University Environmental Law Journal* 22:274–360.

Lidelöw, Sofia, Tomas Örn, Andrea Luciani, and Agatino Rizzo. 2019. "Energy-Efficiency Measures for Heritage Buildings: A Literature Review." *Sustainable Cities and Society* 45:231–242.

Listokin, David, and Barbara Listokin. 2001. *Barriers to the Rehabilitation of Affordable Housing.* Vol. 1 of 2, *Findings and Analysis.* Washington, DC: US Department of Housing and Urban Development.

Listokin, David, Barbara Listokin, and Michael Lahr. 1998. "The Contributions of Historic Preservation to Housing and Economic Development." *Housing Policy Debate* 9 (3): 431–471.

Maldonado, Julie Koppel. 2014. "A Multiple Knowledge Approach for Adaptation to Environmental Change: Lessons Learned from Coastal Louisiana's Tribal Communities." *Journal of Political Ecology* 21:61–82.

Mangin, John. 2014. "The New Exclusionary Zoning." *Stanford Law & Policy Review* 25 (91): 91–120.

Mason, Randall. 2005. *Economics and Historic Preservation: A Guide and Review of the Literature.* Washington, DC: Brookings Institution, Metropolitan Policy Program.

Mazzarella, Livio. 2015. "Energy Retrofit of Historic and Existing Buildings: The Legislative and Regulatory Point of View." *Energy and Buildings* 95:23–31.

McCabe, Brian, and Ingrid Gould Ellen. 2016. "Does Preservation Accelerate Neighborhood Change? Examining the Impact of Historic Preservation in New York City." *Journal of the American Planning Association* 82 (2): 134–146.

McCabe, Brian, and Ingrid Gould Ellen. 2017. "Balancing the Costs and Benefits of Historic Preservation." In *Evidence and Innovation in Housing Law and Policy,* edited by Lee Anne Fennell and Benjamin J. Keys, 87–107. Cambridge: Cambridge University Press.

McNamara, Karen Elizabeth, and Lisa Buggy. 2017. "Community-Based Climate Change Adaptation: A Review of Academic Literature." *Local Environment* 22 (4): 443–460.

Milder, Emily. 2016. "Historically Affordable: How Historic Preservationists and Affordable Housing Advocates Can Work Together to Prevent the Demolition of Rent-Stabilized Housing in Los Angeles." *Journal of Affordable Housing & Community Development Law* 25 (1): 103–131.

Minner, Jennifer. 2013. "Landscapes of Thrift and Choreographies of Change: Reinvestment and Adaptation along Austin's Commercial Strips." PhD diss., University of Texas.

Minner, Jennifer. 2016. "Revealing Synergies, Tensions, and Silences between Preservation and Planning." *Journal of the American Planning Association* 82 (2): 72–87.

Mississippi Development Authority. n.d. *Elevation Design Guidelines for Historic Homes in the Mississippi Gulf Coast Region.*

Mohai, Paul, David Pellow, and J. Timmons Roberts. 2009. "Environmental Justice." *Annual Review of Environment and Resources* 34 (1): 405–430.

Mohl, Raymond A. 2012. "The Expressway Teardown Movement in American Cities: Rethinking Postwar Highway Policy in the Post-Interstate Era." *Journal of Planning History* 11 (1): 89–103.

Munasinghe, Mohan. 1990. "Energy Demand Management and Conservation." *Energy Analysis and Policy*, October, 107–139.

Murray, Alan, Keith Skene, and Kathyrn Haynes. 2017. "The Circular Economy: An Interdisciplinary Exploration of the Concept and Application in a Global Context." *Journal of Business Ethics* 140:369–380.

Nakashima, D. J., K. Galloway McLean, H. D. Thulstrup, A. Ramos Castillo, and J. T. Rubis. 2012. *Weathering Uncertainty: Traditional Knowledge for Climate Change Assessment and Adaptation.* Paris: UNESCO.

National Park Service. n.d. "Renewable Energy Projects, National Historic Landmarks, and the Secretary of the Interior's Standards and Guidelines." https://www.nps.gov/articles/renewable-energy-projects-national-historic-landmarks-and-the-secretary-of-the-interior-s-standards-and-guidelines.htm.

National Trust for Historic Preservation. 2002. *Rebuilding Community: A Best Practices Toolkit for Historic Preservation and Redevelopment.* Washington, DC: National Trust for Historic Preservation.

National Trust for Historic Preservation. 2020. "National Trust for Historic Preservation Statement on Confederate Monuments." https://savingplaces.org/press-center/media-resources/national-trust-statement-on-confederate-memorials#.X9FsTi2ZNQI.

National Trust for Historic Preservation Green Lab. 2011. *The Greenest Building: Quantifying the Environmental Value of Building Reuse.* Washington, DC: National Trust for Historic Preservation.

National Trust for Historic Preservation Green Lab. 2014. *Older, Smaller, Better: Measuring How the Character of Buildings and Blocks Influences Urban Vitality.* Washington, DC: National Trust for Historic Preservation.

New York City Mayoral Advisory Commission on City Art, Monuments, and Markers. 2018. *Mayoral Advisory Commission on City Art, Monuments, and Markers: Report to the City of New York.* https://www1.nyc.gov/assets/monuments/downloads/pdf/mac-monuments-report.pdf.

Noonan, Douglas S., and Douglas J. Krupa. 2011. "Making—or Picking—Winners: Evidence of Internal and External Price Effects in Historic Preservation Policies." *Real Estate Economics* 39 (2): 379–407.

1000 Friends of Florida. 2008. *Disaster Mitigation for Historic Structures: Protection Strategies.* Florida Department of State, Division of Historical Resources, Florida Division of Emergency Management.

Outka, Uma. 2012. "Environmental Justice Issues in Sustainable Development: Environmental Justice in the Renewable Energy Transition." *Journal of Environmental and Sustainability Law* 19 (1): 62–121.

Parkin, Christopher. 2007. "A Comparative Analysis of the Tension Created by Disability Access and Historic Preservation Laws in the United States and England." *Connecticut Journal of International Law* 22:379–381.

Pearsall, Hamill, and Joseph Pierce. 2010. "Urban Sustainability and Environmental Justice: Evaluating the Linkages in Public Planning/Policy Discourse." *International Journal for Justice and Sustainability* 15 (6): 569–580.

Phoenix, T. 2015. "Lessons Learned: ASHRAE's Approach in the Refurbishment of Historic and Existing Buildings." *Energy and Buildings* 95:13–14. https://doi.org/10.1016/j.enbuild.2015.02.034.

Posner, Eric A. 2007. "The International Protection of Cultural Property: Some Skeptical Observations." *Chicago Journal of International Law* 8 (1): 213–231.

Poulis, Ioannis. 2013. "Renewable Energy Plant Development, Historic Environments, and Local Communities: Lessons from the Greek Experience." *Historic Environment: Policy & Practice* 3 (2): 127–142.

Prott, Lyndel V., and Patrick J. O'Keefe. 1992. "Cultural Heritage or Cultural Property?" *International Journal of Cultural Property* 1 (2): 307–320. doi:10.1017/S094073919200033X.

Rico, Trinidad. 2016. *Constructing Destruction: Heritage Narratives in the Tsunami City.* New York: Routledge.

Rizos, Vasileios, Katja Tuokko, and Arno Behrens. 2017. *The Circular Economy: A Review of Definitions, Processes and Impacts.* CEPS Research Report No. 2017/8, April 2017.

Rockman, Marcy, Marissa Morgan, Sonya Ziaja, George Hambrecht, and Alison Meadow. 2016. *Cultural Resources Climate Change Strategy.* Washington, DC: Cultural Resources, Partnerships, and Science and Climate Change Response Program, National Park Service.

Rose, Carol M. 1981. "Preservation and Community: New Directions in the Law of Historic Preservation. *Stanford Law Review* 33:472–534.

Rothstein, Richard. 2017. *The Color of the Law.* New York: Liveright Publishing Corporation.

Ruscavage-Barz, Samantha M. 2007. "The Efficacy of State Law in Protecting Native American Sacred Places: A Case Study of the Paseo Del Norte Extension." *Natural Resources Journal* 47 (2): 969–998.

Ryberg-Webster, Stephanie. 2014. "Preserving Downtown America: Federal Rehabilitation Tax Credits and the Transformation of U.S. Cities." *Journal of the American Planning Association* 79 (4): 266–279.

Ryberg-Webster, Stephanie, and Kelly L. Kinahan. 2014. "Historic Preservation and Urban Revitalization in the Twenty-First Century." *Journal of Planning Literature* 24 (2): 119–139.

Rypkema, Donovan. 2002. *Historic Preservation and Affordable Housing: The Missed Connection.* Washington, DC: National Trust for Historic Preservation.

Rypkema, Donovan. 2005. *The Economics of Historic Preservation: A Community Leader's Guide.* Washington, DC: National Trust for Historic Preservation.

Schindler, Sarah. 2015. "Architectural Exclusion: Discrimination and Segregation through Physical Design of the Built Environment." *Yale Law Journal* 124 (6): 1934–2024.

Scholsburg, David. 2007. *Defining Environmental Justice: Theories, Movement, and Nature.* London: Oxford University Press.

Schupp, C. A., R. L. Beavers, and M. A. Caffrey, eds. 2015. *Coastal Adaptation Strategies: Case Studies.* NPS 999/129700. Fort Collins, CO: National Park Service.

Seekamp, Erin, Sandra Fatorić, and Allie McGreary. 2020. "Historic Preservation Priorities for Climate Adaptation." *Ocean and Coastal Management* 191:1–15.

Seekamp, Erin, and Eugene Jo. 2020. "Resilience and Transformation of Heritage Sites to Accommodate for Loss and Learning in a Changing Climate." *Climate Change* 162:41–55.

Sesana, Elena, Alexandre S. Gagnon, Alessandra Bonazza, and John J. Hughes. 2020. "An Integrated Approach for Assessing the Vulnerability of World Heritage Sites to Climate Change Impacts." *Journal of Cultural Heritage* 41:211–224.

Siders, A. R. 2013. "Managed Coastal Retreat: A Legal Handbook on Shifting Development Away from Vulnerable Areas." New York: Center for Climate Change Law, Columbia University.

Siders, A. R. 2019. "Social Justice Implications of US Managed Retreat Buyout Programs." *Climate Change* 152 (2): 239–257.

Smith, Neil. 1998. "Comment on David Listokin, Barbara Listokin, and Michael Lahr's 'The Contributions of Historic Preservation to Housing and Economic Development': Historic Preservation in a Neoliberal Age." *Housing Policy Debate* 9 (3): 479–485.

Society of Architectural Historians. 2020. "SAH Statement on the Removal of Monuments to the Confederacy from Public Spaces." https://www.sah.org/about-sah/news/sah-news/news-detail/2020/06/19/sah-statement-on-the-removal-of-monuments-to-the-confederacy-from-public-spaces.

Spinelli, Dominic. 2010. "Historic Preservation and Offshore Wind Energy: Lessons Learned from the Cape Wind Saga." *Gonzaga Law Review* 46:741–770.

Talen, Emily, Sunny Menozzi, and Chloe Schaefer. 2015. "What Is a 'Great Neighborhood'? An Analysis of APA's Top-Rated Places." *Journal of the American Planning Association* 81 (2): 121–141.

Thompson, Eric, David Rosenbaum, and Benjamin Schmitz. 2011. "Property Values on the Plains: The Impact of Historic Preservation." *Annals of Regional Science* 47 (2): 477–491.

Tisher, Elizabeth M. 2017. "Historic Housing for All: Historic Preservation as the New Inclusionary Zoning." *Vermont Law Review* 41 (3): 603–634.

UN Environment and International Energy Agency. 2017. *Towards a Zero-Emission, Efficient, and Resilient Buildings and Construction Sector.* Global Status Report 2017.

UNESCO. 2003. *Convention for the Safeguarding of the Intangible Cultural Heritage.*

UN High Commissioner for Refugees. 2014. *Planned Relocation, Disasters and Climate Change: Consolidating Good Practices and Preparing for the Future.*

Upton, Dell. 2017. "Confederate Monuments and Civic Values in the Wake of Charlottesville." *Society of Architectural Historians* blog. https://www.sah.org/publications-and-research/sah-blog/sah-blog/2017/09/13/confederate-monuments-and-civic-values-in-the-wake-of-charlottesville.

Wagner, Jacob, Michael Frish, and Billy Fields. 2008. "Building Local Capacity: Planning for Local Culture and Neighborhood Recovery in New Orleans." *Cityscape* 10 (3): 39–56.

Wagner, Peter. 1998. "Comment on David Listokin, Barbara Listokin, and Michael Lahr's 'The Contributions of Historic Preservation to Housing and Economic Development.'" *Housing Policy Debate* 9 (3): 487–495.

Walkowitz, Daniel, and Lisa Maya Knauer. 2009. *Contested Histories in Public Space: Memory, Race, and Nation.* Durham, NC: Duke University Press.

Webb, Amanda L. 2017. "Energy Retrofits in Historic and Traditional Buildings: A Review of Problems and Methods." *Renewable and Sustainable Energy Reviews* 77:748–759.

Weyeneth, Robert R. 2005. "The Architecture of Racial Segregation: The Challenges of Preserving the Problematic Past." *Public Historian* 27 (4): 11–44.

White House. 2016. *Housing Development Toolkit.* https://www.whitehouse.gov/sites/whitehouse.gov/files/images/Housing_Development_

Toolkit%20f.2.pdf.

Williams, Joanna. 2019. "Circular Cities." *Urban Studies* 56 (13): 2746–2762. doi:10.1177/0042098018806133.

Wolfley, Jeanette. 2018. "Mni Wiconi, Tribal Sovereignty, and Treaty Rights: Lessons from the Dakota Access Pipeline." In *Energy Justice: US and International Perspectives*, edited by Raya Salter, Carmen G. Gonzalez, and Elizabeth Ann Kronk Warner, 141–165. Northampton, MA: Edward Elgar.

World Heritage Center. 2007. *Climate Change and World Heritage: Report on Predicting and Managing the Impacts of Climate Change on World Heritage, and Strategy to Assist States Parties to Implement Appropriate Management Responses.* World Heritage Reports No. 22. Paris: World Heritage Center, UNESCO. https://whc.unesco.org/document/8874.

World Heritage Center. 2008a. "List of Factors Affecting the Properties." https://whc.unesco.org/en/factors.

World Heritage Center. 2008b. *Policy Document on the Impacts of Climate Change on World Heritage Properties.* Paris: World Heritage Center, UNESCO.

Yiftachel, Oren. 1998. "Planning and Social Control: Exploring the Dark Side." *Journal of Planning Literature* 12 (4): 395–406.

Zarhirovic-Herbert, Velma, and Karen M. Gibler. 2012. "Historic District Influence on Housing Prices and Marketing Duration." *Journal of Real Estate Finance and Economics* 48 (1): 112–131.

Ziza, Iva. 2008. "Siting of Renewable Energy Facilities and Adversarial Legalism: Lessons from Cape Cod." *New England Law Review* 42 (3): 591–630.

219

Toward Sustainability and Equity:
Envisioning Preservation Policy Reform
February 6–7, 2020, New York City

▶ THURSDAY, FEBRUARY 6

Opening Remarks and Introductions

— Erica Avrami, *Columbia University*
  Graduate School of Architecture, Planning, and Preservation
— Elliott Sclar and Jacqueline M. Klopp,
  Center for Sustainable Urban Development — Earth Institute
— Bénédicte de Montlaur, *World Monuments Fund*

SESSION 1
Preservation Governance in a New Era
Moderator: Erica Avrami

— Lisa Kersavage, Mark A. Silberman, Cory Herrala –
  NYC Landmarks Preservation Commission: Encouraging Energy
  Efficiency and Resiliency
— Ken Bernstein — *Learning from Los Angeles:*
  Preservation Meets a New Housing Reality
— Louise Bedsworth — *Supporting Sustainable Growth in California:*
  The California Strategic Growth Council

SESSION 2
Heritage, Justice, and the Climate Crisis
Moderator: Jacqueline M. Klopp

— Robin Bronen — *What Does Cultural Preservation Mean in the*
  Context of the Climate Crisis?
— A. R. Siders — *The Role of Heritage in Relocating to Adapt to*
  Climate Change
— Victoria Herrmann — *New Residents, New Heritage, New Policy:*
  Planning for Rural Climate Change Displacement, Migration,
  and Emplacement into America's Cities
— Amanda L. Webb — *Viewing Sustainable Preservation through*
  an Energy Justice Lens

SESSION 3
Heritage, Equity, and Communities
Moderator: Elliott Sclar

— Stephanie Ryberg-Webster — *Preserving the Landscape of Daily Life: Exploring the Intersections of Housing Rehabilitation, Environmental Justice, and Climate Action Planning*
— Claudia Guerra — *Vernacular Architecture in San Antonio: The Original Affordable, Environmentally Sustainable, and Equitable Built Form*
— Lisa T. Alexander — *Vernacular Historic Preservation Law*
— Randall Mason — *Barriers to Equitable Redevelopment*

PUBLIC SESSION
Toward Sustainability and Equity
Moderator: Erica Avrami

A dialogue exploring heritage, justice, and community agency in changing contexts

— Robin Bronen, *Alaska Institute for Justice*
— Lisa T. Alexander, *Texas A&M University*

► FRIDAY, FEBRUARY 7

SESSION 4
Preservation's Purview and Policy Toolbox
Moderator: Erica Avrami

— Sara C. Bronin — *Revisiting the Secretary's Standards*
— James B. Lindberg — *Taking Preservation Policy to Scale: Can Building Reuse Become the New Normal?*
— Jennifer Minner — *Sunrise over Landscapes of Thrift: Toward Circular Economies and Equity Preservation*
— Vicki Weiner — *Policy in the Pedagogy: Preparing the Next Generation to Advance Equity through Preservation Policy Change*

Breakout Discussions

Concluding Discussion and Recommendations

LISA T. ALEXANDER is a professor at Texas A&M University School of Law, with a joint appointment in the school's Department of Landscape Architecture and Urban Planning. She is also a cofounder and codirector of the School of Law's Program in Real Estate and Community Development Law. Her research and teaching focus on housing law and policy, fair housing, historic preservation law, local government law, urban development, and business and social entrepreneurship. She has published in the *Minnesota Law Review, Wisconsin Law Review, Hastings Law Journal, and Georgetown Journal on Poverty Law and Policy*, among other publications. In 2018 she was the first person in the School of Law and one of only twenty-one scholars to receive a Presidential Impact Fellowship—one of the most prestigious recognitions for scholarly impact presented to Texas A&M University faculty. She is the recipient of the 2020 Sadie Alexander Leadership Award by the University of Pennsylvania Law School's Black Law Students Association. She was also a presenter at Texas A&M University's Historic Preservation Symposium in 2020. She received her BA from Wesleyan University and her JD from Columbia Law School.

ERICA AVRAMI is the James Marston Fitch Assistant Professor of Historic Preservation at Columbia University's Graduate School of Architecture, Planning, and Preservation, and an affiliate with the Earth Institute—Center for Sustainable Urban Development. Her research focuses on the intersection of heritage and sustainability planning, the role of preservation in urban policy, and societal values and spatial justice issues in heritage decision-making. She was formerly the director of research and education for World Monuments Fund and a project specialist at the Getty Conservation Institute. Avrami earned her BA in architecture and MS in historic preservation, both at Columbia, and her PhD in planning and public policy at Rutgers University. She was a trustee and secretary of US/ICOMOS from 2003 to 2010 and currently serves on the editorial advisory board of the journals *Change Over Time* and *Future Anterior.*

LOUISE BEDSWORTH is director of the Land Use Program at the Center for Law, Energy, and the Environment at Berkeley School of Law, where is also Senior Advisor to the California-China Climate Institute. At the time of the preparation of this article, Louise served as the executive director of the California Strategic Growth Council, a cabinet-level state organization that coordinates and collaborates with multiple state agencies, local governments, NGOs, and community groups to help realize healthy, thriving, resilient, and equitable communities for all. In this role, Bedsworth harnessed eight years of leadership on climate policy as deputy director of the Office of Planning and Research under Governor Jerry Brown, where she led collaborative research initiatives and innovative climate change adaptation and resilience programs, including the development of the Integrated Climate Adaptation and Resiliency Program and implementation of the state's $70 million grant awarded under the National Disaster Resilience Competition. Immediately before joining the state, Bedsworth worked on climate and transportation policy at the Public Policy Institute of California.

KEN BERNSTEIN is a principal city planner for the Los Angeles Department of City Planning, where he directs the city's Office of Historic Resources. He serves as lead staff member for the city's Cultural Heritage Commission; has overseen the completion of SurveyLA, a multiyear citywide survey of historic resources; and has led the creation of a comprehensive historic preservation program for Los Angeles. He also currently oversees the department's Urban Design Studio and has previously directed other policy planning initiatives, including work on Community Plan updates, housing policy, and transportation planning. He previously served for eight years as director of preservation issues for the Los Angeles Conservancy. He has an MA in public affairs and urban and regional planning from Princeton University's School of Public and International Affairs and a BA in political science from Yale University.

ROBIN BRONEN lives in Alaska and works as a human rights attorney and senior research scientist at the University of Alaska Fairbanks on the climate-forced relocations of Alaska Native communities. She is also the cofounder and executive director of the Alaska Institute for Justice. She works with Alaska Native communities and state and federal government agencies to create a community-led relocation process, based in human rights protections, that fosters community resilience. She has worked with the White House Council on Environmental Quality to implement President Obama's Climate Change Task Force recommendation to address climate displacement. Internationally, she works as an expert on climate-forced planned relocations with the UNFCCC Warsaw Mechanism on Loss and Damage Task Force on Displacement, and she is a member of the advisory group for the Platform on Disaster Displacement, a national government-led process intended to build consensus on the development of a protection agenda addressing population displacement caused by climate change. She has won numerous awards for her work on social and environmental justice issues.

SARA C. BRONIN is a professor at the Cornell College of Architecture, Art, and Planning and an associate member of the Cornell Law School faculty. She has written several books and many articles on property, land use, historic preservation, and sustainability law. She serves as an advisor to the National Trust for Historic Preservation, a board member of the Sustainable Development Code, and organizer of DesegregateCT. She has also previously led Preservation Connecticut and served as vice chair of Hartford's Historic Properties Commission. As chair of Hartford's Planning & Zoning Commission, she led an award-winning zoning code overhaul, housing code rewrite, climate action plan, subdivision and inland wetlands regulations, and the ten-year city plan. A licensed architect, Bronin won three design awards for the rehabilitation of her family's Civil War-era brownstone. She was educated at Yale Law School (Truman Scholar), Oxford University (Rhodes Scholar), and the University of Texas.

ANDREW DOLKART is a professor of historic preservation at the Columbia University Graduate School of Architecture, Planning, and Preservation. He is a preservationist and historian specializing in the architecture and development of New York City, with particular interest in the common yet overlooked building types that line the city's streets. He is the author of several award-winning books, including *Morningside Heights: A History of Its Architecture and Development*, which received the Association of American Publishers' award for best scholarly book in architecture and urban design; *Biography of a Tenement House in New York City: An Architectural History of 97 Orchard Street*; and *The Row House Reborn: Architecture and Neighborhoods in New York City, 1908–1929*, which won the Society of Architectural Historians' prestigious Antoinette Forrester Downing Award in 2012. He is also a cofounder of the award-winning NYC LGBT Historic Sites Project (www. nyclgbtsites.org).

SHREYA GHOSHAL is a recent graduate of Columbia University's Graduate School of Architecture, Planning, and Preservation, and holds dual masters' degrees in urban planning and historic preservation, along with a BS in architecture from the University of Minnesota. Leveraging her multidisciplinary expertise, her research and work focuses on tackling issues of sustainability, equity, and ethics/justice in the built environment. She is driven by a desire to decolonize architecture/planning/ preservation and promote community-centered design.

SCOTT GOODWIN is a writer and researcher focusing on heritage and historic preservation. He is the 2020–2022 Bonnie Burnham Fellow at World Monuments Fund and has served as managing editor of *Future Anterior*, journal of historic preservation history, theory, and criticism. He holds an MS in historic preservation from Columbia University's Graduate School of Architecture, Planning, and Preservation, where his thesis research examined heritage policy and the politics of emotion.

CLAUDIA GUERRA is the city of San Antonio's first cultural historian, a position in the Office of Historic Preservation (OHP). Her work focuses on making the intangible tangible. Guerra is dedicated to fostering the next generation of heritage stewards, as well as including voices who feel disenfranchised from preservation. As cultural historian, Guerra has been conducting oral histories and cultural mapping to capture the cultural story of San Antonio. Using principles from international perspectives on living heritage, her goal is to expand our understanding of heritage and to develop holistic policies that perpetuate tangible and intangible resources. Her work has aided in the creation of a new division in OHP dedicated to living heritage in order to focus on sustainable development, socially inclusive practices, the protection and promotion of community character and cultural heritage, and the revitalization of traditional building crafts and trades. Previously, she worked for the Center for Cultural Sustainability at the University of Texas at San Antonio; her research focused on the connection between spirit of place and spirit of people.

CORY HERRALA is the director of preservation at the New York City Landmarks Preservation Commission, where he has worked since 2007, overseeing a staff of more than thirty-five preservationists and supervisors in the Preservation Department. He participates in interagency initiatives involving resiliency and sustainability and has led efforts to incorporate related work at historic buildings into the commission's regulatory framework. Herrala earned a master of historic preservation degree from the University of Maryland and a professional master of architecture degree from the Savannah College of Art and Design.

VICTORIA HERRMANN is an assistant research professor at Georgetown University's School of Foreign Service, a National Geographic Explorer, and the managing director of the Arctic Institute, a nonprofit dedicated to Arctic security research. As the principal investigator of America's Eroding Edges, she traveled across the country in 2016 and 2017 interviewing 350 local leaders to identify what is needed most to safeguard coastal communities against the unavoidable impacts of climate change. Her current project, Rise Up to Rising Tides, is creating an online matchmaking platform that connects pro bono experts with climate-affected communities. The project seeks to safeguard heritage by connecting national expertise to some of the thirteen million Americans at risk of climate displacement in the coming years. Herrmann teaches environmental communication at Georgetown University and was named one of the world's most influential people in climate policy in 2019. She was previously a Fulbright awardee to Canada, a Mirzayan Science and Technology Policy Fellow at the National Academy of Sciences, and a Gates Scholar at the University of Cambridge, where she received her PhD in geography.

LISA KERSAVAGE is executive director of the New York City Landmarks Preservation Commission (LPC). As executive director of the LPC, the largest municipal preservation agency in the nation, Kersavage oversees the agency's operations and works closely with the commission chair to develop policy and strategic planning agency-wide. Before joining the LPC, she was the project manager of Changing Course, an ambitious design competition to reimagine a more sustainable Lower Mississippi River Delta, in collaboration with Environmental Defense Fund and Van Alen Institute. She also served as the senior director of preservation and sustainability at the Municipal Art Society of New York, public policy consultant to Philadelphia's William Penn Foundation, and executive director of the James Marston Fitch Charitable Foundation and Friends of the Upper East Side Historic Districts. Kersavage received her MS in historic preservation from Columbia University and her BA in art and architectural history from Penn State University.

JACQUELINE M. KLOPP is currently an associate research scholar at the Center for Sustainable Urban Development at Columbia University, a Volvo Research and Education Foundations Center of Excellence in Future Urban Transport. She taught for many years at the School of International and Public Affairs and now teaches in the Sustainable Development Program at Columbia University. Her research focuses on the intersection of sustainable transport, land use, accountability, data, and technology. Klopp is the author of numerous academic and popular articles on land and the politics of infrastructure, with a focus on Africa, and she is increasingly exploring the potential of new technologies to impact transportation for the twenty-first century. She is also a founder of Digital Matatus, a consortium that mapped and created open data for bus routes in Nairobi, Kenya, part of a global movement to create open data for improved planning.

JAMES B. LINDBERG is Senior Policy Director at the National Trust for Historic Preservation. He has more than thirty years of experience in preservation, planning, and sustainable development, including five years as director of the National Trust's Preservation Green Lab. He has led nationally recognized preservation and sustainable development projects including the adaptive use of a former dude ranch in Rocky Mountain National Park and the green rehabilitation of a historic school in Denver. He earned his BA in the Growth and Structure of Cities from Haverford College and his MS in historic preservation from the University of Vermont. He is an adjunct faculty member at the University of Colorado Denver College of Architecture and Planning.

RANDALL MASON plays several roles at the University of Pennsylvania's Stuart Weitzman School of Design: senior fellow at PennPraxis; professor of city and regional planning; former chair of the Graduate Program in Historic Preservation; and founding faculty director of the Center for the Preservation of Civil Rights Sites. Mason was educated in geography, history, and urban planning (PhD, Columbia University). His published work includes *The Once and Future New York*. His professional practice includes projects at many scales, addressing planning, preservation, and public space issues, commissioned by organizations including the Getty Conservation Institute, William Penn Foundation, Brookings Institution, the City of Philadelphia, and the National Park Service. His most recent projects are in Rwanda; Detroit; Washington, DC; and Columbus, Indiana. He lives in Philadelphia and was a Rome Prize Fellow in 2012–2013.

JENNIFER MINNER is an associate professor in the Department of City and Regional Planning at Cornell University. Her research and teaching focus on land use and spatial planning, historic preservation, and community development. She investigates urban change, building reuse, and community memory in all manner of places—from commercial strips to mega-event sites to socially engaged art. She directs the Just Places Lab, a platform for multidisciplinary research and creative action related to place, the built environment, and social equity. Minner

227

earned a BA in anthropology from the University of Washington, an MURP from Portland State University, and a PhD from the University of Texas at Austin.

BÉNÉDICTE DE MONTLAUR is chief executive officer of World Monuments Fund (WMF), the world's foremost private organization dedicated to saving extraordinary places while empowering the communities around them. She is responsible for defining and currently implementing WMF's strategic vision in more than thirty countries around the world and leading a team that spans the globe. Her background mixes culture and the arts, politics, international diplomacy, and human rights. Prior to joining WMF, Montlaur spent two decades working across three continents as a senior diplomat at the French Ministry of Foreign Affairs. Montlaur studied sociology and Arabic at the École Normale Supérieure (Ulm) and public affairs at Sciences Po, Paris. She was a Marshall Memorial Fellow at the German Marshall Fund. She has served on the boards of several cultural and educational institutions and is currently a trustee of the Menil Collection, in Houston.

DAVID MOORE is currently pursuing a master of science in civil engineering at the University of Cincinnati. His research focuses on the spatial distribution of energy burden, as well as the relationships between energy burden and socioeconomic/demographic variables. Moore is a recipient of the US Department of State's Critical Language Scholarship for Japanese; he spent the summer of 2019 in Okayama, Japan, studying Japanese language through an experiential framework centered on the UN Sustainable Development Goals. He holds a BS in architectural engineering from the University of Cincinnati.

MARCY ROCKMAN is an archaeologist with experience in national and international climate change policy. Her research focuses on how humans gather and share environmental information, especially during colonization and migration, which she has used to address situations as diverse as cultural resource management in the American West and homeland security risk communication in Washington, DC. From 2011 to 2018 she served as the inaugural US National Park Service Climate Change Adaptation Coordinator for Cultural Resources. She now works with the International Council on Monuments and Sites as scientific coordinator of a project to improve the incorporation of heritage in reports of the Intergovernmental Panel on Climate Change. She recently served as co-chair on behalf of the International Council on Monuments and Sites (ICOMOS), alongside UNESCO and the Intergovernmental Panel on Climate Change (IPCC), on a project to improve the incorporation of heritage in IPCC reports. Currently she works with Co-Equal, a nonprofit in Washington, DC, to provide climate change research for the US Congress. Rockman holds a PhD in anthropology from the University of Arizona and a BSc in geology from the College of William and Mary.

STEPHANIE RYBERG-WEBSTER is an associate professor in the Department of Urban Studies at Cleveland State University's Levin

College of Urban Affairs. Her research broadly addresses the intersections of historic preservation and urban development. Ryberg-Webster's current work explores the 1970s-era history of historic preservation within the context of Cleveland's escalating urban decline. She has previously published research on preservation and community development, African American heritage, historic rehabilitation tax credits, and preservation amid urban decline. Ryberg-Webster is also the coeditor (with J. Rosie Tighe) of *Legacy Cities: Continuity and Change amid Decline and Revival.* She holds a PhD in city and regional planning from the University of Pennsylvania, a master of historic preservation from the University of Maryland, and a bachelor of urban planning from the University of Cincinnati.

ELLIOTT SCLAR is the codirector of the Earth Institute's Center for Sustainable Urban Development and professor emeritus of urban planning at Columbia University's Graduate School of Architecture, Planning, and Preservation. He is a member of the senior faculty of the Earth Institute at Columbia University. Sclar coordinated the Task Force on Improving the Lives of Slum Dwellers, one of the ten task forces established by the UN Millennium Project to aid the implementation of the UN Millennium Development Goals. He was one of the lead authors of its 2005 report *A Home in the City*, published by Earthscan. Sclar is a nationally recognized expert on privatization. His book *You Don't Always Get What You Pay For: The Economics of Privatization* (Cornell University Press, 2000) won two major academic prizes: the Louis Brownlow Award for the Best Book of 2000 from the National Academy of Public Administration and the 2001 Charles Levine Prize from the International Political Science Association and *Governance* magazine for a major contribution to public policy literature.

A. R. SIDERS is a lawyer and social scientist working to promote fair and effective adaptation to climate change. She is an assistant professor of public policy and geography at the University of Delaware and a core faculty member of the Disaster Research Center. Her latest projects have explored managed retreat—the purposeful movement of people and assets away from risk—and the social justice implications of coastal adaptation. Her research has recently been published in *Science* and featured in the *New York Times*, on *Science Friday*, and on National Public Radio. Siders holds a JD from Harvard University and a PhD from Stanford University. She was previously an environmental fellow at the Harvard University Center for the Environment, an associate at the Center for Climate Change Law at Columbia University, and a Presidential Management Fellow with the US Navy. She is originally from Duluth, Minnesota, and misses the cold.

MARK A. SILBERMAN has been general counsel to the New York City Landmarks Preservation Commission since 1998. Prior to working for the commission, he was a litigation associate at Paul, Weiss, Rifkind, Wharton & Garrison. In the 1980s, he was a lobbyist, organizer, writer, and editor for various environmental and public interest groups in Washington, DC. He is a coeditor of the historic resources chapter of *Environmental Law and Regulation in New York*, edited by William R. Ginsberg and Philip Weinberg (West Publishing, 2001; updated 2019).

AMANDA L. WEBB is an assistant professor in the Department of Civil and Architectural Engineering and Construction Management at the University of Cincinnati, where her research focuses on the energy performance of historic buildings. She was a committee member of ASHRAE's Guideline 34, Energy Efficiency Guideline for Historic Buildings, and she is a US Task Expert for the International Energy Agency's Task 59, Renovating Historic Buildings Towards Zero Energy. She holds a PhD in architectural engineering from Pennsylvania State University, a master's degree from MIT's Building Technology Program, and a bachelor's degree from Yale University.

VICKI WEINER is the academic coordinator of the Historic Preservation master's degree program and an adjunct associate professor at Pratt Institute. She has served as the director of two nonprofit historic preservation organizations in New York City, was the first Kress Fellow for Historic Preservation at the Municipal Art Society of New York, and has provided historic preservation policy consulting services to dozens of community organizations and government agencies. She is the author and coauthor of numerous research reports, briefing papers, and articles on preserving community culture in low-income neighborhoods, and a recipient of the James Marston Fitch Mid-Career Grant. Weiner recently stepped down as the deputy director of the Pratt Center for Community Development, where she was responsible for overseeing the center's planning and policy projects and leading all aspects of organizational management since 2011. Her work at the center included projects that explore connections between preserving culturally important places and creating more equitable communities, as well as heritage conservation studies in such places as Fulton Street Mall in downtown Brooklyn, Manhattan's East Village, and Cypress Hills/East New York in Brooklyn. Weiner has a BA from Drew University and an MS in historic preservation from Columbia University.

Acknowledgments

This is the third volume resulting from the research initiative Urban Heritage, Sustainability, and Social Inclusion, cosponsored by the Columbia University Graduate School of Architecture, Planning, and Preservation; the Earth Institute–Center for Sustainable Urban Development; and the American Assembly. The initiative is generously funded by the New York Community Trust. The need for deep, structural shifts in preservation policy to confront exclusion and the challenges of climate change was the impetus behind the establishment of the initiative. Through a series of symposia and related publications, this research works toward socially inclusive processes that support a just and sustainable built environment so as to inform the next generation of preservation policy.

A two-day symposium in February 2020 convened twenty-two scholars and practitioners in New York City to explore preservation's intersection with questions of sustainability and equity as policy adapts to the era of climate change. This exchange of ideas allowed participants to reflect on and orient their research, and the chapters herein were developed through interviews and participant-authored texts over the course of 2020.

A number of graduate research assistants supported this endeavor. Shreya Ghoshal and Scott Goodwin were crucial collaborators in the development and implementation of the 2020 symposium, and Allison Arlotta and Jenna Dublin graciously returned as team members for the event. Anna Gasha and Katlyn Foster provided administrative and editorial support in the development of the volume, particularly for the interviews. James Graham, managing editor from Columbia Books on Architecture and the City, was a patient and insightful collaborator in pulling together the wide-ranging elements of this book. Erica Olsen has been a keen-eyed copyeditor of the publications in this series, and the graphic design of Common Name (Yoonjai Choi and Ken Meier) has likewise brought a welcome clarity to the ideas of the symposia.

Jacqueline Klopp and Elliott Sclar generously guided and championed this work as part of the Earth Institute–Center for Sustainable Urban Development's scope and mission. We are grateful to the Graduate School of Architecture, Planning, and Preservation, especially Dean Amale Andraos, for continued support. World Monuments Fund (WMF) generously provided the venue for the symposium, and we thank all the WMF staff who provided logistical support over the two-day event. Special thanks go to the New York Community Trust, especially Kerry McCarthy and Salem Tsegaye, for their continued support of and engagement in this project, and for investing in the kinds of threaded dialogues needed to reimagine the future of preservation policy.

Everyone involved in this volume and the initiative deserves special thanks for bringing this book to fruition under the trying circumstances of the COVID-19 pandemic and during a critical moment of racial reckoning. With so many challenges on personal and professional fronts, and so many claims on time and energies, the contributors to this volume nonetheless remained committed to this collaborative endeavor. This book is a testament to their sincere and unwavering dedication to advancing the preservation enterprise to address the needs of the future.

Columbia Books on
Architecture and the City

An imprint of the
Graduate School of Architecture,
Planning, and Preservation

Columbia University
1172 Amsterdam Ave
407 Avery Hall
New York, NY 10027
arch.columbia.edu/books

Distributed by
Columbia University Press
cup.columbia.edu

*Preservation, Sustainability,
and Equity*
Edited by Erica Avrami

Project Editor
James Graham

Graphic Designer
Common Name

Copyeditor
Erica Olsen

Printer
KOPA

ISBN: 978-1-941332-70-2
Library of Congress
Control Number:
2021946762

Director of Publications
Isabelle Kirkham-Lewitt

Associate Editor
Joanna Joseph